A
NORTHWOODS
COMPANION
Fall and Winter

by John Bates

Illustrated by April Lehman

Manitowish River Press, Mercer, Wisconsin

A NORTHWOODS COMPANION
Fall and Winter

Printed in the United States on 50 percent recycled paper.

Editor: Greg Linder
Illustrations: April Lehman
Cover photography: Jeff Richter
Book design: Jerry Lehman
Cover design: Katie Miller

Publisher's Cataloging in Publication Data
Bates, John, 1951-
    A northwoods companion : fall and winter /written by John Bates ; illustrated by April Lehman.
    Includes bibliographical references and index.
    ISBN 0-9656763-1-5 (softcover)
    1. Natural History
    2. Seasons
    3. Nature Study

Library of Congress Catalog Card Number: 97-73781
0 9 8 7 6 5 4 3 2

Published by: Manitowish River Press
               2263 Hwy. 47
               Mercer, WI 54547
               Phone: 715-476-2828
               Fax: 715-476-2818
               E-mail: manitowish@centuryinter.net

For my family,
and for those who love the Northwoods.

Books get produced through the cooperative efforts of a series of talented people. This book wouldn't have happened without the following people and their superior skills: Greg Linder's editing and advice, Jerry Lehman's interior design, April Lehman's illustrations, Katie Miller's cover design, Stepheny Freedman's proofing and Jeff Richter's photography. My deep thanks to all of you.

Thanks must also be given to all of the individuals who have hiked, canoed, birded, botanized, sea kayaked, snowshoed, cross-country skied, and just plain talked and hung out with me over the years. Your insights and camaraderie have made all the difference, and will continue to make all the difference.

My most profound thanks must always go to my wife Mary for both her groundedness and her willingness to leap.

III

Grateful acknowledgment is made to the following for permission to reprint previously published material:

Anderson, Tom. © LEARNING NATURE BY A COUNTRY ROAD, by Tom Anderson, reprinted with permission of Publisher, Voyageur Press, Inc., 123 North Second Street, Stillwater, MN 55082 U.S.A. 1-800-888-9653.

Isherwood, Justin. From "Snow," Wisconsin Natural Resources Magazine, © by Justin Isherwood. Used by permission of Justin Isherwood.

Isherwood, Justin From "What Cold is Good For," Wisconsin Natural Resources Magazine, © by Justin Isherwood. Used by permission of Justin Isherwood.

Kappel-Smith, Diana. From WINTERING. © 1979, 1980, 1982, 1983, 1984 by Diana Kappel-Smith. Reprinted by permission of McIntosh and Otis,Inc.

Leopold, Aldo. From A SAND COUNTY ALMANAC: AND SKETCHES HERE AND THERE SPECIAL COMMEMORATIVE EDITION by Aldo Leopold. Copyright © 1949. Used by permission of Oxford University Press, Inc.

Olson, Sigurd. From LISTENING POINT, reprinted by permission of Alfred A. Knopf. Copyright © 1953 by Sigurd Olson.

Peattie, Donald Culross. From AN ALMANAC FOR MODERNS, reprinted by permission of Curtis Brown, Ltd. Copyright © 1935, 1963 by D.C. Peattie.

Steinhart, Peter. From "Pull of the Moon," Audubon Magazine, September, 1989, by Peter Steinhart. Used by permission of Peter Steinhart.

Vukelich, George. From NORTH COUNTRY NOTEBOOK, Vol. 2, © 1992, by George Vukelich, reprinted by permission of Prairie Oak Press and Helen Vukelich.

Wendorf, Susan. From HARVEST MOON: A WISCONSIN OUTDOOR ANTHOLOGY. © 1993. Used by permission of Susan Wendorf.

Contents

INTRODUCTION

The word "season" comes from the Old French "saison" and the Latin "sation," both of which mean the act of sowing. The fundamental act of planting was tied so directly to how well one could read seasonal signs that the word and the act became one! Not only was one's survival hitched to reading the signs for when to plant, but it was also tied to understanding the whens, whys, and hows of a myriad of other seasonal signs, from when various species of fish began to spawn, to when geese and ducks migrated, to when various fruits came ripe, to when to strip bark and cut wood for making tools and implements.

Our need for recognizing the variables and nuances of seasonal changes has fallen by the wayside as the U.S. has become 94 percent urbanized. Still, paying daily attention to what the world has to offer has both a practical and sublime side. George Vukelich in his *North Country Notebook, Vol. 2,* gets humorously to the heart of the practical matter: "When you live up in the North Country in winter, you just naturally keep track of things, because you could wind up freezing your buns if you don't." Justin Isherwood writes of the sublime side: "After a 10,000-foot fall, snow can land with every crystal, every cornice and gable intact. Snow waltzes down a December sky like a debutante down a Danish staircase."

We are blessed to have such seasonal changes to enjoy. How could one fully appreciate the revolution that spring represents without first experiencing a northern winter? The ruggedness of life in the North Country can best be understood by looking at the individual lives and extraordinary adaptations of the species of animals and plants that live here. Michael Link, author of *Outdoor Education,* wrote that the "northern states are the theatres of the seasons, the variety act of geography." How true.

A Northwoods Companion is a phenological guide, meaning it's a picture of the orderly timing and progression of natural events. Each chapter brackets natural events into two-week time periods when it is reasonable to expect the events may occur. But every year has its own personality, its own sense of drama, timing and delivery of its lines.As with all forecasting, the future will undoubtedly offer itself in unanticipated ways. Enjoy the variability, make note of it, and try to find the patterns and the reasons behind it all.

A NorthwoodsCompanion was written over the last eight years from a series of simple outings designed around exploring and discovering the natural world. The act of discovery appears to me to be wrapped up in the art of staying still long enough that both experience and understanding have a chance to catch up to you and reveal themselves. In my naturalist guiding, if I can make a one-mile hike last three hours, and if the time feels as if it flew by, then we've probably had a terrific experience. It takes time for questions to form, to be voiced, for curiosity to take hold and be acted upon; and then more time for observations to be ground into possible "answers". To go as slow as possible in quiet observation is the fastest way to learn about the natural world. There's no short course. I've tried, and I've come home empty every time. I suggest you stop and look around every few steps. Get your knees and hands dirty, and learn to explore where you are rather than try to catch a glimpse of the world as you stride purposefully by.

One last note. Aldo Leopold writes in the July chapter of A *Sand County Almanac*, "We only grieve for what we know". The message is clear: the loss of a species is relatively painless to us if we have little connection to it. The writings of Wallace Stegner and Wendell Berry further refine this thought. Berry believes that if you don't know where you are, you don't know who you are. He refers to himself as a "placed person", in contrast to a displaced person who is mobile, unsettled, and rootless. Berry isn't talking about knowing what street you live on, but rather the knowing that occurs when you work and play in all the weathers a place can bring to bear, suffering and loving and valuing a place because of all that you put into it and all that you get out of it.

Stegner writes that it's probably time we as a culture settled down. That it's time "we looked around us instead of looking ahead". He argues that a place "is made a place only by slow accrual, like a coral reef", that we need to grow up in a place, live in it, know it, and leave it to our children who will do the same.

I hope this book helps you in better "knowing" the Northwoods. The more we talk with one another about natural events like the goldfinch at our feeders, the depth of snow in our yards, the deer tracks we saw in the woods, the more we learn about the Northwoods, and hopefully the more we value it. Eventually we may get to where we know enough to grieve for the loss of just about anything (with the possible exception of mosquitoes) that lives here. When that happens, we will truly belong here and share a common sense of place.

This is a book for generalists written by a generalist. In this age of specialization, I have chosen to broadly wander, both experientially and intellectually, in hopes of finding a greater understanding of the whole picture. I've tried to open my eyes to anything and everything the Northwoods has to offer, and the result is a potpourri. But then, so is the natural world. *A Northwoods Companion* is for the generalist who wishes to think about it all, and then to see if she can find her place in it.

Even in a country you know by heart,
it's hard to go the same way twice.

Wendell Berry
Traveling at Home

X

SEPTEMBER

The Ojibwe word for September is *wasebugogizis,* meaning "shining leaf." The process of color change in leaves works like this: Light-absorbing, green-pigmented chlorophyll masks the other color-producing substances in a leaf during the summer. In the fall, the trees stop producing chlorophyll, the masking effect is eliminated, and the yellows and reds (carotenoids, carotenes, xanthophylls, and anthocyanins) that were hidden under the green chlorophyll become visible.

Each tree species contains a different balance of these substances, thus producing different colors at different times. Even trees of the same species may exhibit different coloration in different geographical areas. Some trees, like alders and black locusts, have very little pigmentation, so they change very little. Other trees, like birches, sugar maples, and aspens, are usually rich in carotenoids, which produce a brilliant yellow. Red maples, red oaks, and sumac are usually rich in anthocyanins, which create deep reds.

As always, science serves the intellect well but speaks little to our sense of aesthetics. In isolation, science has the same dampening effect on our experience of beauty that chlorophyll has on leaf colors. The natural world needs to be understood through equal avenues of head, hands, and heart. Using one without the others begs a deeper insight.

birch

maple

HORICON MARSH

Migration

of the Monarch!

MinkTracks

turtlehead

gel ©97

SEPTEMBER 1-15

Sumac

Locust

September 1 to September 15

Migration: Fattening Up

Major bird migrations begin in early September. Three of the best areas for seeing hawks and other birds in huge numbers (sometimes 40,000 a day!) are Duluth's Hawk Ridge, the Apostle Islands (particularly Outer Island), and the Whitefish Point Bird Observatory near Sault Ste. Marie, Michigan. A good northerly or westerly wind, and dry conditions, often move birds south in a hurry. Don't bother looking for migrating birds if the wind is coming out of the south--most birds sit tight rather than fight a head wind.

On a full-moon September night, keep an eye open and a pair of binoculars handy for migrating birds silhouetted against the moon. Nearly all of our insect-eating birds migrate at night. Larger, secretive birds like woodcocks and rails also use the cover of night. Some birds, including loons, geese, ducks, and herons, travel both by day and by night.

> ### September Musings
>
> *The increasing scarlet and yellow tints around the meadows and river remind me of the opening of a vast flower bud. They are the petals of its corolla, which are of the width of the valley. It is the flower of autumn, whose expanding bud just begins to blush.*
>
> —Henry David Thoreau

Migratory birds need to fatten up for their journeys. Through the action of several hormones, fat is accumulated just under the skin in order to provide energy for the long, often nonstop flights. Blackpoll warblers double their weight in September, ballooning from 12 grams to 23 grams. The added bulk gives them enough fat reserve to fly 85 consecutive hours over the Atlantic Ocean to South America. Male ruby-throated hummingbirds may distribute nearly one-half of their weight into fat reserves--up to two grams of their four-and-a-half gram total body weight. The added weight fuels their 26-hour flight over the Gulf of Mexico to Central America.

Nonmigrating birds have no need to undergo the same hormonal changes, and thus don't gain weight in the fall to the extent of migrants. Nor do they have the same ability to replenish their fat reserves if exhausted. Of approximately 215 nesting birds in the Upper Midwest, only about 25 are permanent residents. In other words, nearly 90 percent of "our" birds are either in the process of migrating or preparing to depart. Over 100 nesting birds in the United States will travel abroad, wintering in the West Indies, Central America, or South America.

4   Woodpeckers

Our three migrating woodpeckers--the northern flicker, the red-headed woodpecker, and the yellow-bellied sapsucker--begin their southward journey by the middle of this month. The lack of insect life on the ground makes travel south a dietary requirement. Our other northern woodpeckers--the pileated, hairy, downy, and black-backed--find winter meals by drilling into trees and exposing over-wintering adult insects, larvae, and eggs.

The woodpeckers' winter stay is highly beneficial to human society, because they consume a huge amount of insects. An old saying goes, "Eat one in May, kill a thousand a day." If an insect can be eaten before it reproduces in spring, the effect of its death is multiplied dramatically. The same holds true all winter, so it's fair to say that woodpeckers may be our best natural insecticide.

Feeding Hummingbirds in the Fall

Should you take down your hummingbird feeders in September, so the hummers won't stay here too long? Many people have heard this myth, but it's absolutely not true. Hummingbirds have an acute instinct that tells them when to migrate south. They will leave whether you provide them with free meals or not. Hummers coming to your feeders in September may be birds migrating through from Canada. They need to build up body fat in order to make the flight to Texas and ultimately across the Gulf of Mexico, so keep feeding the hummers until they stop coming through.

Hummers Tanking Up

Carol Christensen from Lac du Flambeau called one September to report that the last of her hummingbirds had departed on Saturday, 9/17. She should know, since 40 to 60 hummers keep her busy filling feeders throughout the summer. During the last two weeks of August, when hummingbirds "tank up" for their migration, Carol puts out about two quarts of nectar every day. Friends who visit her often hand-feed the hummers by quietly holding a small feeder in their hands. The hungry hummers come right in--sometimes so close that Carol says you can feel the breeze from their wings.

5

Monarch Butterfly Migration

Another migration is currently in progress--that of the monarch butterfly. The difference between the monarch migration and bird migration is that monarchs are a generational migrant, while birds are individual migrants. This means that, while the same individual birds will return the next year, the next *generation* of monarchs return--not the same individual butterflies. The monarch adults that are now migrating to Mexico will head north in spring, laying eggs along the way. Though most of the adults won't make it all the way back to northern Wisconsin, the next generation will finish the northward migration and lay new eggs.

The round-trip distance to Mexico and back totals 2,500 to 3,000 miles. With a northerly wind, the monarchs will migrate at high altitudes, taking advantage of the tailwind and the energy savings. One tagged monarch was recovered after 18 days of its migration. It was 1,000 miles from the tagging site, having averaged about 55 miles a day.

Monarchs get concentrated into narrow migration corridors just like hawks, so most hawk-watch areas are also good for monarch watching. The monarchs begin leaving in late August; the exodus peaks in September, though some are seen hereabouts into October. Hundreds or even thousands may gather together at their nightly roosting spots.

Monarchs live as far north as central Canada, and are the only northern butterflies that migrate. Millions of buckeye and painted lady butterflies, both common to southern Wisconsin, drift south in September, too. Buckeyes are known for the large, dark "eye-spots" on their brown wings. The most famous migration flight of butterflies involved three billion painted ladies that passed through a California site in 1924!

Cormorants

Bob and Ruth Kesselhon from the Manitowish Waters area wrote to tell me about a cormorant they observed in September on Papoose Lake. Theirs was a rather rare sighting for our inland lakes region-- cormorants most often nest along the Great Lakes or on major flowages. Cormorants are large, with wingspans reaching four-and-one-half feet, and are nearly all black except for a yellow-orange throat patch. They can reduce their specific gravity by squeezing air out of their plumage and bodies, allowing them to sink into the water. Thus they appear to swim low in the water, and are often visible only from the neck up. Cormorants spend a lot of time in trees or on stumps with their wings hung out to dry like summer laundry. For some counterevolutionary reason, their wing feathers are not waterproof, so they have to climb out of the water frequently to catch some drying rays.

Cormorants are superb swimmers, able to dive down 100 feet or more and remain underwater for over a minute while they search for fish. They most commonly prey upon rough fish like suckers, carp, and bullhead, so they are little threat to sport or commercial fishing. However, many fishermen would have you believe otherwise.

Historically, cormorants were reported to undertake spring migratory flights in huge numbers. According to a 1926 article in the *La Crosse Tribune,* one flight "continued for two-and-one-half hours . . . there were always from a dozen to hundreds of large flocks in the air...The number of birds is variously estimated at from 100,000 to 1,000,000."

However, cormorant populations were systematically destroyed during the 1950s, due to the belief that they ate far more than their fair share of fish. That slaughter, coupled with habitat loss and DDT proliferation, meant that only a few breeding colonies remained in all of Wisconsin by 1960.

The cormorant was protected under the Endangered Species Act in 1973, and populations have since made a comeback. By 1985, these birds had been removed from the endangered list--in large part because hundreds of artificial nesting platforms had been placed in suitable areas like the bay waters of Green Bay and the Mead Wildlife Area.

Populations in the Chequamegon Bay region over the last decade illustrate how quickly cormorants recovered. Only 21 birds were seen in Chequamegon Bay in the spring of 1981; by 1986 and 1987, 439 were being observed during an average spring.

Fall migration generally peaks in the first two weeks of October, but individuals may be seen until ice-up.

Geese and Marshes

The first flights of geese come through in early September. Soon, long "Vs" of geese will be sailing on tailwinds, carrying the last vestiges of summer south with them. The sound and beauty of their flights always impress us, but the *magnitude* of their flight is equally impressive. When Canada geese leave their nesting grounds in northern Canada, they often fly the entire journey to a stopover like Horicon Marsh in one day. That's an 800-mile flight! With a good tailwind, a goose can raise its airspeed to 70 miles per hour from its average of 40 miles per hour, making the journey in less than 12 hours.

If you're not familiar with Horicon Marsh (near Waupun, Wisconsin), Horicon is the largest cattail marsh in the United States. To give you an idea of how many birds utilize Horicon, the fall 1989 migration population of Canada geese peaked at 700,000 in the marsh. Nearly 80 percent of the 1.1 million Canada geese in the Mississippi Valley population stop off annually in the vicinity of Horicon.

Obviously, those of us in the Lakeland area will see far fewer geese. The only significant site that attracts migrating honkers is Powell Marsh, which brings in 500 to 4,000 birds during any given fall, depending in large part on how many goslings were produced that year. The young birds require rest during migration, so they often stop for a meal and some down-time. Other than Powell, we have very little good goose habitat in the northwoods. Geese are grazers, eating the soft shoots, leaves, and buds of various grasses, as well as cultivated crops and various meadow plants. They like wild rice, something we do have our share of, but we certainly don't have the enormous stands necessary to support large numbers of geese. An average Canada goose weighs in at seven to 10 pounds and eats about half a pound of food per day, so we would need good-sized rice beds to hold many geese.

At 12,800 acres, Powell Marsh is certainly big enough to attract large numbers of waterfowl. But Powell is not really a marsh. It's a sedge-leatherleaf bog, which may not matter to non-botanist types, but matters greatly to the appetites of various waterfowl. Still, large flocks of geese have traditionally been attracted to Powell after major burns occurred in the summer. The DNR-conducted burns produce succulent sprouting grasses and sedges in the fall, but the department's efforts to burn sections of Powell annually are often frustrated by the lack of proper burn conditions. Suitable conditions occur just once every three years or so, and even then only several hundred acres may be ready for burning.

As a result, Powell will never become a Horicon, but perhaps that's a blessing for those of us who value living near a great birding area that is not inundated by hordes of people. On a typical hour poke-around one early September in 1996, I saw an American bittern; a flock of double-crested cormorants; three sandhill cranes; several marsh hawks; two otters munching on a school of fish that were trapped in a receding pool; numerous geese and ducks; and a black tern. To me, that's as great a spectacle as thousands of geese.

Mink

My wife Mary and I observed numerous mink tracks one September along the exposed shoreline of the Turtle-Flambeau Flowage. The flowage was drawn down several feet, and shoreline feeders like mink were probably in seventh heaven. Mink can catch fish and crayfish in the water, catch mice, rabbits, birds, and frogs on land, or catch muskrats anywhere in between. Think of mink as the utility baseball players of the natural world. They may not be the best at any one skill, but they're able to play all the positions and make a very good living.

Fully grown mink are two feet long and look much like weasels. They are chocolate brown in color, except for some white blotching under their chins. Mink are quite common, but because they feed mostly between dusk and dawn, they are not often seen. They're very curious animals. While ice-fishing, a friend of ours was able to coax a mink close enough to eat fish from his hand.

Great Blues

Early one September Mary, our daughter Callie, and I kicked up six great blue herons, all feeding in one small slough on Powell Marsh. Though they're common, great blue herons, like deer, seem to withstand the human "boredom" test. We often lack appreciation for frequently seen wildlife species, but few people tire of the beauty of herons. Their beauty, though, can inspire different perceptions. Here are two examples:

I wasn't looking for great blues particularly, but all day long I couldn't take my eyes off them; patient, gangling, serene, with their dark-browed warrior's eyes and beaks like swords . . . In one place I spent an hour and a half sitting on a stone, watching a great blue up to his ankles in water, and he was doing what passes for hunting...When he stretched his long neck it seemed to spread out from him smoothly, like a cat on the prowl. When he walked it was with a jerk-and-stop . . . jerk-and-stop motion.

—Diana Kappel-Smith

9

A great blue heron thinks it hears the polished leather of an officer and snaps to attention; instinct of an ensign. The canoe drifts, the bird goes back to feeding, tracking the shallows with the attitude of those who clear mine-fields by listening. Instead of Claymores it detects frogs and shiners and a snorkeling shrew. The head and neck are serpentine, a separate entity from the body, coiling like secret weaponry from the narrow fuselage of a night fighter.

—Justin Isherwood

Hummingbird Moths

Hummingbird moths are most often seen in early September. These moths are actually mistaken for hummingbirds, because they have the same general body shape and size as their avian counterparts. They also hover in the same helicopterlike flight, produce a "humming" as their wings beat at better than 60 strokes a minute, and drink from the same nectar-rich flowers. Their mouths are long, flexible tubes used for sucking nectar from deep within flowers, serving the same function as a hummingbird's beak. Unlike the rigid inflexible beak of a hummer however, the moth can coil its proboscis under its head like a spring.

Hawk moths (the family to which hummingbird moths belong) range throughout the state. They are most visible in late afternoon and at dusk feeding in flower gardens.

Look for their larvae, called hornworms, in your garden--they're often seen slinking near your tomato plants. These green, two- to three-inch-long worms use a projection on their "tails" to dig into the loose soil. There they form protective chrysalises, later emerging as moths.

10

Ricing

Mary and I went ricing one September weekend with Jim Meeker, a professor at Northland College and wild rice researcher. We'd never tried harvesting rice before, assuming that we needed an "expert" along to show us the ropes. Jim is certainly that. But we were surprised to learn that the process of ricing requires few skills, though there's clearly an art to doing it efficiently. When the rice is ready, the grains simply fall into the canoe when knocked with a wooden rod. It's as easy as that.

We assumed our ricing roles, one becoming the "knocker," the other serving as the "poler." The knocker sits in the canoe, holding in each hand a 30-inch-long wooden rod. He or she sweeps the long stalks over the side of the boat with one rod, while tapping the stalks with the other rod. The rice is swept in alternately from each side of the canoe, in order to efficiently harvest a path through the rice bed.

The poler stands at the other end of the canoe, wielding a 14-foot-long pole with a metal duckbill on the end, which spreads wide to prevent the pole from simply sinking into the muck. The trick in poling is to maintain a straight course and just the right speed. The best speed allows the knocker time to sweep both sides of the canoe, but not enough time to closely examine the rice worms crawling up his leg. The knocker should not have to work too feverishly to keep up.

For me, the art of ricing lies primarily in the poling. When I poled, we moved along in a series of fits and starts, in a direction best described as a random curve. Fortunately, our winter food supply is not dependent on my current ricing skills. If it was, the family would thin down considerably.

As the grains fell, many of them stuck onto my pants and shirt, then to our carpet later that night. Each grain has a long "tail" of sorts with tiny barbs along its length, easily noticeable under a hand lens. The barbs probably serve to lodge the grains securely into the muck bottom of a river or bay, so they can germinate.

Wild rice is the only cereal grain native to North America. Along with maple sugar, it served as a critical food source for the estimated 30,000 American Indians who lived in the wild rice district of northern Wisconsin and Minnesota. According to estimates, wild rice provided 25 percent of the total calories in their diet. The Menominee Indians took their name from this native grass, *menominee* meaning the "wild rice people."

The native people moved their camps to the best rice stands every fall, then spent the better part of a month harvesting and processing rice. In her book *Chippewa Customs,* Frances Densmore explains that each group of people had its own share of the rice field; the women established the boundaries of each group by going to the rice field in midsummer and tying some of the rice into sheaves. The women also did the harvesting, though a man often poled the canoe through the rice while the woman used her ricing sticks to knock the rice from the stalks. Wild rice matures unevenly, coming ripe over a period of several weeks, so the harvesters returned many times to the same site in order to gather rice.

Not only did the rice feed the native people, but it also fed countless waterfowl that descended into the rice stands for easy foraging. Wild rice is rated today as the top duck food in the northeastern United States (from Maine to Minnesota). It is a particular favorite of the mallard, coot, blue-winged and green-winged teal, wood duck, redhead, sora rail, bobolink, and various blackbirds and sparrows. Some of the best autumn bird-watching can be done from the margins of a wild rice stand.

In our area, certain lakes that are known for their good rice crops must be posted before anyone can harvest the rice. These lakes are "opened" and posted by the tribes. In Vilas County, these lakes include Allequash, Little Rice, Irving, West Plum, Nixon, Aurora, Devine, West Ellerson, Mickey's Mud, Frost, Sand, the Sugarbush Chain, and Rice Lake. If you're interested in harvesting rice, call the Department of Natural Resources to find out which lakes are currently posted.

11

You'll need a permit for harvesting, which covers you and anyone in your immediate family. Note also that rice can only be harvested in nonmotorized canoes that are no longer than 17 feet and no wider than 38 inches.

There are numerous other good ricing sites in our northern counties, where you can harvest without worrying about whether they are posted. Only those lakes listed as requiring a posting must be posted. Keep your eyes open for a rice bed, check with the DNR to determine whether it needs to be posted, then get a license and try your hand at ricing. It's remarkably easy, and a thoroughly pleasant way to spend a few hours on an autumn afternoon.

12

Turtlehead

While we don't usually think of fall as a good time to see wildflowers, many species are still found in abundance along roadsides, in fields, and in marshes. One of my favorites is turtlehead, an oddly shaped, creamy white flower that can easily be imagined as the head of a turtle. However, others have thought it resembled a fish, giving rise to its other common names, "cod-head" and "fish-mouth." Look along wetland edges and stream banks to find it, where it usually grows singly or in a small bunch.

Turtlehead is a member of the snapdragon family. The inch-long flowers are two-lipped and tubular, and the entire plant often stands three feet tall, giving it a rather coarse appearance. The bisexual flowers grow in an unusual spike. The lowest flowers exhibit their final female phase, while the upper, unopened, younger flowers exhibit the pollinating male phase.

Turtlehead is the most important larval food for the Baltimore checkerspot butterfly, a black, orange-spotted butterfly that emerges from hibernation in the spring and feeds on the leaves, eventually laying its eggs on the leaf undersides.

Sumac Colonies

Easily seen on roadsides, staghorn sumac has usually turned a brilliant autumn scarlet by September 15. Enjoy the color display, but also note the shape of each colony of sumacs. Most of them will be tall in the middle and slope off on each side, like a dome. Each dome represents a clonal colony of sumac, with "Mom" in the middle and the younguns spreading on either side. Each individual could be named Junior, since they are all identical.

How and why does sumac do this? While the large, conelike seed structures turn red in the fall and provide plenty of cross-fertilized seeds for next spring's growth, sumac hedges its reproductive bets by cloning itself asexually. Many of its roots eventually bend up and away from "Mom," a process called "root suckering." As each root surfaces, it grows into an adult plant. Because each clone is younger than the original, they become shorter and shorter-hence the camel hump appearance of sumac.

Notice also the great variation in sumac colors. Some have shiny green, butter yellow, vivid orange, flaming red, and deep purple leaves, all on the same shrub. As one author wrote, "Probably no tree in the country, perhaps in the world, may exhibit so many and such contrasting shades and tints, such frosty coolness with its fire."

13

Prairie Vestiges

While driving Upper Midwestern roads in the autumn, keep an eye out for tall, native prairie grasses like big bluestem and Indian grass. I spent a weekend one early September driving around southern Wisconsin, looking at prairie remnant sites. I gradually learned how to identify remnants of the prairie community that once covered two million acres in Wisconsin. Prairie made up 6 percent of the Wisconsin landscape, but only 2,000 acres or so remain, scattered hither and yon. To have seen an original tallgrass prairie in its full magnitude, with waves of ten-foot-tall grasses in which one could get lost, is a vision that's no longer possible in Wisconsin. However, it's one worth dreaming about.

While true prairie was rare in the northwoods, dry sites that are consistently burned or mowed can mimic the habitat conditions of a southern prairie, offering us tiny, prairielike vestiges here and there. Look along Highway 70 west of Minocqua, where some of the tall prairie grasses stretch and flower today.

Bracken Fern

Bracken ferns usually frost off in the last weeks of August or early September, and their brown skeletons lace many highways now. Though they appear dead, they are perennials that will revive with great vigor next spring. Their roots extend some 10 inches deep into the soil, where they are well-protected from excessive cold. They also clone themselves through horizontal rhizomes in order to produce large colonies. Expect their resurrection in May.

Portage Trails

14

One of the requirements for becoming a French voyageur was the inability to swim. It seems the fur companies didn't want anyone abandoning the canoes when the waters got threatening. What better way to keep your crew on board than to guarantee their death if they gave up the ship?

The fur traders used our lake area extensively for travel until the middle 1800s. The remarkable fact that 20 percent of the land surface of Vilas County is water--a percentage exceeded by just three other areas in the world--helped make this area a veritable switchyard of canoe trails. Most of these trails are long since obliterated, but their whereabouts are reasonably well-documented in the original surveyor records, and in the assorted maps and writings of the first traders and explorers to visit our area. We should mark these old trails and clear them again wherever possible. When Mary and I have walked on old portage trails that are preserved in the western part of the state, we have felt a unique reverence and excitement seldom experienced on less historically significant sites. One way to breathe life into our history is to bring back the trails that the native people once followed. By literally walking in their footsteps, we might better understand the world from their perspective.

Biodiversity Issues

My family and I enjoy fall hiking in the old-growth, state natural area between Star Lake and Plum Lake in Vilas County. The amount of deer browsing on the maple and hemlock seedlings in this area is always dramatic. The vast majority of seedlings are dead, though hemlock reproduction is unaccountably strong in a number of areas. Still, we always wonder what this stand will look like in a few centuries, when the mature trees topple and few seedlings of the old-growth hemlock are available to reproduce themselves.

This stand of trees covers more than 560 acres, which means it's probably the largest old-growth stand left in the state. Yet its size can't protect it from the appetite of overwintering deer, which yard up here in years of heavy snow. The reach of deer into this old-growth stand is only part of the problem that must be faced if we are to protect the biodiversity of the stand. The taller trees in the natural area are unprotected from the wind by the much smaller trees around them, and so are subject to being toppled by a major storm.

15

To protect the biodiversity of natural areas, we need large blocks of intact ecosystems in order to ensure survival. Whether the ecosystems are prairies, coastal rain forests, sand dune communities, or old-growth stands, we must set aside larger blocks of each community than we have generally done to date.

The decline of interior woodland bird species has been well-documented in recent years. Unless forest stands are large enough, edge species like blue jays and cowbirds can fly into the interior of a forest and devastate the reproductive success of deep-forest birds. Until this era of forest fragmentation, these birds had never needed to evolve defenses against such aggressive species.

To keep larger blocks of forest whole, I have come to endorse a concept I never believed I would endorse. In order to preserve biodiversity and still harvest timber-types like aspen, which require clear-cutting, we may have to concentrate our clear-cut areas into large blocks. Our current practice of clear-cutting small patches of forest creates the fragmenting effect, making rich habitat for species that live on the edges of forests and fields. If we wish to maintain stands of hemlock, cedar, and Canadian yew, all of which are like candy for deer, and if we wish to maintain birds of the interior like ovenbirds and various warblers and thrushes, we need to rethink how we log our forests. If this change is to occur, foresters and wildlife managers must work more closely together on songbird species we haven't considered important in the past.

One major difficulty will lie in convincing the hunters that we have far too many deer, in large part due to our fragmentary forestry practices. Another difficulty will involve convincing the public that clear-cutting, which must be done to continue production of aspen, should be done in larger blocks, even though clear-cutting is an aesthetic nightmare.

In order to maintain ecosystems in their natural condition, another concern that must be addressed is the maintenance of dead trees. Eighty-five species of North American birds are dependent for nesting in cavities in old trees. Contrary to most current advice, I argue that families using wood heat should cut live trees for firewood, leaving the dead behind for use as cavity trees. While considered unsightly by some, the wildlife value of these "snag" trees is exceptionally high, and their gradual breakdown into the soil adds nutrients to the system. The community of insects that helps break down fallen trees is also a rich source of food for many woodland animals.

What Are We Seeking?

It's the time of year when what's left of the garden harvest is frantically gathered in before the first night of hard frost. Giving up the garden for the next seven months of winter is hard on many people. Minnesota writer Paul Gruchow asked the following question in one of his essays: "Why is gardening the most widely practiced hobby in the United States? When you can't resist planting a few peas in the backyard on the first warm day of spring, what is it that you crave? Peas?"

I would ask an analogous question: What is it that the 60 million feeders of birds in the United States crave? Another sighting of a black-capped chickadee?

I don't believe we seek peas or chickadees. Instead, we seek something much larger. There is a sense of loss within us that seems best filled by interacting with wild things and experiencing the beauty they represent. While no amount of natural beauty will fulfill us completely, I am convinced that it is a component of life we cannot do without. The discovery that we are part of a living, mostly non-human community has value and purpose in itself; it often leads to a necessary loss of personal importance, which is the first step to gaining acceptance into the larger natural community. I find it a concept difficult to articulate, but easier to experience. Feeding birds and growing gardens put us in

16

touch with natural beauty, giving us a consistent connection with the natural world--a connection that our technological society obliterates.

So while gathering the harvest of another year's garden this fall, give some thought to the other factors, besides a good salad, that draw you into the garden.

The Larynx of the Wind

There is no natural sound I enjoy more than the wind in tall pines. John Eastman wrote in *Natural History* magazine: "Pine is the larynx of the wind. No other trees unravel, comb, and disperse moving air so thoroughly . . . They are the receiving stations to which all winds check in, filtering out their loads of B-flats and F-minors, processing auditory debris swept from all corners of the world."

Only wind in pines can at different moments soothe me, inspire me, or send chills along my spine.

September Musings

People need beauty as well as bread.
—John Muir

Night Sky

Astronomy is a means of communing with nature on the grandest scale. You can cover with your fingernail a cluster of 500 galaxies, each of which is of similar size to the Milky Way. The light reaching us tonight from most stars is so old that it has been traveling since the time of our dinosaurs. While I find a world that's more than large enough to study right here in the northwoods, I don't believe anything can stretch the mind like the study of the night sky.

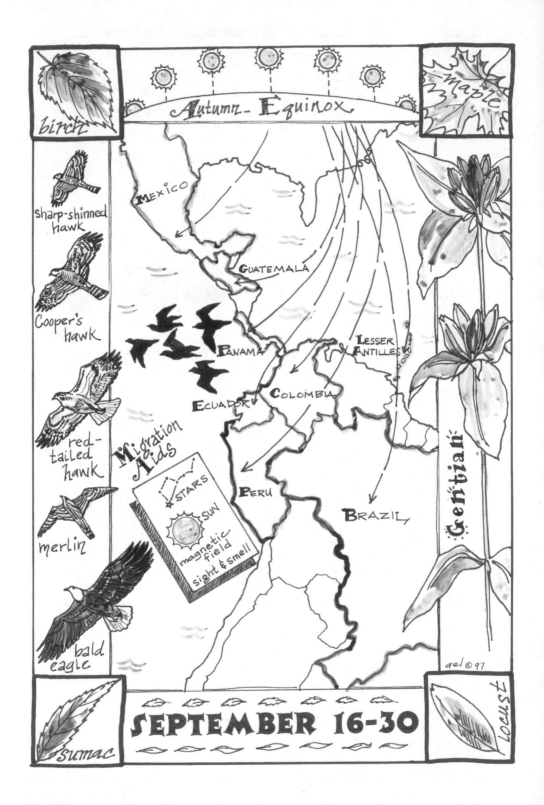

Autumn Equinox

birch

maple

MEXICO

GUATEMALA

sharp-shinned hawk

Cooper's hawk

PANAMA

LESSER ANTILLES

ECUADOR

COLOMBIA

red-tailed hawk

Migration Aids

STARS

SUN

magnetic field

sight & smell

PERU

BRAZIL

merlin

Gentian

bald eagle

ael © 97

sumac

locust

SEPTEMBER 16-30

September 16 to September 30

Equinox

Autumn equinox occurs on or about September 21st, marking the official beginning of fall. On this day the sun rises and sets precisely in the east and west. From this day forward, the sun will rise south of due east on the horizon until the sun pendulum swings back during the spring equinox in March.

The fall equinox was once a time of great celebration; the harvest was in, and the winter posed grimly on the horizon. But we are less in tune with such cycles these days. We pay little heed to natural events unless they have a direct impact on our lives. Whether we pay attention or not, winter is on the march, and the shorter days and longer nights signal its advance.

Wintering Sites of Wisconsin Migrators

Where do the birds that breed in Wisconsin go during the winter? An article in the Fall 1990 issue of *The Passenger Pigeon,* the journal of the Wisconsin Society of Ornithology, describes where Wisconsin's 133 neotropical migrants overwinter. "Neotropical" refers to regions south of 25° North, including both Central and South America.

The majority of Wisconsin neotropical migrants winter from central Mexico to central Colombia and eastern Venezuela; southern Mexico hosts the highest number of wintering species. If you aren't up on your

Late-September Musings

Out of the clouds I hear . . . the honk of geese, invisible, but coming on. The flock emerges from the low clouds, a tattered banner of birds, dipping and rising, blown up and blown down, blown together and blown apart, but advancing, the wind wrestling lovingly with each winnowing wing. When the flock is a blur in the far sky I hear the last honk, sounding taps for the summer.

—Aldo Leopold

geography, Colombia and Venezuela are in the northern regions of South America. Thus most of our neotropical migrants are not dependent on the areas most associated with tropical forest clearing, such as Brazil. In order to find explanations for the declining numbers of Wisconsin's neotropical migrants, it appears we should look instead for environmental changes in both Wisconsin and the northern neotropics.

We know where some of "our" birds winter. The least flycatcher suns in southern Mexico to northern Colombia, while the veery winters wholly within South America, south into Paraguay. The upland sandpiper pushes down into Bolivia, southern Brazil, and Argentina. Returns of bands on ospreys breeding in Wisconsin over the last 24 years (25 out of 554 bands were returned during that time) show ospreys wintering in Ecuador, Colombia, Panama, Brazil, Peru, Guatemala, and the Lesser Antilles.

Some birds seem positively masochistic in their choice of winter homes. The blackpoll warbler, a Canadian breeder, flies four days nonstop over the Atlantic Ocean, until it reaches Antigua in the West Indies. That's 2,000 miles without a rest. One naturalist compared such a feat to human efforts, finding this flight equivalent to running 1,200 consecutive four-minute miles.

Most of our neotropical, insect-eating birds--sparrows, vireos, thrushes, wrens, warblers, orioles, and others--migrate at night. Experiments with indigo buntings revealed that they get their bearings by using prominent stars and northern constellations, including the Big Dipper, the North Star, and Cassiopeia. Buntings raised in labs without a view of the night sky aren't able to navigate by the stars. Night migrators apparently imprint on star patterns when they're young, then use that information later when they migrate.

Daytime migrators like crows, doves, swifts, swallows, herons, geese, ducks, loons, hawks, and gulls orient themselves by using the sun's position as a compass. They also have an internal clock to compensate for the sun's movement throughout the day. In an experiment with starlings, a stationary light was substituted for the sun. The birds' bearing shifted 15 degrees per hour, in exact correspond-ence with the expected movement of the sun across the sky.

Then there are those experiments that simply defy explanation, no matter how good the navigational systems. Eighteen albatrosses were captured on the Midway Islands in the Pacific Ocean, and were transported to places like the Hawaiian Islands, Japan, the Philippines, and the coast of Washington. Fourteen of those birds returned to their nests, one of them traveling 4,120 miles across unfamiliar territory to reach its home!

Migration Dates

Migration is in full swing for many birds now, while other birds have not yet to begin preparations. There's a phenology for autumn migration, just as there is for wildflowers in the spring. I've culled the following bird migration departure dates from Dick Verch's book, *Chequamegon Bay Birds*. Because Chequamegon Bay is in the Ashland area, the dates should hold reasonably true for the northern Wisconsin region. Here's a partial list of those birds that have just departed, or will be departing in the next few weeks:

21

Species	*Departure Time*
black tern	leaves by September 1
brown thrasher	uncommon to see in September
Canada goose	third week September, peaks mid-October
catbird	gone by end of September
chipping sparrow	mid-August to mid-September
common loon	begins mid-September, peaks mid-October
common merganser	early September, peaks early October
coot	late August, peaks mid-October
flicker	mid-September to mid-October
great blue heron	many gone by September 1, but may stay into October
hooded merganser	mid-September, peaks early November
junco	mid-September, peaks mid-October
killdeer	mid-September to mid-October
kingfisher	mid-September to late October
kinglet	early September to end of October
mallard	mid-September, peaks mid-October
pied-billed grebe	mid-September, most gone by mid-October
red-eyed vireo	mid-September
robin	mid-September to early November

Species	Departure Time
rose-breasted grosbeak	begins early September, gone by end of month
ruby-throated hummingbird	mid- to late September
spotted sandpiper	mid-September
warblers (most species)	begin mid-August
woodcock	September to mid-October

Some birds are long gone already--like upland sandpipers, which began migrating in late July and are seldom seen after August 17. Nighthawks are usually departed by late August. Swallows and martins should all be gone by now, as well as Nashville warblers and redstarts (most gone by September 1); mourning warblers (early August); indigo buntings (no sightings recorded after August 17); and northern orioles (no sightings after September 1).

There are other birds whose departure date Dr. Verch isn't certain about, including whip-poor-wills, green-winged teal, American bitterns, kingbirds, winter wrens, sedge wrens, and a host of warblers such as chestnut-sided, black-throated green, magnolia, and yellow. Any information you can offer on the departure dates of these species would be much appreciated. Drop me a note or call, and I'll pass the information up the line.

Later Migrations

Here are more migration dates to begin noting over the next few weeks:

Species	Departure Time
black duck	end of September to early November
blue-winged teal	late September to mid-October
cedar waxwing	by October 1, but may remain later
red-headed woodpecker	late September
ring-necked duck	October 1 to mid-November
saw-whet owl	late September
scaup	October 1, peaks November 1
song sparrow	September, but seen into December

22

Species	_Departure Time_
white-crowned sparrow	mid-September to end of October
wood duck	end of September to end of October
yellow-bellied sapsucker	late September to late October

Disclaimers

Good friend that she is, Carol Christensen called to let me know she had seen a great blue heron on White Sand Lake on September 19. I had written that they were usually gone by September 1. Carol's call reminded me why I should emphasize the following sayings: Never say never and never say always. Most great blue herons *are* gone by September 1, but stragglers may remain all the way into mid-December if the weather stays mild and the marshes remain open. I've noticed that our wild residents don't religiously read my writing. They have this habit of acting independently, ignoring my predictions. So please take these dates with a grain of salt.

Why Flock?

A number of bird species are flocking together in preparation for the migration south. Individual birds of species like blackbirds, geese, and sandhill cranes now happily socialize. They have lost the territorial aggressiveness that was evident earlier in the year, when they fought and postured over a small piece of marsh or a cluster of trees. This change in philosophy reminds me of watching football players hugging each other and telling stories after a game, as if they hadn't been trying to tear each other's heads off just a few minutes earlier.

It's assumed that flocking helps birds find food through the group's collective effort, and that flocking helps assure the safety of individuals by shielding them within a large group. Though this gregariousness is not fully understood, the extra sets of eyes and ears certainly must help identify food and predators. Flocking is also thought to increase feeding efficiency, because flocks can usually overcome the territorial defenses of individual birds.

A study in two Ohio woodlots attempted to test the theory that flocking is related to the amount of available food. The more food, the less flocking should take place, according to the theory. Researchers left one woodlot undisturbed, but stocked the other with sunflower seeds and suet. Far fewer birds of different species flocked together in the stocked stand, supporting the theory that the species flock together in order to increase feeding efficiency.

Within the flock, individuals seem to lose their identity and behave in the same way as the other individuals, a process called "social facilitation." For example, when one bird utters an alarm cry and flies away, all of the birds follow instantly. Flocks of shorebirds and blackbirds are so tuned in to the group mind that they often fly only a few inches apart, synchronously twisting and turning in flight as if they knew one another's thoughts. It's a remarkable aerial ballet arranged around a spontaneous reaction, and it may be the best improvisational theater one could ever watch.

Sometimes the flocking appears elastic and responsive to the situation. One observer watched a flock of 25 cedar waxwings being pursued by a Cooper's hawk. Every time the hawk made a pass at the waxwings and was about to seize an individual, the previously loose formation suddenly tightened up, forcing the hawk to veer away. Eventually the hawk gave up and flew off. Flocks of starlings will ball up in the same manner when attacked by a peregrine falcon. Because the falcon could hurt itself trying to dive through a bunched-up flock, it seldom tries to take one of the starlings.

Kettles and Funnels

Many hawks have begun migrating south. Mid-September is the prime migration time for broad-winged and sharp-shinned hawks, plus American kestrels, merlins, and peregrine falcons. Broad-wings tend to "kettle," meaning that they fly together in large, circular formations often numbering in the hundreds. The other hawks usually migrate singly, darting along at fairly low altitudes.

Duluth's Hawk Ridge is the primary midwestern fall migration route that the hawks funnel through. Record numbers for September sightings there include: nearly 49,000 broad-wings on September 15, 1993; 1,683 sharp-shinneds on September 24, 1993; 545 kestrels on September 3, 1988; 57 merlins on September 16, 1991; and 18 peregrines on September 30, 1988.

The larger hawks, like harriers, goshawks, red-tailed, and rough-leggeds, tend to come through in greatest numbers later in October, though some do migrate over the ridge in September.

Duluth is a funneling point because the North Shore of Lake Superior is so long. It attracts enormous numbers of hawks (and passerines) that are unwilling to fly over the big lake. Once the birds have been forced along the shoreline into Duluth, the high ridge encourages the hawks to come right up the hillside, following the thermals. As a consequence, many fly right at an observer's eye level. If you hit the day right, the numbers are overwhelming, even astonishing.

Hawk Ridge is a nature reserve owned by the City of Duluth and operated by the Duluth Audubon Society. During the fall, the resident naturalist and many other hawk experts from around the country are up on the ridge counting hawks. They're often available to answer questions if you're uncertain about what to look for or what you're seeing.

25

A Good Day On Hawk Ridge

On Sunday, September 17, 1995, the official count reached 26,599 raptors, including:

25,679 broad-winged hawks	13 American kestrels
725 sharp-shinned hawks	9 peregrine falcons
60 red-tailed hawks	8 northern harriers
45 turkey vultures	7 merlins
30 bald eagles	6 Cooper's hawks
14 osprey	1 golden eagle, goshawk, and Swainson's hawk

Many of the kettles of broad-wingeds were quite high as they passed, so observers needed binoculars in order to see them. A few kettles included 250 hawks! Just two days earlier, a group of Lakeland area residents and I had visited Hawk Ridge, but we didn't quite require the calculator necessary on the 17th. A strong southerly wind and light rain grounded the hawks, so we saw a grand total of two during our three-hour vigil. The Great God of Daniel Greysolon, Sieur Du Lhut didn't smile on us that day, but the experience amply demonstrated the principle that observation times are chosen by wildlife, not by humans. If you visit Hawk Ridge this fall--and you really should if you want to see one of the most remarkable bird spectacles in the country—call ahead to get the Duluth weather forecast. The large hawk flights move most consistently when the winds are coming from the northwest and the west. They move less consistently when the winds come from the north and southwest, and generally don't move at all when the wind's out of the south, east, or northeast. The professional bird counters on the ridge hasten to offer the caveat that there are no guarantees. On some days with "good" weather, the hawks may be few, while on some days with "bad" weather, they may stream through.

"Things hoped for have a higher value than things assured," conservationist Aldo Leopold once wrote. We were skunked on that Friday, but we can take solace in the fact that if the hawks were as accessible as animals in a zoo, our appreciation of their spectacle would be greatly dampened. That is the curse and joy of wildlife viewing--we require rarity in order to assign value to our experience, yet seeking rarity ensures that we will often come home with empty hands and unfulfilled visions.

One More Time,
If at First You Don't Succeed...

A year later, September 18, 1996, I was one of 47 intrepid birders who traveled by bus to Hawk Ridge, in hope of witnessing the traditional mid-September migration of hawks. We spent a beautiful, sunny day up on the ridge, but a moderate southeast wind put a lid on our dreams of witnessing large flights. Still, we saw a good diversity of big raptors, including sharp-shinned hawk, Cooper's hawk, red-tailed hawk, rough-legged hawk, merlin, American kestrel, bald eagle, osprey, and turkey vulture. Remarkably, we failed to observe a single broad-winged hawk, although we had arrived hoping to see tens of thousands.

We were not graced with vast numbers, but perhaps that was a partial blessing, because we had time to look at each bird in detail. I was struck by the effortlessness of the hawks' flight, particularly in the face of the headwinds that day. The hawks were still somehow able to find thermals (updrafts of warm air) to ride, and they made their jour-

26

ney south appear almost casual. Some came across the ridge and were gone in a flash, while others sailed above us in a leisurely manner.

If we could have watched their flight over many miles, we would have seen them spending about half their time climbing and the other half gliding. Hawks usually fly at altitudes between 700 and 1,600 feet, ascending a thermal in a series of spiral climbs as if they were winding their way up a watch spring, then power-gliding downward. If a thermal is strong enough, raptors can climb nearly straight up within it. They repeat the process over and over, climbing and then gliding long distances until they must climb again. By late afternoon the air cools, the thermals dissipate, and the hawks land for the night.

27

Hawks can also use the updrafts created when wind is deflected off a ridge. If a ridge is long, hawks are able to glide at right angles to the updrafts. That practice seemed to work well the day we were at Hawk Ridge. The wind was out of the southeast, perpendicular to the ridge, and the hawks were gliding on a southwest tangent.

Sharp-shinned hawks don't need to wait for the thermals. Instead, they may use old-fashioned wing flapping, or what's called "powered flight." Thus they can leave at dawn and fly at low altitudes, regardless of the wind direction or the strength of the thermals. We saw far more sharpies on Hawk Ridge than any other hawk--an indication that they were using the deflected wind off the ridge to make progress, while other hawks were mostly grounded.

Migrating for the First Time

The vast majority of birds don't have a hawk's ability to soar and glide, so most migrate at night and fly by using powered flight (continuous wing flapping) or a variation thereof. Some fly in bounds, winging in short bursts to gain altitude, then descending with their wings folded against their bodies. Warblers, vireos, thrushes, orioles, and small woodpeckers use this method. Others, like crows, large woodpeckers, herons, and some hawks, undulate, flapping several times to climb, then stretching their wings out to glide.

Birds need both a compass and a map. They also have to know how far to go and when to stop in order to get to their wintering site. Young-of-the-year that migrate without their parents are thought to be genetically programmed to migrate in a given direction for a specific period of time. How else could one explain the first migration? Several experiments have verified this theory. For one study, researchers took 11,000 banded adult and immature starlings that were captured in the Netherlands, and transported them to Switzerland during their autumn migration. When released, the immatures ended up in northern Spain, while the adults flew to the northwest coast of France, or continued on to England where they normally winter. The experiment showed that the adults can truly navigate, while the immatures seem to follow an instinctual time and distance formula. Birds that make it into their second year of life have a profound advantage over first-year birds, because they now possess a rudimentary map from which to steer the next autumn.

28

Paul Kerlinger, author of *How Birds Migrate,* theorizes that birds may have three stages of navigation. The first stage is the innate, time-distance program utilized by young-of-the-year. The second stage may involve the use of magnetic or olfactory cues, which direct the bird once it is within several hundred miles of its destination. The third stage may include the use of topographic features as a road map for getting to the bird's winter home.

Shorebird Stitching

The last of the shorebirds should be through our area by mid-September. One naturalist said about sandpipers, "Their running feet (are) a constant stitching of the sea and land."

The Tabasco Cure

Harriet Woods of Minocqua wrote me one fall, reporting that she had a squirrel eating the paint off her garage door and wondering what she could do to discourage the little beast. A later note from Harriet indicated that a new paint job and a liberal dose of Tabasco pepper sauce on the area had driven the squirrel away. All's well, then, as long as it doesn't return someday with a bunch of friends, a bag of chips, and a quart of tequila.

Practice Makes Perfect

I received a call in mid-September from a woman who had been watching two bucks and a doe in her backyard when one of the bucks and the doe began mating. The caller wanted the answer to the obvious question of what they were up to, given that deer don't usually begin reproductive activity until later in October. The answer? They were practicing. Bucks attempt to establish dominance at this time of year, and while no actual mating takes place, their exhibitions demonstrate which of them may be the most capable when the real season begins.

29

Falling Leaves

Autumn leaves turn color and eventually fall to the ground, based on the declining length of daylight (called the photoperiod), the temperature, and the amount of available moisture. Warm and wet conditions in August and early September team up to encourage the trees to hang onto their leaves later than usual. From a tree's standpoint, why drop your leaves if it's warm and moist enough to photosynthesize? Indeed, some broadleaf trees in tropical climates never lose their leaves, because there's no point in doing so. On the other hand, a cold, dry spell will rapidly stimulate autumn colors, and a strong wind will drop the fragile leaves.

If you're interested in traveling to see fall foliage, the U.S. Forest Service maintains a fall color hotline. You can reach it by dialing 1-800-354-4595.

Closed Gentians

One of the very last of the woodland wildflowers comes into bloom in September--the bottle (or closed) gentian. The unique, deep blue petals stay closed in a shape akin to a bottle, but the bottle can be opened. Mary and I watched a bee land on top of one of the blossoms. The bee forced its way in for some nectar, performing a little pollination service during its visit.

The Art of Seeing

Ezra Pound once observed that "Genius is the ability to see ten things where most people see only one." I'm unaccustomed to quibbling with the likes of Ezra Pound, but I'm not so sure seeing is a matter of genius. To me, keen observation is a matter of paying attention. A summer woods may be a sensory blur to many, but to the botanist it is a wealth of plant species. The cutaway bank along a roadside may appear to be so much dirt and rock to a motorist, but to a geologist it offers a revelation of glacial travel. Likewise, the morning spring cacophony of birdsong is a lot of noise to the late sleeper, but it presents a symphony of individual musical instruments, easily identified and enjoyed, by the avid birder. The night sky provokes fear and darkness in the average urbanite, but it offers an ordered composite of stars, galaxies, nebulas, and black holes to the trained eye of the astronomer.

It's a simple axiom: The more you pay attention, the more you see and eventually know. And the more you know, the more you realize how *little* you know, and therefore the more you need to pay attention. So the cycle of discovery continues. Lord knows how many times I've made the most obvious of discoveries right under my feet, then reeled in amazement at my own natural illiteracy, at the recognition of how much I miss every day and every minute because I haven't taken the time to truly see. Helen Keller wrote that "The worst thing in life is a person who has sight, but no vision." How many of us, in whatever endeavors we undertake, pay enough attention to find actual vision?

Wilderness

Jim dale Vickery, the author of *Open Spaces,* writes that in time he has learned to "judge his standard of living not by what he has, but by the quality and size of open space around him." He believes that wilderness is a gift to the spirit--not a luxury, but a necessity. Open spaces, he writes, are "not superfluous playgrounds, but commonly held homes for the needy freedoms of man."

Those of us who live in the northwoods--and those who can only visit here--do so to transform ourselves, to be awakened, to see the world with less shadow and more clarity. Vickery asks in his writing,

"Does a person ever lose the trees, animals, skies, and sunrises of his or her outdoor hours? Or do these things forever provide us with a living mosaic of natural beauty which nourishes awe, if not hope, during mankind's sometimes grim search for meaning?"

Vickery believes in the intrinsic value of outdoor experience, and so do I. Lands and lakes without homes on them, without obvious signs of continual human use, are places I seek out, places where solitude and historical context can momentarily be touched.

The Northern Highlands/American Legion State Forest, found within Iron, Vilas, and Oneida counties, contains 902 lakes, totaling over 50,000 acres and comprising 9 percent of all the lakes in Wisconsin. Oneida County includes 1,132 lakes totaling 69,874 acres; Vilas County has 1,321 lakes (the most of any county in Wisconsin) totaling 92,232 acres. Even though ski slopes are found in its northern half, Iron County still contains 494 lakes, accounting for 29,368 acres of water. In the three-county area then, 2,947 lakes cover 191,474 acres.

Only 19 of these lakes, covering 3,664 acres, are designated as wilderness lakes, and all are within the Northern Highlands Forest. In other words, less than 2 percent of the total acreage of water in the three counties is wilderness; only 0.6 percent of the lakes are so designated.

I believe this is too little to meet our needs for wilderness and the needs of the flora and fauna, which have so little voice in this political debate. The question of wilderness set-asides comes down to the heavily value-laden question of how much wilderness is enough. To arrive at an answer, we must ask whose value system shall be used as the measuring stick. Should we respond to the 59 percent of the people who, in a 1986 DNR recreational survey, said they had gone fishing in the last 12 months? Should we listen to the 58 percent who had gone on nature hikes? How about the 32 percent who had gone hunting, or the 32 percent who had been out canoeing or kayaking? What about the 19 percent who snowmobiled, or the 76 percent who just walked for pleasure?

My value system says we don't have enough wilderness lakes. The NH/AL State Forest is visited by over a million people every year; 19 lakes are intended to serve the needs of the 32 percent of visitors who kayak and the 58 percent who fish, many of whom desire an experience apart from jet-skis and 100-horsepower bass boats.

Here is one vote for maintaining more areas where homes, logging, and motors are prohibited.

31

The Incongruity of Jet-Skis

New Hampshire has implemented an outright ban on the use of personal watercraft on lakes that are 75 acres or smaller. Sections of some larger New Hampshire lakes are also off-limits to jet-skis.

"People regarded jet-skis as intrusions on their lakes and intrusions on the silence," said Charles Knox, a spokesman for the New Hampshire Department of Environmental Services. "Having these machines on ponds seemed incongruous with the reason most people visited these areas."

32

In the meantime, Wisconsin townships must one by one draft ordinances to try to control these mechanical mosquitoes.

September Musings

Leaves are rustling below and above. As is true sometimes in higher circles, they seem to grow loquacious with age; the slightest occasion, the merest nudge of suggestion, the faintest puff of the spirit sets them off. For me they will never talk too much. I love their preaching seven days in the week. The driest of them never teased my ears with a dry sermon.

—Bradford Torrey

OCTOBER

The Ojibwe word for October is *binakwegizis,* meaning "the month of the rake or comb." If I had to pick my favorite two months of the year, I'd choose May and October. May takes first place because it presides over the extraordinary life-awakening metamorphosis that the northwoods undergoes after a long winter. But October comes in a close second. October acts as the flip side to May, sending birds scooting back south, and finalizing much of the botanical world's work for the season in a truly glorious finale--another metamorphosis. It's a fireworks display far more tuned to my sensibilities than a Fourth of July celebration. October's leaf-fall is a celebration of another season of life successfully composed and performed, the final concert orchestrated in carpets of color.

I like, too, the transformation that each plant species offers in its autumn departure. For instance, in summer I don't perceive blackberry, maple, and hazelnut leaves as unusually beautiful. In autumn, though, the understory of red blackberry leaves is brilliant among the taller, golden hazelnut shrubs, and both are overarched by red or sugar maples, each maple expressive in shades ranging from yellow to orange to scarlet. I am forced to reexamine my perception of each species. There's far more here than I had realized in early summer. Not only is autumn a visually stunning performance piece, but the artwork serves important ecological functions, laying the groundwork for the forest community to thrive next spring after winter quiescence.

October also has qualities that apply purely to humans. The cool air allows me to bring out the clothes I favor most, like flannel shirts and heavy jeans (I've never been a shorts kind of guy). You can work or play hard in October without suffering from the heat. The insufferable mosquitoes have returned to their aquatic ways; the tables are finally turned, and they are now the ones subject to predators. We build our first woodfires and again smell woodsmoke. And the Indian summer days are truly appreciated as gifts, because we know what's on the horizon. The feel of October transcends most of our words. It's a time of transition when the trees and shrubs give us the best of both the aesthetic and practical worlds. For that we should be out every day, giving our thanks.

33

AMERICAN BEECH

Black-
eyed
Susan
Mabel
Eileen

Stream
Ecology

OCTOBER 1-15

October 1 to October 15

Color Season

Here's your handy-dandy northwoods roadside guide to identifying fall foliage colors at 55 miles per hour:

Reds
- red maple
- sumac
- silver maple
- red oak (turning brown)
- maple-leaved vibernum
- blackberry
- dogwood

Yellows/Golds
- birch
- aspen
- sugar maple (may be orange)
- elm
- ash
- tamarack

October Musings

I don't believe there is a wind that has more responsibilities than one conceived in autumn ... Some folks would disagree, claiming that the winds of March carry the greater load of chores... But it is in the fall that the winds most need to hurry and get their jobs done. The passengers on these winds are many. Sailing away are summer's dreams, while winter's promise rides the same wind.

—Tom Anderson

Oaks and ironwoods will hold onto their leaves all winter, so look for their raggedy brown leaves rustling in the December winds.

Early hard frosts don't improve coloration as some believe; rather, these cold spells can injure or kill the leaves before they reach full color production. Cool evening temperatures, like 45°F, help bring out color by slowing the movement of sugars from the leaves to other parts of the tree. The sugars help increase the formation of anthocyanin, which produces the red color in leaves.

But any explanation of autumn leaves begs the point. Fall colors are on the verge, the air is crisping up, the groundlayer is dying back. It's a time to be out walking.

Preserving Autumn Color

My wife Mary gathered a beautiful "bouquet" of autumn leaves for our table, but within a day or two the leaves had wilted so badly that we had to toss them out. So I called Medicine Man Joe, a friend and pharmacist from Minocqua, for his glycerin trick, which is supposed to keep leaves looking spunky for a week or two. Joe advises taking a small hammer, laying the branch and leaves on a newspaper, and pulverizing the base of the branch to which the leaves are attached (don't use branches bigger than one-eighth of an inch—these are thin branches, not firewood). Beat the bottom several inches of the branch flat, then immerse the branch end in a vase containing a mixture of one part glycerin (available at any pharmacy) and two parts hot tap water. The flattened branch will increase the surface area of the stem, allowing the glycerin to be absorbed more easily into the leaves. The leaves should now stay pliable much longer, although they may undergo a slight color change. Joe refuses to guarantee how long the leaves will keep, saying it depends on variables such as how dry your house is, whether you picked leaves on a dry day or a wet day, how quickly you get the leaf into the solution, and so forth. Give it a try--the brilliant colors of October are worth preserving.

Rake or Mulch?

Many people start to rake their yards as the autumn leaves begin to accumulate. Why not put a mulching blade on your lawn mower, and mulch your leaves into your soil? The nutrient cycle was meant to be completed, not circumvented by raking, bagging, and removing. Do your back and your soil a favor this fall, and keep the leaves where they belong.

Working Soil

Forest hikes are all the more beautiful now, due to the sometimes brilliant, sometimes subtle carpet of downed leaves, courtesy of all the rain and wind that usually occurs in the first week of October. While the leaves heighten the color of forest trails, one of their functions is, of course, to improve soil conditions. But not all leaves provide equal benefits. Maples store few nutrients in their roots over winter, choosing instead to pump nutrients into their leaves prior to leaf-fall; hence they are designated as "nutrient pumpers."

On the other hand, oaks store their nutrients in their roots throughout the winter, making their leaves nutrient-poor when they fall. Oak leaves decompose very slowly, usually taking several years to break down fully due to their high acid (or tannin) content.

Hemlock needles are worse yet. In fact, the fall rain of hemlock needles actually *degrades* the soil through a process called "podzolization," which results in leaching out of nutrients and acidification of the soil. Bacteria, the primary decomposers of the leaf litter, don't like acid conditions, so decomposition takes place very slowly beneath hemlocks.

Oak leaves and conifer needles create a "mor" humus, a surface groundlayer characterized by low bacteria populations, high fungi populations (fungi are slower decomposers than bacteria), low earthworm numbers, low nutrient content, highly acidic conditions, and a mat of leaves.

Nutrient pumpers like maple create a "mull" humus, characterized by high populations of bacteria, earthworms, and other soil organisms, and well-mixed, granular leaf particles.

Thus the leaf litter of different forest communities creates very different groundlayers. The original settlers of the northwoods didn't know "mull" from "mor," but they surely knew that the forest to clear for the new farmstead was maple, not pine, oak, or hemlock.

Leaves also improve the soil structure. Fifty percent of an ideal soil is composed of air spaces. Decomposing leaves are cemented into particles called "crumbs," which provide a host of air channels. These channels allow oxygen to reach the roots, allow water to percolate through the surface down to the roots, and they make movement easier for earthworms and other soil organisms. Not only does the water percolate down better, but it is also absorbed better by the loose soil.

The groundwater is then gradually released over time. This slow release greatly contrasts with the feast and famine approach that characterizes a compacted soil like hard clay. Rainwater runs off the clay surface in sheets. It is deposited into the nearest stream, often carrying the top layer of soil with it if the soil is exposed directly to the rain. A forest leaf layer shields the soil from direct runoff and high temperatures, and it slows evaporation, which helps seedlings survive.

We lament autumn in many ways because it represents the end of the luxuriant life we enjoy in summer, but without autumn leaf-fall, the nutrient well would soon run dry and the forest floor would repeatedly wash away.

Stream Ecology

In the water-rich northwoods, what happens to leaves that fall into a stream? The leaves are broken down through a rather fascinating process. A stream not only transports leaves downstream, but along the way, a progression of specialized aquatic insects and decomposers (fungi and bacteria) processes them, until the leaves have been effectively recycled.

A leaf is first chewed into smaller pieces by a "shredder" insect, such as a cranefly or various caddisfly larvae. The smaller leaf parts are then worked on by bacteria and fungi, and begin to decompose. The smaller particles are then filtered out and further reduced in size by "collector" insects like black fly larvae and some mayfly larvae. Or the smaller leaf particles may be eaten off rocks and logs by "scraper" insects, including water penny beetles and the "water boatman," a water bug with long, oarlike legs. By the combined efforts of all these insects and the decomposition work of bacteria and fungi, the leaves eventually are fully broken down.

The three categories of insects--shredders, collectors, and scrapers--not only help recycle leaves, but they also serve as prey for various other aquatic insects like stonefly, damselfly, alderfly, and dragonfly larvae, as well as larger predators such as frogs, turtles, and fish.

Small headwater streams usually contain high numbers of shredders. Here the initial work of breaking down full-size leaves begins. The small streams flow into larger streams, which flow into small rivers, which flow into large rivers…you get the idea. As rivers widen and slow down, the community of aquatic insects changes from shredders to a population dominated by collectors and scrapers, which process the fine leaf particles created by the shredders into even smaller particles. A family of insects like caddisflies may include individual species that perform in each feeding category. In other words, certain species of caddisflies act as shredders, others are collectors, while still others are scrapers.

Unlike forest communities, which in the same area undergo successional changes over time, a natural stream community remains stable in any given area. The stream's insect community instead changes predictably along its entire length, as the stream becomes wider and slower.

39

Aquatic stream communities assimilate most deciduous leaves rather quickly. Acidic conifer needles are processed more slowly, as are oak leaves, because of their high tannin content. Leaves that contain tannic acid, including oak, hemlock, and tamarack, stain the waters brown--hence the root beer coloration of many local streams and lakes. The pH of the water is also affected by the tree species that live along the banks of the stream. Maples will decompose rapidly, and are more neutral; pines will decompose slowly and increase the acidity of the water. Thus, if you want to learn about the water quality of a river, lake, or stream, look first to the forest community (or lack thereof) that feeds the water community. The character of the entire watershed has a profound impact on the quality of the water.

Hazelnut

Mary and I often mountain bike into the pine uplands of the Manitowish River Wilderness Area. The old trails have grown up into blackberry and hazel brush, so we usually have to leave our bikes behind to follow the paths. Hazelnut and pine must enjoy one another's company, because the hazel is a virtual monotype beneath the pine. At times, we have to "swim" our way through the hazel switches to make any progress. With difficulty, I have pulled up the roots of hazelnut brush and found a thick, horizontal stem that led straight to its neighbor. The neighbor, I discovered, was similarly attached to its neighbor--and on they went, holding hands beneath the soil and interlacing branches above the soil. This low, dense growth form offers good cover and nesting sites for birds. Hazel also provides a great deal of food for various animals. Squirrels and chipmunks eat the nuts; grouse eat the catkins (the flowers); rabbits, deer, and moose browse the whole plant.

The leaves turn a pale yellow at this time of year, but their beauty is offset by their branches, which often whip unsuspecting hikers across the face. The stems also play havoc with snowshoes in the winter, so Mary and I avoid snowshoeing amidst this ubiquitous shrub whenever we can.

Hardy Black-Eyed Susans

A number of flowers remain in bloom in October, unfazed by frost and "old age" as measured in flower time. They offer an impressive display of hardiness. Still blooming in places are ox-eye daisy, hawkweed, aster, goldenrod, yarrow, purple knapweed, clover, bladder campion, and even dandelion.

Black-eyed Susans still light up many an open roadside or field. The center "eye" is rarely black, although it turns blackish after it goes to seed. The common name should really be brown-eyed Susan--or maybe brown-eyed Mabel or Eileen. I've yet to come across an explanation for the honoring of someone named Susan. If anyone can tell me the origin of the name, I'd like to know.

The black-eyed Susan is a cousin of the ox-eye daisy. However, the daisy originated elsewhere, while the black-eyed Susan is native to prairies in the U.S. It was supposedly transported to this area in hay from western clover fields. As a biennial, it forms a rosette of leaves in the first year only, then produces its flower in the second year.

Beech Trees

One October weekend, I traveled through the eastern Upper Peninsula of Michigan. While hiking, I did several double takes at the sight of a tree I'd forgotten I would find in that region. It was American beech, and it was abundant. The tree's smooth, gray bark and jagged leaves are a dead giveaway for identification purposes--particularly in older forests, where beech benefits from the shaded habitat it tolerates so well.

Beech is found as far west as the Wisconsin counties along Lake Michigan and Green Bay, and throughout most of the U.P. It's absent from the westernmost counties, and it hasn't quite made it into north central Wisconsin. It may well get here in time, but time appears to be the key. The rather limited distribution of beech in the Midwest (it is found throughout the East) has to do with Wisconsin's last glacial retreat. After the ice sheets had withdrawn, the denuded landscape began its healing. At first the climate and the landscape resembled Arctic tundra, with lichens and mosses, stunted willow, and birch. As the climate warmed, spruces and sedges gradually replaced the Arctic communities, and the forests resembled the boreal forests found today in Canada. In fact, little fingers of boreal forest still reach into Wisconsin. As warming continued, habitats that were once covered by mile-thick ice sheets regained oak, pine, and maple, and the northwoods took on more of its current appearance.

41

However, beech never extended its range beyond the easternmost counties of Wisconsin. Botanists calculate that beech re-invaded New York state some 7,000 years ago, then worked its way west through slow seed distribution to Wisconsin, arriving in our state some 3,000 years ago. Here it has stalled--or at least its movement is so slow that it's barely appreciable.

I hope beech someday finds its way into our region, though I'll need more than a few rounds of reincarnation to see it. We already have more than our share of beauty, but who doesn't wish for more? Beech is as beautiful a tree as any you're likely to meet, and its nuts are highly valuable to wildlife. The now-extinct passenger pigeon once fed extensively upon beechnuts.

Beech isn't the only tree that has trouble extending its range westward through Wisconsin. Eastern hemlock ranges only as far west in Wisconsin as western Sawyer and Bayfield counties, while yellow birch quickly diminishes in abundance as it nears the eastern Minnesota border.

Woodcock

Woodcock hunting takes place in October. I don't hunt them with a rifle, but I often hunt for them with my eyes. Woodcocks have evolved some remarkable adaptations worth appreciating. To find food, they plunge their long bills full-length into wet soil, probing for worms. The upper mandible is flexible and highly sensitive, and the woodcock can apparently feel about for worms, then open the tip of its bill to seize its prey.

The woodcock has a rounded head. Its eyes are placed about where our ears are, allowing them to see in virtually any direction. When the bird is facedown, poking around in the soil, it can still watch for predators behind it.

The woodcock's mottled brown coloration blends perfectly into autumn's fallen leaves. To kick a woodcock up, you nearly have to step on one. Without dogs to flush woodcock, I suspect that hunters would have much less success.

42

More Migration Dates

Many later migrating birds are just starting to migrate through. Watch for the following species, which are presently leaving or will be passing through in the next few weeks:

Species	Departure Time
pintail duck	mid-October
double-crested cormorant	early October
veery	seen until mid-October
hermit thrush	seen until mid-October
palm warbler	late October
fox sparrow	mid-October
snow bunting	first seen in mid-October and may stay
tundra swan	mid-November until freeze-up
snow goose	early October to mid-November
golden-eye	begins October 20, peaks second week of November
bufflehead	begins mid-October, peaks mid-November
snipe	seen into late November
white-throated sparrow	September through mid-November
song sparrow	September through early December
white-crowned sparrow	mid-September through end of October

I saw my first snow buntings one October 12th, on the shores of Lake Superior in Bayfield County. To demonstrate how some birds just can't be pinned down on migration dates, greater yellowlegs begin migrating in mid-July, but may keep filtering through until mid-October. I saw dozens of them, along with thousands of migrating ducks and geese, one October on a variety of lakeshores in the Agassiz National Wildlife Refuge in northwestern Minnesota. During peak migration, 100,000 ducks of a dozen species may funnel through this spectacular refuge.

Of Sieges and Exaltations   43

If you happen to observe bunches of birds of various species this fall, you may be uncertain about whether to call them "flocks," "coveys," or something else. Dorothy Bendrick from Boulder Junction kindly sent me the now-archaic, but correct terms for many species of birds. These wonderfully descriptive terms add a bit of poetry to our otherwise diminishing vocabulary. Here are a few: a *charm* of finches; an *exaltation* of larks; a *murmuration* of starlings; a *murder* of crows; a *siege* of herons; a *staring* of owls; an *unkindness* of ravens; a *whisp* of snipe; and, oddest of all, a *mutation* of thrush. Note the bad rap crows and ravens have suffered in the past--a reputation that they maintain today in the minds of many.

1994 Crane Count

The sandhill crane count in 1994 tallied a record 12,124 sandhills in Wisconsin, up nearly 4,000 from 1993's wildly wind-blown count. Wisconsin's crane count began back in 1982, and the long-term population trend continues to move upward. There have been several "blips" in the annual data. Deviations like the 1993 count demonstrate again the need to collect information for many years before trying to draw any conclusions. Wisconsin, and those who take part in the count, should be proud of this effort. The sandhill crane count is one of the largest single-species surveys done in the entire world.

Beaver Lodging

Water levels are often high in the fall. The Manitowish River may be two feet above normal, creating a floodplain of sorts. I canoed a stretch of the river one October when the water was high, and I thoroughly enjoyed the new access I had into wetland areas that are usually unnavigable. The river channel had lost its definition, in the process gaining an uncertainty, a new identity. This added dimension allowed me to feel a new sense of potential for discovery on a river that I canoe often enough to pretend I "know" it. I'm sure the ducks and geese migrating through, the resident muskrats and beavers, and the river's fish were even more appreciative of the new access to food sources.

I pulled up alongside an active beaver lodge where the inhabitants had been busy creating an underwater cache of branches for winter feeding. Fresh cuts of willow and alder, the leaves still projecting, were stashed under the water with only the surface branches sticking out. The cache was within 10 to 15 feet of the lodge, as most are, providing easy under-the-ice access during the winter.

This lodge was not particularly big, but some are impressive structures. One lodge in Bayfield County, measured in 1919, was 16 feet high by 40 feet wide, with walls four feet thick. A six-foot-tall man was able to stand upright in the interior room. An ordinary lodge is three to five feet high and eight to twenty feet wide. Six or more beavers commonly hole up for the winter in a lodge, so they need relatively large accommodations. The Bayfield County lodge must have been the beaver equivalent of a Holiday Inn.

Beaver populations remain high in the northwoods. When my daughter Callie was four years old, she underwent her preschool screening. When asked to identify a picture of an ambulance, she didn't know what it was. The next morning though, she looked at a book I was using to obtain background information on beavers, and she identified a beaver lodge from a picture. When people ask me why I live in the north country, this story is one of my best answers.

44

I'm Stuck on You

Amour arises among porcupines in October. If you have wondered how porcupines manage to express affection without injuring each other, well, so have I. As a precursor to mating, the male "sings" in a low-pitched meow or a high-pitched falsetto, in an attempt to woo the female. The pair may rub noses and touch each other's face and head with their forepaws as part of the courtship. Eventually they will mate, in a manner similar to other mammals of equal size. Fortunately, the underside of the female's tail does not have quills, so the male can lean against her and proceed without getting "stuck on her."

After mating the female soon loses interest in the male and goes her own way. Seven months later, a single precocial "porcupette" is born with its eyes open and its body well-furred. The porcupette's quills are soft at birth, but they dry and harden within several hours. The mother is protected from injury at birth because the baby emerges headfirst within a birth sac. It will nurse for over three months, but it's quite active and eating solid food after just nine days. The porcupette sets off on its own in the fall, before its mother comes into estrus again.

45

Porcupines: Evolutionary Genius

One October our Siberian husky, Keena, managed to engage a porcupine in combat for the second time in her life. Why she doesn't learn is surely one of the mysteries of life, but we humans also do a fine job of repeating mistakes. So, while I am tempted to compare Keena's brain to a snow pea, I must humbly decline given our species' preeminent status as repeat offenders.

I nevertheless had a few unkind words for her when she loped up to me with a cheek full of quills after one of her five-minute disappearing acts into the woods. I recalled that some enterprising (or insane) person once counted every quill possessed by an adult porkie, arriving at the rounded figure of 30,000. I decided I was actually thankful that Keena didn't empty the whole quill tank upon herself.

But why attack a porcupine in the first place? The average porkie weighs in at 18 pounds; the world record holder weighed 42 pounds! That's not terribly massive, but it's all contained in a short mound that looks like a muskrat hut made from hypodermic needles. The hump bristles like a World War II machine gun nest, so what's the likelihood of biting your way to victory? And how would Pavlov, the dean of behavioral psychology, salivating dogs, and reinforcement theory, explain why dog learning does not take place in the face, as it were, of such negative rewards?

"There's a reason," I said to my dog, "that God and evolution conspired to make a creature's maximum speed just two miles per hour."

"Think before you bite!" I yelled at her. "Think!" But she cowered, not keen on intellectual advancement, interested only in the removal of the barbs that bit her like incessant, sharp puppy teeth. If I didn't pull them out immediately they would sink into her at the rate of a millimeter an hour, due to the fishhook barb at the end of each quill.

46

October Musings

What finer occupation is there in the wide world than that of packing apples of a bright autumn day with a light west wind blowing and scattered white clouds floating fleecily across the deep blue sky?
—John Kieran

They came out easily, but the first time Keena encountered a porcupine I had the pleasure of taking them out of her paws after she had walked a mile back to the house, the quills pushing inward with every step. Those came out with much more difficulty and a lot more whimpering.

Playful Insects?

Longtime Boulder Junction resident Paul Brenner dropped me a note to describe a sighting he had while working in his garden. He wrote: "A large downy seed, probably a Canadian thistle, came floating by. A large dragonfly caught it in the air; almost immediately another dragonfly made him drop it and caught the thistle. Within seconds, the first dragonfly made a pass and made him drop it, too, then picked it up and flew out of my sight."

Paul wondered whether the dragonflies were fighting over what they thought was a large insect, or if perhaps they were "just playing." I'd never considered the possibility that insects could "play," because play is considered a highly evolved behavior characteristic only of higher mammals. I'd be curious what an entomologist would say to the possibility of insect play, though the concept of playful mosquitoes or blackflies is not one I wish to contemplate for too long.

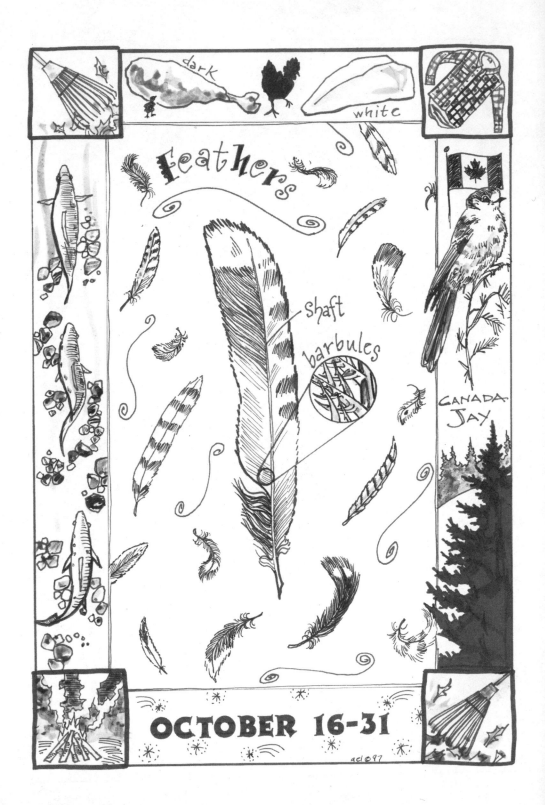

dark

white

feathers

shaft

barbules

CANADA JAY

OCTOBER 16-31

acl©97

October 16 to October 31

Tamarack Gold

By mid-October the bogs have become a muted blaze of dusty gold, courtesy of that confused conifer, the tamarack. In the summer, most of us take little notice of the blue-green of tamarack, as it blends in with the life around it. But in mid- to late October, tamarack offers the final brilliance of an autumn season in decline. All of its needles will soon drop, carpeting the reddish sphagnum moss in gold for a few weeks before winter snows transform the landscape into a white panorama.

No one seems able to explain why tamaracks drop their needles. I have a theory that since tamarack branches don't bend well, they can't tolerate heavy snow loads. So they evolved to minimize the amount of snow they might collect in a winter, a key trait being to lose their snow-holding leaves. Whatever the reason for their deciduous form, tamaracks are perceived as fence-sitters, unable to decide which botanical party to belong to--the conifers, or the deciduous hardwoods. They borrow characteristics from both affiliations, and we are the fortunate recipients of their autumn ambivalence.

Seed Spaceships

The white pines in our yard produced a bounty of cones in 1996. I spent one morning pulling many of the cones apart to collect their seeds. Each scale of the cone contains two single-winged seeds that fit perfectly into indentations within each scale. I nearly sealed my fingers permanently together with all of the pine pitch exuded by the cones, but the effort was worth it. I'll plant some of the seeds inside in pots, and put the other seeds in the freezer to plant some spring, in the understanding that pines may require freezing and thawing of their seeds before they will sprout.

Pines aren't the only trees currently sending out seeds. Much of the plant world is in the midst of sealing itself up for a long winter and simultaneously seeking new worlds. Since the adult plants can't explore new lands themselves, they must send their embryos. The plant usually surrounds its embryos with a large food supply, then protects the embryos with laminations of tissue that will withstand extremes of temperatures, decay, pressure, and soil chemistry. Within those layers are sensors that will detect and respond to the right combination of temperature, light intensity, oxygen and moisture when they occur, and then initiate growth. The plant puts on a final gift wrap over the whole thing. The wrap may be bright, colorful, and sweet-tasting to ecourage travel by way of digestive systems. Or it might be sticky or bristly in order to hitch a ride to another town. Or it might be an aerodynamic appendage like a silk parachute or a winged helicopter. Or it might be a waterproof coating that acts like a PFD and floats the embryo down the lengths of rivers to final deposition on silty shore-lines. Whatever the strategy, it's clear that NASA couldn't have designed a better spaceship than the seeds of most plants.

Once in their new world, the seeds may not germinate for years until their sensors detect the right conditions. Clover and mustard seeds can wait over 50 years in the soil for the ground to be plowed before their "on" button will engage. The plow kills competition, opens the ground to sunlight, and churns in oxygen.

How long can seeds remain viable? An alpine vetch (pea family) seed was found in a fossil rodent burrow deep in the permafrost, and was radiocarbon-dated at over 10,000 years old. Supposedly one of the scientists planted it, and it grew. That's patience.

Crows

Cal LaPorte from Manitowish Waters asked me: Why during the coldest weather of winter are crows seldom seen, but if the weather moderates, they appear as if by magic? Since I wasn't sure, I called Jim Baughman, an expert birder from Eagle River. His educated guess was that the crows remain close to their roosts during extreme cold in order to conserve energy, and thus are seen far less afield. But if the weather moderates, they will forage more widely, and be seen more commonly. Another reason may be that flocks of crows roam widely in winter, and may travel up to 50 miles a day in search of food. So it may be possible that crows wintering in central Wisconsin might travel north during warm spells in order to try to take advantage of unexplored feeding opportunities.

The fact that we have crows in the winter at all is a rather recent phenomenon. Crows were observed in the winter north of Highway 64 first in the 1950s, and their winter expansion into more northern counties proceeded slowly. It wasn't until 1964 in Oneida County and 1968 in Bayfield County that crows were counted on a Christmas bird count. Now crows are consistently found in every county of Wisconsin during Christmas bird counts.

Historically, the common crow was considered quite uncommon in Wisconsin in the mid-1800s. In response to increased human settlement, the crow population grew proportionately, and by 1890, crows were abundant in southern Wisconsin. Today, winter roosts of 200 and more are common in southern and central Wisconsin; Whitnall Park in Milwaukee hosts up to 15,000 crows some winters!

During a cold winter, the crows in our area are most likely visitors from further north. But if our winter is mild, breeding crows often remain in the area. If our crows do migrate, the largest flights are between October 1 and November 15. They return as one of our first spring arrivals in late February.

Cardinals

Two Minocqua residents told me they had cardinals nesting in their backyards during the summer of 1996. Cardinals have moved north gradually over the last century, somewhat akin to the previous crow story, though certainly in much more modest numbers. In the 1800s, cardinals only ranged as far north as southern New York, and were always considered nonmigratory. During the early 1900s, cardinals began inching northward across eastern North America, and ultimately established themselves as far north as southern Canada. Today they are common as far north as the Wausau area. The first cardinal sighting ever reported in Vilas County didn't happen until 1958, although one was spotted in Iron County in 1912. The cardinals' gradual expansion northward has been exceeded only by the extraordinary advances of the introduced house sparrow and the European starling. If

51

the cardinals' northern acclimation continues over the next decade, they may become relatively common visitors to northwoods feeders.

What brought them north? Probably three things. Winter feeding of backyard birds has certainly extended the northern winter range of many species of birds. Our climate has been warming as well. But most important has been our altering of the original forest into agricultural lands interspersed with an enormous amount of forest edge. Add in our manicured landscaping of our homes with shrubs and the concentrated availability of corn and grain, and we offer the perfect habitat requirements of cardinals. Cardinals live along the forest edge, nest in dense low bushes, and roost in dense thickets. We couldn't have designed a better management strategy for their increase than our forest clearing and settlement patterns.

It remains to be seen how much farther north, and in what numbers, cardinals will expand. I'm certainly hoping to see them at one of our feeders some winter.

Goose Dinner

Bob Kovar from Manitowish Waters reported a remarkable sighting. A flock of geese was flying over a cranberry marsh when a mature eagle intercepted the flock, taloned one of the geese, and landed on a dike and ate it. It was soon joined by another eagle, who must have been invited to the dinner.

Migration

The October 1996 issue of *Natural History* has six articles on the migration of raptors. I have tended over the years to rave about Duluth as one of North America's best sites for watching the fall hawk migration. But worldwide, there are sites that are better yet. The largest autumn hawk migration in the world occurs over Veracruz, Mexico, where one fall 20 species and over four million birds were counted, including nearly two million broad-winged hawks, 1.5 million turkey vultures, several hundred thousand Swainson's hawks, 50,000 Mississippi kites, and assorted other raptors.

If trans-Atlantic travel is your passion, at Elat, a resort town and Israel's only port on the Red Sea, the spring migration is incredible. Thirty-five species of raptors, as well as storks, cranes, and pelicans soar in the thermals over Elat. An estimated three million raptors migrate through the Middle East, the majority of which cross at Elat after a 2,500 mile flight over desert terrain. A half million honey buzzards, 40,000 Levant sparrowhawks, and at least 30,000 steppe eagles are the most numerous.

Puffballs May Inherit the Earth

Puffballs are round mushrooms ranging in size from a large softball to a small pumpkin. A single large puffball contains so many spores that if every spore germinated to an adult for two generations, the resultant mass would be 800 times the volume of the earth.

53

Horicon Marsh

My wife Mary and I hiked several trails in Horicon Marsh one early October, hoping to see the beginning of the massive waterfowl migration that attracts over 400,000 observers to the area every year. Unfortunately, we arrived before the major waves of birds; they typically peak in mid-October. Nonetheless, we saw many small skeins of geese, along with individuals of species like pied-billed grebes, great egrets, harriers, red-tailed hawks, and various ducks.

Horicon covers 31,000 acres, filling in what was once a shallow, glacial lake bed. It is now the largest freshwater cattail marsh in the United States. More than 260 bird species have been sighted in Horicon, so it is arguably the best place to watch birds in Wisconsin--possibly the best in the Midwest. For rare-bird seekers, species such as white-face ibis, white pelicans, and red-necked phalaropes have been recorded here.

Two-thirds of the marsh is a national wildlife refuge with limited access; the remaining third is a state wildlife area under the management of our Department of Natural Resources. Exploration by canoe is by far the best means of seeing the marsh, and Mary and I hope to get back there soon to do some paddling and muddling.

Junco Flocks

Flocks of northern (or dark-eyed) juncos migrate through the northwoods in mid- to late October, scavenging along roadsides for seeds. In a strong migration year, I can kick up a flock every few hundred yards as I drive. Each flock usually sheers off into the adjoining woods, then comes right back to the road after I've gone by. Look for the junco's characteristic outer tail feathers, which flash white as they fly away.

I often see numerous sparrows mixed in with the juncos. Those moving through with the juncos include white-throated, white-crowned, American tree, and chipping sparrows. Yellow-rumped warblers also migrate in mid-October, and I have watched many of them hawking insects all around our property. Yellow-rumpeds are usually the earliest warbler to arrive in spring and the last to leave in fall.

Dark and White Meat

If you've ever wondered why some bird meat is light while other meat is dark, here's the short answer. In avian physiology, the "dark meat" found in a bird is the musculature that provides long, sustained energy for efforts such as migratory flight. The muscles are dark red because their fibers contain red, oxygen-carrying compounds, and because they are richly supplied with blood. The "white meat," on the other hand, is the musculature used for quick bursts of high energy that, once expended, can't be quickly replenished. These lighter-colored muscles are predominant in pheasants, grouse, and quail, and are capable of sustaining heavy work for only a short period. Thus, if a grouse is flushed several times, it's often too exhausted to keep flying, so it resorts to running along the ground.

The pectoralis or "breast" of a chicken is white meat. These muscles are used for rapid, short flight. The chicken's legs or "drumsticks" are red meat, because these muscles are used for walking about all day long.

Feathers

As geese "V" their way overhead in what appears to be a nearly effortless journey, I marvel at the architecture of a feather. Only birds have feathers--no other creatures are so blessed. Feathers perform a wide array of functions, including signaling courtship, providing camouflage, protecting birds from the elements, and enabling flight.

Birds possess a variety of feather types, ranging from fluffy to stiff. Hence you can sleep on them or write with a stiff feather quill. Down feathers, which comprise the bird's undercoat, are the finest, lightest insulation known. Each down featherlet has its own tiny muscles, which serve to hoist the featherlet so it can gather and hold air for insulating purposes. Between the down feathers and the flight feathers are feathers called semiplumes. These act as padding along the contours of the body. The stiff, outer flight feathers are like oiled shingles, shedding water and wind, although (like any jacket) they have their limits. Too much wind or water drives a bird to shelter or, in some cases, to death.

Pick up a feather sometime and look at it closely. A feather is given its rigidity by a hollow shaft that runs through its entire length. On either side of the shaft is a fine veining, or ribbing. Each "rib" extends diagonally backwards, and is called a barb. Every barb is much like an individual feather, for it too has a central shaft that is ribbed or fringed. The fringes on the barbs are referred to as barbules. Whoever came up with the term "barb" was quite literal-minded. The barbules bear microscopic hooks, but only on one side of the barb. The other side has flanges. Think of them as the two sides of a zipper. They can split apart, yet come back together in an airtight weave that supports flight. The interlocking veins of a flight feather were probably the inspiration for the human material we call "Velcro."

55

The flight feather of a raven or another large bird may contain 500 barbs on either side of the feather shaft and 500 barbules on either side of every barb. If the ribbing of the feather is pulled apart, a bird can simply pass the edges through its beak to rejoin the barbs, a process similar to running the slide of a zipper up and down.

For all that feathers do for a bird, they generally comprise just 4 to 12 percent of the bird's total weight. A tundra swan has over 25,000 feathers, while a hummingbird has 900 to 1,000. Our wintering birds are currently growing more feathers, just as mammals grow more fur, in order to weather the cold. A chickadee adds 25 to 30 percent more feathers as a means of reducing heat loss.

Trout Spawning

Brook trout spawn in mid-October, some of them engaging in a futile attempt to spawn under the bridge at the far south end of Fallison Lake Trail, which is located within the Northern Highlands/American Legion State Forest in Vilas County. Fallison Lake was chemically treated to remove all fish in 1977; it was then stocked with brook and rainbow trout in 1978. The rainbow trout failed, but Fallison supports a good population of brook trout. However, the DNR must stock yearling brook trout annually, because the brookies are unable to reproduce successfully in Fallison.

Brook trout create their nests in gravel near upwelling springs, and they require cool, well-oxygenated waters. Springs are essential for keeping the water cool in summer and warm in winter. These habitat requirements are most often met in headwater spring ponds and spring-fed streams, but brook trout can be found in lakes, too. Peak spawning occurs in mid-November in Wisconsin, but it begins as early as October 15 in the north.

Brook trout are the only stream-dwelling trout native to the Great Lakes region. If you want to try your hand at catching some brookies, Vilas, Oneida, and Forest counties are a trout fisherman's paradise. The three counties contain nearly 300 trout streams--almost 40 percent of the state total.

Brook trout also go by the name of speckled trout. Their vivid spawning colors in fall are remarkable.

Muskrats

Muskrats build their winter lodges in October, in preparation for the cold. Muskrats combine cattails, rushes, and mud to raise a round hut that extends three to four feet above the marsh. Tom Anderson, an excellent nature writer, notes that the muskrat performs an act that is rare in the autumn; while everything around it is falling, the muskrat is busily raising a new home.

Young muskrats, as well as grouse, undergo a seasonal dispersal called "the fall shuffle." The young must move out and find their own, unoccupied territory for the winter. Some are forced to travel a considerable distance to find the right habitat and a lack of competition, and many fail to survive the move.

Trapping Muskrats

Before daybreak one late October, I accompanied Jeff Wilson onto the Flambeau Flowage, in order to check the muskrat traps he had set the day before. I'm not a trapper, but I had long wanted to see how the process works and, hopefully, to learn some natural history in the bargain. Jeff works for the Mercer office of the DNR, and he has been a trapper for many years. He has a strong love of the flowage and knows it well. It was a fair deal--I offered my help in paddling the canoe, which made Jeff's job much easier, and Jeff shared his understanding of muskrats.

I learned a great deal that morning. For one, I hadn't known that the sloughs were already iced over; we had to do our best impression of a Coast Guard icebreaker to reach many of the muskrat houses. I also hadn't known how prolific the muskrats were in the marsh area where we were working. Over 40 muskrat houses had been built in the preceding weeks, in hopes of creating protection from the winter. I learned that mink are voracious predators of muskrat. We found one muskrat lying headless on top of its house, and we guessed that the culprit was probably an owl or a mink. We found duck feathers on top of another muskrat house, and again the predator was probably a mink. While I knew that muskrats are rapid breeders, I hadn't really known how prolific they are. Northwoods muskrats typically have two litters of four to eight young in a year, and the first litter is potentially able to breed before winter sets in.

57

Many of the muskrat houses we saw were built on top of stumps or logs in the water. One was on top of a rock, making the plunge hole exit a trick neither Jeff nor I could decipher—how does one escape through solid rock?

Muskrat houses are quite small compared to beaver lodges, and are constructed of cattails, bulrush, and various aquatic vegetation mixed well with mud. We saw muskrat feeding platforms as well, these resembling smaller houses with an obvious hollow on top where the muskrat sits.

Because muskrats eat the stems and rootstalks of large aquatic plants like cattail, they help maintain openings in marshes that might otherwise fill in with cattail. Those openings provide water for ducks, herons, and a host of other waterfowl, allowing them to loaf and feed. If your favorite swimming hole is being invaded by aquatic vegetation, import a few muskrats--they will greatly reduce marsh or shoreline vegetation.

While in a canoe for many hours with a friend, there is time for talk. Did we discuss the ethics of trapping? At some length. Did we agree on the need for trapping? No. But Jeff knows his wildlife biology and population dynamics, and clearly his trapping was not significantly depleting the muskrat population of the Flambeau Flowage. When he asked if we are better off making much of our clothing, like nylons and polypropylenes, from petroleum products instead of using renewable furs on a limited basis, I didn't have an answer. We didn't plumb the larger question of animal rights, perhaps because neither of us really knows what is true regarding that debate. But we did share an equal appreciation for the beauty of the area and its wildlife, and both of us knew there were few places we would rather have been that morning than the Flambeau Flowage.

Sightings

If snow falls in the area by the end of October, bears may begin entering hibernation; bucks start scraping and rubbing amorous "initials" into the ground and onto the trees; snowshoe hares and weasels turn white; lakes "turn over," and water temperatures drop below 40°F; wild cranberries are ripe.

Canada (gray) jays usually show up at our feeder and fly around the house in late October. Roger Tory Peterson says they look like huge, overgrown chickadees. Gray jays are a bird of the spruce/fir boreal forests of Canada, and our area represents the southernmost edge of their range, because it includes scattered areas of boreal forest.

Woodchucks should be underground and in hibernation by now. As soon as the green plants that feed them have frosted out, they retire underground, blocking their holes with soil.

Montreal River Gorge

Jeff Richter, a friend and a local photographer, took us north and west of Hurley to the Montreal River Gorge, a spectacular canyon area cut by the Montreal River. While the gorge is just 30 miles north of where we live, the topography differs dramatically from the generally level lake and bog region we call home. The rock faces of the gorge spill straight down for over 100 feet to the whitewater of the Montreal--furious rapids that only experts generally attempt. The native name for the river was *Kawasiji-wangsepi*, meaning "white falls river." The French didn't bother trying to paddle it. Instead, they traversed 42 miles of the Flambeau Trail to get from Lake Superior to Long Lake north of Mercer, where lake and river travel became easier.

Two dams at former high waterfall sites control the flow of the river now, but the Montreal still looks more than imposing.

About 1.5 billion years ago, a mountain range as high as the Rockies stretched from northern Minnesota across northern Wisconsin and as far east as New York. Stream erosion later cut gaps in what was left of these mountains. The Montreal Gorge is only one of nine water gaps crossing the Penokee Range. These gaps are concentrated in a 30-mile stretch between the Bad River and the Montreal, creating northwoods terrain that's remarkably different from what most of us are used to. I know precious little about geology, but I do know how to appreciate geological beauty. This area provides what may be the most beautiful rock formations we have in northern Wisconsin.

59

1994 Frog Populations

Every year, frog surveys are undertaken in nearly every Wisconsin county, in order to determine the long-term population trends of our native frogs. Each survey route visits 10 sites, and each route is run during three time periods yearly--April 8 to April 30, May 20 to June 5, and July 1 to July 15. The DNR has coordinated the volunteer survey since 1984 as a means of looking at the possible decline in the health of wetland habitats. Because frogs and toads are considered good indicator species of the overall health of an area, their long-term increase or decrease may tell us much about the status of wetlands throughout the state.

We have only 11 species of frogs and one species of toad (the American toad) in Wisconsin. In the northwoods, we have fewer yet--eight species of frogs and the American toad. One frog species, Blanchard's cricket frog, is endangered statewide, while bullfrogs and pickerel frogs are listed as species of "special concern."

Data from 1994 indicated that only wood frogs, spring peepers, and green frogs were present in numbers above their long-term averages, adding some fuel to the fire for those who are concerned about the decline of frogs and toads in Wisconsin and nationwide. The report also revealed highly fluctuating populations for each species over the 11 year survey period. This long-term information gives us reason to be very cautious before jumping to any conclusions. Perhaps 1994 was just a "bad year," not a real indicator of general decline. Clear trends are hard to determine, and we have more questions than answers. Many years of additional data will be needed before anyone can say what's happening with specific species of frogs and generally what's occurring in our wetlands.

Full Moon

The full moon in October is called "the hunter's moon" by the Algonquin Indians, "the moon of the changing seasons" by the Sioux, and "the moon when the water freezes" by the Cheyenne. The moon rises one hour later every subsequent night; gradually, over the next two weeks, it fades to a new moon. The "harvest moon" occurs on the date of the closest full moon to the autumn equinox.

These are beautiful nights to be out. The weather is not too cold yet, and bugs are only a "fond" remembrance.

Halloween

The anticipation of Halloween usually has our youngest daughter in a tizzy. She loves costumes, likes the candy, and is scared witless by much of the rest. She once asked me why we had Halloween, and I hadn't the foggiest idea.

As it turns out, like most contemporary celebrations, Halloween has its historical roots in the natural cycles. The celebration of Halloween was an ancient Celtic tradition marking the midway point between the autumn equinox and the winter solstice. Not only did the winter season begin on this day, but it was believed by the Celts to be a sort of "crack in time," the one day of the year when the dead could revisit the living. To ward off evil spirits that might return, a new and sacred fire was lit, from which all other fires in Ireland were supposed to be lit. Our current traditions of lighting jack-o'-lanterns and bonfires are all that remain from this practice. According to the Irish tale, the "Jack" in jack-o'-lantern was a man barred from both heaven and hell who was condemned to walk the earth with his lantern until Judgment Day.

During the Middle Ages, officials of the Christian church transformed the occasion into All Saints' Day; they regarded the day preceding it as bedeviled, because it was the prelude to the former Celtic/ pagan feast day. Trick or treating apparently arose from a theater tradition, in which actors on All Saints' Day and All Souls' Day dressed up in disguises, begging for rewards in return for their prayers on behalf of the dead. The prayers and the astronomy are long forgotten, of course, but the costuming, the lit pumpkins, and the begging for treats remain.

Evil Flora?

When Halloween comes around, many of us engage in nonsensical tomfoolery intended to scare one another. It makes me think how we have a long history of seeing evil or frightening things in various plant species too. Wood anemones were a symbol of illness to some Europeans—they knew to hold their breath and run fast if they came upon a field of anemones because the wind that blew across the flowers was poisoned. Harebells were called "witches thimbles" by ancient Scots, who thought witches could transform themsleves into hares. Hares were thus thought to be a "black" meat that would cause nightmares and depression. Heather was linked to anyone not believing in the Church. Because missionaries had a difficult time crossing the heaths to try to bring the word of God to the back country people, the people were referred to as heathens, people of the wastelands unprotected by the salvation of the Church.

On the other hand, some plants were given positive supernatural powers. Columbine was thought by some to symbolize the Holy Ghost. "A stalk of columbine," writes Mary Durant, author of *Who Named the Daisy? Who Named the Rose?*, "with seven blooms was symbolic of the seven gifts of the Holy Ghost—the spirit of the Lord, the spirits of wisdom, understanding, counsel, might, knowledge, and the fear of the Lord." Common wood betony was believed to drive away evil spirits if worn as an amulet or planted in a graveyard. It was so powerful that snakes placed in a circle of betony were suppposed to lash themselves to death. Garlic was thought to guard one against werewolves and befuddle the powers of a magnet. Geraniums were thought by Islamic people to be a gift from Allah through his prophet Mohammed. Mohammed went for a swim one day leaving his shirt upon some weeds. When he came ashore and picked up his shirt, the weeds had become geraniums. Ginseng was thought to bring immortality to those who drank it in ancient China.

61

Whether a plant is a trick or a treat depends on who is looking at it and from what bias. A weed is a plant without a press agent. We place a princess or a werewolf mask upon the plant dependent on whether it fits our current needs. A tomato in the flower garden is bad, as is a rose in the pea patch. Part of the trick in life is to see past the costumes society or individuals place on anything and see the real thing, whether plant or person. Come to think of it, maybe there's symbolism in how close Halloween is to Election Day.

October Wind

There is both a smell and a feel to an autumn wind that sets it apart from all other winds. It has the equivalent effect for the woods walker that the sniffing of ammonium has for the faint--it makes the world clearer. Details take on a sharpness, pricking the senses and replacing the haze and softness of summer.

The autumn wind invigorates. It speaks with no hesitancy in its voice and even less room for procrastination.

Late-October Musings
Two Views

No, it is not because I am filled with obscure guilt that I step gently over, and not upon, an autumn cricket. It is not because of guilt that I refuse to shoot the last osprey from her nest in the tide marsh. I possess empathy; I have grown with man in his mind's growing. I share that sympathy and compassion which extends beyond the barriers of class and race and form until it partakes of the universal whole. I am not ashamed to profess this emotion, nor will I call it a pathology. Only through this experience many times repeated and enhanced does man become truly human. Only then will his gun arm be forever lowered. I pray that it may sometime be so.

—Loren Eiseley

I thank you on behalf of all the hunters and fishermen who have learned that an outdoor experience goes beyond setting a hook or pulling a trigger--that it reaches further than open season or legal limits--that it increases our awareness of ourselves and the world around us . . . It is on your home ground that many of us have tasted the land and the freedom it offers.

—George Vukelich

(excerpted from a letter written by a hunter to a landowner in thanks for the opportunity to hunt his land)

NOVEMBER

The Ojibwe word for November is *guckudinogizis*, meaning "the month when it freezes." Ice-up on our northern lakes usually occurs by mid-November. Nearly 50 percent of the surface waters in the northern hemisphere freeze every winter, creating some 19 million square miles of ice, give or take a mile. For the next five months, nearly all life in our northern waters will take place under the seal of ice. Under this lid, life forms practice the kind of deficit spending of nutrients and oxygen that would make our government proud. Not until spring, when the revenues of sunlight and oxygen fill the aquatic treasury once again, will our waters be rich and thriving.

As the November ice thickens, sunlight and air are reflected back into the sky, and the dissolved oxygen supply begins to decline. Even though plant photosynthesis can continue, it does so at a bare minimum, because so little light penetrates to fuel the process. The respiration of animals, from fish down to bacteria, will gradually reduce the oxygen supply. Organic waste products will build up on the lake bottom as the recycling bacteria shut down for lack of oxygen. Not even Ross Perot could find a way to reverse this debt, though the amount and kind of debt varies from lake to lake, due to a host of factors. One way or another, it's out of our hands. We can only hope that, when the ice recedes in late April, enough oxygen has held out to sustain the aquatic organisms through the winter.

November 1 to November 15

First Snow

I am always awestruck by the way the first big snow changes the landscape so dramatically that it's like being on a different planet. The

snow dampens sound and movement to such an extent that on a short walk into the woods, it becomes easy to think you have the place all to yourself, that everything has gone somewhere else. Of course, most everything is still out there (except the many birds that have migrated south), but where are they? What are they up to?

To me, the art of enjoying winter in the northwoods seems bound up in seeking answers to those two questions. And as with most questions in the natural world, seeking the facts often leads to a dozen new questions-- many without clear answers. The mysteries keep us knee-deep in wonder and reverence, emotions I think are essential to a continued, healthy discourse with the world around us.

The first snowfall offers beauty in many forms, like the snow-laden branches of our evergreens, hanging low with the weight but primed to spring upward when the snow shifts and falls. There's life in that flexibility. By contrast, the stark hardwoods seem resigned to accepting their lot and waiting out their time. I've given thought to the wintering strategies of deciduous and evergreen trees. Given the po-

November Musings

I go Up North as often as I can but it never seems to be often enough. My soul resides there; it is the place of the "other me" in much the same way, I suspect, as is the life forming within the womb of a pregnant woman. There is there a sacredness, a wholly otherness that I've found nowhere else. Those who know Up North know we take life from the depths of its water and breath from the far reaches of its open skies and peace from the quaking serenity of its birches.

—Susan Wendorf

litical winds that blow (and blow and blow) in November, I've come to regard the evergreens as conservatives--Republicans, if you wish; I think of the deciduous trees as liberals--Democrats, if you will. Actions by both parties are taken in defense against winter thirst, wind, and cold. The winter wind dries things out, much like a desert wind. It also blows sharp ice crystals that have the shredding power of sand. To maintain a leaf under such circumstances would be foolhardy, unless a tree's defense budget was greatly increased. A forest economics policy is thus drawn by both parties, the currency measured in energy units.

66

The evergreens invest heavily in the status quo, and in their defense department. As a security measure against winter, they have adapted their leaves into short needles, retaining the needles by sealing them with an extra layer of resiny wax. I can hear them softly chanting, "Hold on. Hold on." They spend very little on progressive ecological strategies like improving the soil through the release of nutrient-laden leaves. "Tighten your belt," they say. "Grow slow, but grow long." They offer an impassive face and speak in hushed tones. Pessimists to the end, they will grow in their poor soil and impoverish the soil further with their acid needles, but they will hold on.

The deciduous trees take another tack. Liberal in their generosity, they are willing to give abundantly. They invest in the future, speculating rather wildly on the next season. They drop their dry, broad leaves, often pumped full of nutrients, in order to enrich the soil for coming generations. Then they seal the leaf scars with corky cells, caulking the seams. They are big spenders in the perennial, optimistic belief that next year can only be better. They are risk takers, these deciduous folks--believers in making big gains through big efforts. They give their coats away; they speak colorfully and evocatively; they believe that spring will heal them in a burst of flowers and warm, favorable winds.

A few independents stand to the side, borrowing traits from both camps. The tamarack sidesteps its coniferous mates and drops its golden needles, the last deciduous act that occurs in the forest during any autumn. Though the needles don't particularly enrich the bog, they are a show of independence that seems more symbolic than useful.

Then there's the red oak, which behaves like a southern Democrat. It drops its acidic leaves but invests them with very little nutrient content. The red oak plays the conservative among the liberals in its party. It even holds onto many of its dried-up leaves, which are of no value unless perhaps the red oak shakes them at other trees in defiance, as if to say, "I'll play by my own rules."

Meanwhile, now that all the rhetoric of the trees is accounted for, there is the winter itself to contend with. Winter usually has the final say regarding who thrives in the spring and who doesn't, and the season is ultimately the issue all trees must address, whatever their politics.

If only the stakes for our politicians in Washington were equally high.

Snow Depth   67

Nine inches of snow are needed to adequately insulate the ground. Diana Kappel-Smith, a Vermont naturalist and writer, describes this as the "winter threshold, and then the underworld begins a time of sheltered calm and darkness." In terms of insulation value, light snow is comparable to dry peat or blown cellulose, because of all the air spaces it contains.

Twelve feet down into the soil in a normal snow year, it is warmer in January than in June. The stored solar heat and the geothermal heat rising from the core of the earth is trapped by the snow layer. This heat vaporizes the bottom of the pack, creating "depth hoar," a delicate, crystalline space in which small animals can move about. Here, the temperature stays near or above freezing, regardless of the surface temperature.

As if to prove the point, our husky caught a meadow vole under the snowpack one November day. I watched her pounce with both feet into the snow, then listen as the vole tried to escape. The vole tunneled back under her several times, running away behind her before she knew it. Eventually the vole lost the battle, but only after several minutes of momentary escapes, tunnelings, and sprints for freedom.

Snow Job

A book entitled *The Great Eskimo Vocabulary Hoax* (Geoffrey Pullum, U. of Chicago Press, 1991) discounts the long-held belief that Eskimos use 20 or more words to describe snow. Words like *qamaniq* for "the-shadow-under-trees-where-little-snow-lies;" *qali* for "snow-caught-in-trees;" or *siqoq* for "snow-moving-over-the-ground" may not be valid says the book. If this is true, it's too bad. These words provided an excellent example of how language can be used—or not used—to alter our perception of reality. The theory held that because we lack a vocabulary to describe the real differences between types of snow, we fail to perceive those differences. One essayist remarked that if this theory is true, perhaps we could unlearn all the names we use to describe different races, and by so doing eliminate our prejudices.

We do use some snow terminology—words like "dusting," "hardpack," "powder," and "blizzard"—but we still lack appreciation for the many forms that snow can take, and our limited descriptive vocabulary reflects our limited perception.

68

To take a closer look at snowflakes, find a piece of black cardboard or velvet and allow it to become thoroughly chilled. Now let snowflakes fall on the surface. While you're outside, use a hand lens or a microscope to examine the crystal structure. The International Snow Classification System divides snow into 10 different categories, including the familiar six-sided stars called stellar crystals, as well as needles, capped columns, plates, columns, spatial dendrites, irregular crystals, graupels, ice pellets, and hail.

Last of the Migration

The last migrating birds of the season may be seen until mid-November (and some even later). They include the snow goose, ring-necked duck, bufflehead, scaup, golden-eye, hooded, red-breasted and common merganser, mallard, black duck, and tundra swan. Not only the big water birds are left. Early November can still turn up yellow-rumped warblers, song and tree sparrows, cedar waxwings, Cape May warblers, fox sparrows, and flocks of snow buntings.

North Shore Birds

I spent three days at the beginning of one November birding with a group of folks who were members of the Wisconsin Society for Ornithology. We traveled along the North Shore of Lake Superior from Duluth to Grand Marais looking for the last of the autumn migrants. I spotted a number of "lifers," like boreal chickadees, surf scoters, lapland longspurs, and a Pacific loon. Unfortunately, we missed by a week a record migration day at Duluth's Hawk Ridge. On that memorable day, they nearly doubled their previous records for bald eagles (322) and golden eagles (23). If you're not familiar with Hawk Ridge, it is widely considered the second-best site in North America for watching fall migrations, and their count numbers prove it. Record days are particularly astounding.

But the birds aren't tethered at Hawk Ridge, or any other wildlife hot spot for that matter. We visited on a Friday afternoon; unfortunately, we were accompanied by a south wind, which stops most migrants dead in their tracks. Only one hawk had wandered through that morning, though we got to see upwards of ten that afternoon (mostly sharp-shinned and red-tailed hawks). The last three times I've been on Hawk Ridge, the action has been downright slow, but if wildlife appeared on demand, we'd be bored silly with the show. Humans have a disturbing habit of disdaining that which is common and easily experienced. I don't begrudge the downtimes; they provide the anticipatory stage for those moments of glory when you're somehow blessed by being in the right spot at the right time.

69

You can support Hawk Ridge by becoming a "Friend of Hawk Ridge." For a $15 annual donation, you get visiting privileges at the banding research station observation blind, which is ranked among the top few in the country, banding nearly 3,000 hawks and owls every fall. You receive an annual report and a summer newsletter, and you have the satisfaction of helping this fine program continue its work. Write to: Friends of Hawk Ridge, Duluth Audubon Society, c/o Biology Department, University of Minnesota, Duluth, MN 55812.

Bohemian Waxwings and Mountain-Ashes

During the North Shore birding trip, I was impressed by the number of American mountain-ashes laden with scarlet berries all along the Lake Superior coast. Most people think of mountain-ash as a short tree that's planted as a cultivar in yards, and as one that produces orangish berries. Actually, that's the European mountain-ash. But American mountain-ash belongs in natural communities, too. It is most at home in the boreal forests of Canada, reaching southward into northern Wisconsin, Minnesota, and Michigan only to a limited degree.

The fruits form large hanging clusters, and each cluster may contain over a hundred berries. The berries hang on until the spring unless a flock of waxwings or robins strips them in a gluttonous splurge. On a November afternoon, when most leaves are down and color is hard to come by, those berries are a neon blaze amidst the dark forest branches. While they are not the most nutritious of fruits, many a bird is drawn to them. We were graced with a flock of Bohemian waxwings, a species I'd never seen before, that was making its way down the coast, feasting on the berry bounty. Whatever berries are left from the autumn season will be consumed throughout the winter by birds like sharp-tailed grouse and evening or pine grosbeaks.

In winter, mountain-ash is easy to identify. Its gummy, red, long, cone-shaped buds really have no imitators. The bark is purplish-gray with large lenticels (breathing pores) all along the branches. It looks quite a bit like the bark of an alder to me, but mountain-ash grows mostly on upland slopes, while alder is seen in low-lying areas. Mountain-ash will grow on wetter sites, too—just to spite us, so we can't use its habitat as a character reference. Moose browse the fragrant inner bark heavily throughout the winter, providing the basis for the tree's colloquial names: "missey-moosey" or "moose-miss."

Snowy Owls

Snowy owls don't usually arrive before November 20 in non-invasion years, but invasion years often bring owls into northern Wisconsin by early November, or even the last week of October. Halloween is the usual arrival date in the Ashland area, where as many as six snowies may overwinter in an invasion year. Christmas bird counts throughout Wisconsin yield an average of 12 to 15 snowies in eight to 10 areas. Lean years offer five or fewer snowies, while invasion years usually result in 20 to 25 individuals.

In the Lakeland area, Mary Lou Fisher called one November 8th to tell me she had found a dead snowy owl under a large hemlock tree near the shore of White Sand Lake in Vilas County. She saw no wounds on the bird; when she took it to the Northwoods Wildlife Center, the staff there couldn't find any sign of injury, either. The owl apparently died of natural causes. Perhaps it exhausted itself during its flight here from the Arctic and was unsuccessful in its initial hunting.

My wife Mary and I saw our first snowy owl of 1994 on November 14th. It was perched atop a dead snag in the midst of hundreds of acres of bog in the Powell Marsh. The late afternoon sun hung on the horizon, its deepening horizontal rays illuminating the owl so brightly against the darkening sky that it looked like the beam of an island lighthouse. We worked our way as close to the owl as the bog would allow, and still the snowy sat tight, rotating its head frequently in the 270-degree arc that only owls can manage. Eventually it flew across the marsh and disappeared into the woods, swooping low and looking like a white barrel with wings.

Examination of birds that have been shot (yes, some Neanderthals still illegally shoot snowy owls) has proven that their diet consists primarily of meadow voles. Look for snowies in open areas where they can hunt voles, such as along shorelines, fields (airports are good locations), roads, and bogs. Snowies tend to perch conspicuously on poles, fence posts, and even TV aerials, so an observer has to be nearly blind to miss them--although they also stand on lake ice, where their coloration blends in with the ice. If you're fortunate enough to find one in its roosting or hunting area, it will most likely remain there until its departure in March for the Arctic.

71

Tundra and Trumpeter Swans

In early November, Mary, our daughter Callie, and I drove to southwestern Wisconsin, in order to witness the migration of tundra swans along the Mississippi River. There is a backwater of the Buffalo River three miles north of Alma, at a spot just before the Buffalo flows into the Mississippi. This shallow pool, called Rieck's Lake, harbors thousands of tundra swans in November. The swans thrive on the rampant arrowhead tubers and wild celery offered by the lake. We probably saw 1,000 or more while we were there, but 10,000 have been observed on peak days.

Few superlatives can quite describe the sight of translucent white flocks of swans against the blue sky, coming in for landings, taking off, or just flying over. If you're looking for one last major birding spectacle before the winter halts most such activity, the swans often remain on Rieck's Lake until just before ice-up, giving you ample time into December to witness their beauty.

Tundra swans were formerly called whistling swans, in case you have an older bird book. They nest in the high Arctic, then split up. Two-thirds of them migrate south and west to California; the other third (some 70,000 birds) sweeps south through the Dakotas, then heads nearly due east all the way to the Chesapeake Bay on the Atlantic. Flying as long as 10 hours a day at speeds up to 60 miles per hour, tundras may cover 600 miles in a day. Once they reach this portion of the Mississippi though, they're in no hurry to move on.

Tundras can be distinguished from trumpeter swans by their smaller size. An average tundra weighs 18 pounds, compared to 28 for the average trumpeter. Tundras have black facial skin that tapers to a point in front of their eye and is punctuated by a yellow spot that is often (but not always) noticeable. In contrast, the black facial skin of a trumpeter extends all the way around the eye. At a distance this distinction can challenge or frustrate most birders, so knowledge of their calls helps considerably. The high-pitched, quavering call of a flock of tundras has been described as "what seems like a group of distant, barking dogs" by Sam Robbins (*Wisconsin Birdlife*). According to John Terres (*Encyclopedia of North American Birds*), the call is "suggestive of Canada goose call, like distant baying of hounds, but also more like soft, musical laughter, *wow-how-ow*."

A trumpeter's call is lower and more buglelike; it's been described as a "short, far-reaching *ko-ho*, like the sound of an old-fashioned French taxi." If you aren't up on your French taxi sounds, the best way to learn the difference between them is through personal experience. Trying to put bird songs into an English alphabet (or any alphabet) is a tough business. You're better off experiencing them for yourself in the field.

Northwoods Swans

The northwoods is not part of a main migration route for tundra swans, but now and again they are seen. One November four tundras were observed on Hasbrook Lake, just outside of Lake Tomahawk. The lake had frozen overnight, and the two adults and two young landed on the newly formed ice, where they remained for several hours.

While tundra swans will continue southeast to the Chesapeake Bay, mute swans sometimes winter over on the open water of the Manitowish and Trout Rivers. The mute swans are nesting pairs originally from Chequamegon Bay near Ashland. Mutes were introduced to the area in the 1940s as an ornamental species for parks and estates. Wildlife managers appreciate the swans' beauty, but frown on their territorial aggressiveness and their substantial uprooting of aquatic plants.

An effort was made in the late 1980s to substitute trumpeter swan eggs for mute swan eggs in the mutes' nests, in the hope that the mutes would raise trumpeter cygnets. Very few cygnets made it to adulthood, however, so the use of mute swans as surrogate parents to help restore trumpeter populations was discontinued. Efforts are now under way to possibly remove mute swans from our waters before they do any further wetland damage. Hopefully, these efforts will be successful. Sometimes beauty bares previously invisible teeth after a relationship has begun. Such is the case with mute swans.

73

Immature Eagles and Otters

A gentleman who lives in the Manitowish Waters area wrote one early November after seeing 10 immature eagles, all perched together fifty yards from his house. "There were six sitting on the big log, two on the dead head perch, and two more on the bog by the beaver house... No two looked alike. Their feathers were at all different stages of color. They were all within 30 yards of each other... As we were watching these eagles, otters came swimming over, and we actually saw one leap out of the water at an eagle that was standing on the bog. It seemed the otters were a little overwhelmed with this crowd of teenagers. The eagles stayed for most of the day, flying here and there. It was like [the Alfred Hitchcock film] *The Birds.*"

Loons and Ice

I seem to receive a phone call or two every November from distraught lakefront residents who observe a common loon trapped in the ice. One such call came from a gentleman who lives on Payment Lake, just outside of Mercer. An immature loon had been trapped when a pool of open water in the lake iced up overnight. I called Warren Burns, director of the Northwoods Wildlife Center, to see if his crew could get to the loon. Warren anticipated my question before I even asked it, saying he had already received several calls from other areas where loons were iced in. Because it was already late in the afternoon, the loon rescue had to wait until the next morning. Unfortunately, the loon was gone in the morning, and the lake was sealed tight with ice. Because loons can't run on ice in order to take off, this one almost certainly perished.

The rescue of these loons is a tricky business. One person has to push a canoe with another person in it over the ice, until the canoe breaks through, whereupon they get to paddle very briefly till they are stopped by ice again. Usually acres of thin ice lie ahead, so the team leapfrogs from hole to hole, hoping to avoid a hypothermic November swim. Even when the team does reach a loon, it often dives continuously in an effort to escape what it perceives as a threat. On 12 occasions during one year, iced-in loons were lost when Wildlife Center personnel simply couldn't make the rescue. One difficult rescue effort, which took over three hours, was nearing success when an eagle swooped down and took the loon right from in front of the rescue team.

The loons still remaining in November are usually immatures. Most adult loons have long since left for the Atlantic Coast, where they winter without their breeding plumage and refrain from their haunting vocalizations. Southerners don't get worked up about loons like we do, because "our" loons lead a quiet lifestyle during the winter season.

Snow Buntings

I must admit that there aren't a huge number of natural events in November that I look forward to, but one event I do await is the arrival of the snow buntings from their high Arctic nesting grounds. These beautiful birds nest further north than any other land bird. Their black-and-white wings distinguish them from all other birds in our area. Overhead, snow buntings appear almost completely white. In winter flight drifting over a large field in a typically big flock, snow buntings appear "like giant snowflakes" writes John Terres, author of many books on the natural world. While the males are totally black and white in their summer breeding plumage, they display a rusty brown cap along with a streaky cinnamon-colored back in their winter plumage.

Snow buntings appeared in our area during the last two weeks of October, wheeling in tightly knit flocks along roadways and fields. Their very sharp, strong bills can easily break apart the seeds that they forage from weeds along the ground and from low shrubs like alder. They are gregarious in the winter, often associating in large flocks (up to 2,000!) with horned larks and lapland longspurs.

The "snowbird" usually doesn't remain in the Lakeland area, but if our snow cover isn't too deep, some may stay the winter. Our heavy forest cover isn't their habitat of choice, but it's not due to their lack of hardiness. They can handle severe cold down to -58°F. Like ruffed grouse, they may burrow in the snow to keep warm. They even are known to snow-bathe in the winter.

To find snow buntings, search in fallow fields where weed tips remain above the snow, or in farm fields where fresh manure laden with undigested seeds has been spread.

75

Snow buntings, like nearly all of our winter visitors, are irruptive in nature. They may be seen in large numbers in the north one year and be absent the next.

One resource I have notes that snow buntings were once shot for market—one city reportedly had 80,000 snow buntings in cold storage. Apparently they are still eaten by native tribes in the far north.

Insects

Many small invertebrates like spiders and centipedes are now in hibernation, as are the northern reptiles and amphibians. One of the only terrestrial insects that maintains its body temperature through the winter is the honeybee. Thousands of these bees cluster together in a compact ball to conserve heat, achieving an average temperature of 64°F in the center and 50°F on the periphery.

Nearly all other insects must allow their body temperatures to plummet. Some insects, like some trees, have the ability to supercool by purging their bodies of impurities around which ice crystals could form. They then synthesize glycerol, which allows them to chill down to -50°F without freezing. Caterpillars and the pupae of moths and butterflies can tolerate some freezing, as long as the freezing is confined to the fluids surrounding their body cells.

The Magnitude of the Night Sky

By November 12 we will experience only nine hours and 38 minutes of daylight. As a result, it makes sense to enjoy the nightlight. Note that I didn't say night*life,* so this should not be taken as an excuse to visit a tavern. Instead, take an early evening walk and look at the stars. Depending on the year, Venus may be the brightest object in the night sky—so bright that it can be seen in the daytime. Venus reaches a magnitude greater than -4, which is exceptionally bright given that a first-magnitude star is considered the brightest. Sixth magnitude is the dimmest.

Each step of magnitude represents a factor of 2.5, so a first-magnitude star is actually 100 times brighter than a sixth-magnitude star. Sirius, the brightest star in the sky, is a -1 magnitude. Only Jupiter (-2), Mars (-2 to +2), and Venus (-4) are brighter. Historically, the brilliance of Venus has caused Earth's inhabitants to mistake it for a variety of other objects. A remarkable example occurred in 1945, when Venus was so bright that Allied bombers over Japan tried to shoot it down, believing it was an enemy plane. I suspect they missed.

I don't do near as much stargazing as I should, partly because I have to walk a quarter of a mile to leave behind the streetlights that stand within several hundred yards of my house. I have little to complain about, though, compared to city dwellers who live in an electric wonderland of nightlight. Most people simply can't see the Milky Way. Some cities have now seen the light, as it were, and are directing their lighting downward to prevent light pollution. Tucson, Arizona, requires that all outdoor signs illuminated from below must be turned off by 11 p.m. For street lighting, the city now uses low-pressure sodium bulbs, which emit a narrower spectrum of light.

Even if you are a novice at understanding the night sky, you can get a humbling perspective on the universe. In order to reach you, the light you see from an average star has been traveling 670 million miles per hour (186,000 miles per second) since the time of dinosaurs. The Milky Way alone contains one trillion stars, covering an area that is 100,000 light years in diameter.

Smells

The autumn woods smell wonderful into early November, if the snows haven't arrived. The cornucopia of wet leaves is the apparent source of the smell. It's odd how few words we have to describe smells; I can't find the right ones now to capture the aroma of an autumn woods. In her book, *A Natural History of the Senses,* Diane

Ackerman says we can detect 10,000 different odors, but "smell is the mute sense, the one without words."

Our lack of vocabulary is all the more remarkable given the fact that we breathe some 23,000 times a day; each inhalation brings in a constellation of smells, and each exhalation changes the air around us. We do have deep and poignant memories of smells—links that shoot us back in time to a moment in a kitchen, a walk in the woods, a new car, or a member of the opposite sex. As Ackerman says, "Hit a tripwire of smell, and memories explode all at once."

Smells even improve learning and retention. Children who are given smells to associate with word lists recall and retain the words much more easily than they do without the olfactory cues.

Each of us has our own identifying smell, like fingerprints, as any bloodhound can attest. Christopher Columbus said that the Indians he first met on Hispanola could identify one another by the scent of their footprints in the sand. Helen Keller said that she could tell the profession of a person by his or her smell. Jean-Jacques Rousseau, the 18th-century French philosopher and writer, could identify 100 plants by their smell. One person in a hundred today has extremely sensitive olfactory cells--500 times more sensitive than the average person.

Most animals are far better at detecting scents than we are. Salmon can smell their original spawning waters and return there over hundreds of miles. From over two miles away, male moths can smell the pheremones of a female seeking a relationship. And all kinds of mammals leave their scent on just about every standing object, their calling cards as clear as messages on our telephone answering machines. "At the sound of the beep, just urinate here."

My point, you ask? Breathe deeply. Draw in the northwoods and all of its aromas while you can, because the snow is coming.

The Cookstove

Mary and I hooked up her old wood cookstove one fall, after it had been in storage for 13 years. The stove hails from the 1930s. While beautiful to look at, it is something less than airtight. But I like that. A yellow blaze and crackle emanates through the cracks, warming the mind as well as the body.

The stove sprawls outward, with a water reservoir to one side and warming ovens above, but the wood box is small. I'm sure it was designed to reduce overheating while baking in summer kitchens. I must split the wood many times so it will fit inside the box, but I'm warmed twice over for the work. And the heat is somehow warmer and more comfortable than heat provided by our modern, 92-per-cent-efficient gas furnace--our backup heat source. We've heated for years with wood, and while the work of cutting, splitting, stacking, and hauling is sometimes a burden, the feel, smell, and sound of a fire more than compensates for the sore backs.

Canoeing

I took my last canoe trip of 1992 in mid-November, exploring a stretch of the Manitowish River I'm very familiar with, but one that I had never seen from a canoe at that time of the year. Wearing a blaze-orange vest and cap was my concession to any crazed deer hunters who might mistake me for a buck that was out for a Sunday swim. During the first part of my journey, I did in fact hear one hunter who was baying incessantly like a senile bloodhound. I hope he was trying to drive deer; if not, he needs psychiatric help. But silence gradually reclaimed the river and became my companion the rest of the way.

Although I realize it's a contradiction in terms, not enough can be said for silence. Precious little broke the stillness beyond the dip of my paddle and the sound of the wind in the brittle grasses. Two mature eagles eyed my progress from their shoulder to shoulder perch in a dead tree, but they offered no voice or action. No animals waited around river loops to be surprised into sudden flight or a deep dive. The colors along the river were muted, too; only the ruby splash of red osier dogwood punctuated the somber deep greens, grays, and browns. The wind even stayed behind me, a miracle of sorts to any-one who has spent much time on a winding river. Its voice was quiet too as it helped speed me to the pullout.

What did I enjoy most? The swirling of water around me, a sound that would soon be hushed by ice.

Sightings

Club mosses are "fruiting" in November. Tap the candelabras (the strobili) that extend upward from the plant, and a yellow cloud of spores will issue forth. Ants should by now be in torpor inside wood. If you find some, you can warm them up and watch them become active, although I have no idea why you might want to do this. Frogs and turtles should be well-buried in mud, dirt, or cavities, waiting out the cold.

Nearly all the leaves have fallen from our deciduous trees--except oak and ironwood, which tend to hold onto some leaves throughout the winter. Only tamarack may yet have some leaves (needles, in this case), and these will soon come down. Bears should be denning up. Winter mammal coats are just about full, and hares and ermines are changing color. The ground cover is withered by frost, and greenery is hard to come by. Beavers are finishing the caches of branches in front of their lodges. Deer and moose are rutting. Squirrels are fattening up and caching seeds for the winter. Snow buntings have arrived. Ice is on some of the shallow ponds and sloughs.

79

> ### November Musings
> *The last trees have traded their leaves against a winter thirst. Winter isn't only too lightless and too cold for most plants' chemical machinery; it is a drought of momentous proportions...*
> —Diana Kappel-Smith

It's quiet in the woods, except for the racket we make by walking on dry leaves. Everyone's settling in.

Grackles, starlings, nuthatches, evening grosbeaks, white-throated sparrows, juncos, blue jays, red-winged blackbirds, chickadees, and hairy and downy woodpeckers are working over November feeders. Grackles and various blackbirds usually flock just before sunset in some black ash trees below our house, then fly in a congregation to their communal roost. Soon they should be on their way south, but while the weather stays soft and the feeders are full of sunflower seeds, they must be asking themselves, "Why not stay awhile?"

merganser

19 MILLION SQUARE MILES OF iCE

Orion

Betelguese

Rigel

NOVEMBER 16-30

November 16 to November 30

Black Bears

On the opening morning of the 1995 deer season, Tim Fitzgerald, the station manager at the DNR's Mercer office, was waiting quietly
for a buck to come by when he heard the approach of a large animal. Gradually a black bear came into view, heading directly toward him and unaware of his presence. When the bear got within 30 feet, Tim became, shall we say, a bit uncomfortable with the bear's beeline path in his direction, so he made a noise. The bear froze instantly in its tracks, then quickly made a wide circle around him before continuing in the same direction.

A week later, Annette Tellefson from Manitowish Waters called to ask me what

> ### Late-November Musings
> *The gnawing lack of the basic necessities of life makes itself gradually felt through the autumn months, and spring comes slowly also, so that winter is a turning rather than a coherent event.*
> —Diana Kappel-Smith

sort of creature would make tracks eight inches long and five inches wide in the woods near her home. I drove over to take a look, and though I'm no expert on animal tracks, the tracks in the snow were clearly left by a black bear.

Annette was quite surprised that a black bear would be up and about in late November, but some bears--particularly males--are traditionally seen during the deer hunting season. The movement of black bears in late November appears to be on the increase for three reasons:

1. Male black bears don't often go into dens. In fact, over one-third of adult males sleep right on the ground, on a nest of bunched-up grasses. Another one-third may crawl under downed treetops, but they're still aboveground. The last third of the adult males use more traditional den sites, like hollow logs and tip-up mounds. The males can be easily aroused from their torpor. During hunting season, when

the woods are significantly disturbed by humans, it's not uncommon for a black bear to be moving around--presumably trying to find some peace.

2. Bear numbers are quite high, so the chances of seeing one are increased. Good tracking snow like we had in 1995 provided much more evidence of their presence.

3. The large increase in deer feeding and baiting provides longer seasonal eating opportunities for bears, so they're able to stay out much later into the winter. Gut piles from hunting season add to the table fare.

Female black bears may den up as early as October 1, but no bear actually hibernates. They go into torpor, a significantly reduced state of activity and metabolism, from which they can easily be "awakened."

82

Deer Hunting and Biodiversity

The current deer hunt is an extravaganza--glorious to some and odious to others, but seldom nonpartisan. I have treaded neutral waters on the hunt for a long time, but given the current numbers of deer, one has little choice but to favor huge deer harvests. We have created high deer populations by three major actions--chopping forest habitats into small blocks, which provide supermarket conditions for deer by increasing forest edge; by farming virtually everything inbetween and raising crops deer love; and by reducing big carnivores like wolves to a near phantom presence.

High deer densities can literally reverse forest succession. The understory is so overbrowsed in some areas that the woodlands are reduced to what author Jared Diamond describes as "visiting an apparently thriving country and suddenly realizing that it is inhabited mainly by old people, and that most of the infants and children have died."

The population explosion makes indirect losers out of understory nesting bird species, butterflies that depend on understory plants, and birds that feed on the fruits, seeds, and nuts of trees that are browsed to death as seedlings. Because large carnivores are absent, and because we continue to create optimal habitat for deer, humans have little choice but to control the deer through hunting. We have dramatically affected our forest communities, so we must accept responsibility for managing its imbalances.

Acorn Crop

The 1995 acorn crop was a total failure in the Lakeland area. That's normal, periodic "behavior" for oak trees. The production of periodic mast crops is thought to be a common "strategy," employed by trees in order to escape the ravages of seed eaters. A poor year will typically reduce the population of jays and squirrels, which rely on the acorns. The alternation of good and bad years ensures that, in the good years when seed production is high, the limited predator population will be unable to utilize all of them. Some seeds will escape predation, then will hopefully encounter the right conditions for germination and ultimate survival. One author refers to high mast years as "flooding the market," which is a good analogy.

Deer seem to cope well without winter acorns. Gray squirrels are probably the most affected species, although they can probably compensate by working the local bird feeders for sunflower seeds.

Acorns rate at the top of the wildlife food list and are of major importance to animals in Wisconsin other than deer and squirrels, including wood ducks, ruffed grouse, pigeons, prairie chickens, wild turkeys, flickers, white-breasted nuthatches, red-headed woodpeckers, black bears, raccoons, fox, chipmunks, and various mice.

83

Feeding Birds: Can I Take a Vacation?

As winter closes in, chickadees flock to our feeders every morning. The appearance of friendly feeding is deceptive, however. A classic pecking order rules feeder etiquette, and many birds consistently lose encounters with the top dogs. In the strict, energy budgeting world of a northern winter, actions must result in greater benefits than costs, and those shunted away from the feeders may lose their lives. Up to 80 percent of the chickadee population dies in a given year, most before they are a year old. Such statistics often make bird lovers become slaves to their feeders, afraid to leave on a Christmas vacation for fear of killing off the resident flock. If you're a concerned feeder of birds, take heart. During most winter weather (when temperatures are above 10°F), chickadees obtain only about 25 percent of their daily energy requirements from feeders, picking up the rest from fields and woods. When experimenters have withheld seed, the feeder-habituated chickadees survived just as well as those that never visited feeders.

When temperatures drop below 10°F, though, the survival rates of backyard feeder birds nearly double those for wild foragers. Below-zero temperatures mean that a chickadee must find the equivalent of 250 sunflower seeds per day in order to survive. That's a lot of foraging. Chickadees need at least 20 times more food in winter than in summer.

The bottom line? Feeding birds in average winter temperatures makes little difference, but feeding them over a prolonged cold spell may make a great difference.

Bird Banding

James Audubon became the first person to band birds in America in 1803, when he banded a brood of phoebes. Since the early 1920s, the management and operation of systematic bird banding has been coordinated by the U.S. Fish and Wildlife Serv-ice. All bands placed on birds now read: "Notify Fish and Wildlife Service, Wash., D.C." If you ever find a band, simply place it in an envelope addressed USFWS, Wash., D.C., and it will get there. Include notes on when and where you found the band, the condition of the bird, and any other pertinent information.

Bird banding has provided data essential for the study of migration. It has helped us learn about locations where birds summer and winter, home ranges, avian life spans, and flyway routes. This essential information has helped provide the basis for the sound conservation practices now employed to help preserve birds in a world environment that is increasingly hostile to all animals.

All records of bands placed on birds and the subsequent recaptures of birds are sent to the USFWS, where it is possible to review the recorded history of birds ranging from hummingbirds to bald eagles.

Bird banding does take place locally. Major research projects in recent years have resulted in local banding of common loons, bald eagles, merlins, and ospreys, as well as "backyard" birds like chickadees, goldfinches, and nuthatches.

Common Mergansers

While in the Alma, Wisconsin, area one November, we headed north and crossed into Minnesota just below Lake Pepin (of Laura Ingalls Wilder fame). In late November, before freeze-up, common mergansers gather by the tens of thousands on the southern end of the lake. Bald eagles concentrate here as well; in 1993, the number peaked at more than 500 in early December. This was probably the highest concentration of eagles to be found anywhere in the lower 48 states.

Common mergansers aren't all that common in Wisconsin's northwoods, because we're at the southernmost edge of their nesting range. I have seen them in summer on several large lakes, including Star Lake in Vilas County and the Flambeau Flowage in Iron County. Like wood ducks, they nest in tree cavities. The newly hatched chicks must make like fuzzy little paratroopers and jump out of holes that may be 50 feet off the ground. Upon landing, they scurry after the hen to reach open water.

85

The adult drake's markings are unmistakable, although at a first, distant glance you might mistake it for a loon. The male's head has the coloration of an old, deep green medicine bottle. The drake's back is black, but the remainder of the body (except for the red legs and feet) is pure white, tinged with a peach color. The reddish bill is edged, with sawlike teeth that can grab and hold onto slippery fish. The common merganser typically feeds on "rough" fish like suckers and carp, but it can pump its webbed feet at such a speed while swimming that it can take trout and salmon fry as well. The notion of a bird that can outswim a fish will always be remarkable to me.

Common mergansers have been known to stay a winter on open waters, and they often stay at least until ice-up, so you may see a few in late November. Many choose to winter on lower Lake Michigan.

Varied Thrush

Gil Willms from Lac du Flambeau called on November 28, 1994, with a most unusual sighting. A male varied thrush had been visiting his feeder throughout the day, feeding on sunflower seeds and wild bird mixed seed alongside several mourning doves. If you have never seen a varied thrush, there's a reason why--varied thrushes breed and winter on the Pacific coast and as far east as western Montana. For one to wander some 1,400 miles to Gil's feeder is quite unusual. Three to 12 varied thrushes are reported in Wisconsin during any given winter, and most remain at the same feeding location for several weeks. The first storm of the 1994 winter season, which occurred just a few days earlier, probably provided the air express routing for this robin-sized thrush's journey to the northwoods.

Wintering Birds, Diseased Trees, and Cavities

Wintering birds show up at our feeders in significant numbers by late November--goldfinches, evening grosbeaks, purple finches, chickadees, nuthatches, and blue jays, along with those wanna-be birds, the red squirrels. The chickadees often flit into a white spruce right in front of our window, probing the cones for seeds; alternately, the chickadees join the nuthatches in probing the bark of our trees for wintering insects and their offspring.

The insect gleaning brings to mind Aldo Leopold's November essay in *Sand County Almanac,* entitled "A Mighty Fortress." Leopold wrote of the virtues of disease and insects, without which we would not have "a treasury of eggs, larvae, and cocoons" for the chickadees' table. Those losses of the summer season, the trees dead from a host of possible mortalities, may in death be more valuable to wildlife than when they were living, Leopold observed. A disease like heart rot provides cavities for barred owls, wood ducks, squirrels, and tribes of other species. As Leopold concluded, "Dead trees are transmuted into living animals, and vice versa."

By the way, in my view, there is no better book to give a nature lover for Christmas than *Sand County Almanac.*

Project Feeder Watch

The Cornell Lab of Ornithology conducts the largest backyard bird study in North America, utilizing observers in all 50 states and 12 Canadian provinces and territories. Compiling observer reports from regions throughout North America helps researchers to understand the movements of birds in the winter and to project their overall population increases or declines. For example, the winter of 1994-95 was exceptionally mild. Feeder observers in northeastern and north central states reported fewer normal resident birds like hairy woodpeckers, blue jays, and northern cardinals than had been reported in previous years. But feeder counts for those resident species were steady in the normally mild southern states, indicating that birds up north were simply ignoring feeders because natural food was readily available.

Another example of how regional data can be used to demonstrate the effect of winter weather on feeder visits occurred in the same year. Low numbers of white-throated sparrows, white-crowned sparrows, and rufous-sided towhees were reported in the southeast. Those three species usually migrate into the southern states for the winter, but as it turns out the mild weather allowed them to stay up north.

Boreal species like finches, redpolls, and nuthatches, which often wander from their home ranges southward into our area, were generally down in 1994-95, too. Harsh winters send them scampering our way for food, but counters in Alaska reported high numbers during this particular winter. Apparently we were low here because the boreal species could afford to stay farther north.

More than 12,000 backyard bird-watchers are enrolled in Cornell's Project FeederWatch, and nearly 1,000 of them are educaters who make FeederWatch into classroom projects. To join, call 1-800 843-BIRD, or write to Project FeederWatch, P.O. Box 11, Ithaca, NY 14851-0011. The project is funded through its participants, and the cost to join in is $15. You'll receive complete instructions, data forms, the newsletter *Birdscope,* and a beautiful bird calendar.

Which Birdseed?

Different species of wintering birds prefer different kinds of food, but if you wish to choose one kind of seed that will attract the greatest number of species, use black-oil sunflower seeds. Numerous studies show that these seeds are the favorite of the majority of species that visit backyard feeders. Buy the black-oil seeds, not the striped sunflower seeds. The striped seeds are bigger and thicker, making them tough for smaller birds to handle and crack.

Every so often, I think I need to provide other seeds for our backyard birds. More often than not, the birds kick out or ignore the varied tablefare, and I'm left with a feeder full of millet, milo, and whatever else is in the mix.

Certain species do prefer seeds other than sunflowers. Blue jays like whole corn; doves like corn, milo, and millet; small finches like niger seed, which is too expensive for me. Here's a chart that provides general guidelines:

88

	chickadees/ nuthatches	finches	grosbeaks cardinals	jays	wood- peckers	doves
sunflower	•	•	•	+	+	
safflower	+	+	+			
corn				•		•
millet		+				+
milo				+		+
niger	•					
suet	•			+	•	
• = preferred + = also eaten						

Peanut butter works well as a suet substitute; peanuts and popped popcorn are appreciated by numerous birds also. Table scraps may be put out as long as they aren't moldy or spoiled.

Blue Jay Gluttony

I've watched blue jays take sunflower seed after sunflower seed at our bird feeders, apparently swallowing them whole. I watched one jay swallow 53 seeds before it flew off. They're not really swallowing the seeds; instead, they're filling up their gullets, just as a chipmunk fills its cheek pouches. After taking their fill, the jays fly to a quieter spot, where they regurgitate the seeds and crack them open. Because they're aggressive and gluttonous, blue jays can be perceived as a nuisance at feeders, but to their credit, they are the first to sound the alarm if a predator comes near. The warning benefits all birds in the vicinity.

White Pelicans

The "Most Remarkable Sighting Award" for November of 1995 went to Terry Peck at the Sunrise Resort on Presque Isle Lake. While taking out a dock, Terry saw a white pelican some 100 feet away on the lake. He coaxed the pelican to within 50 feet by trying to feed it bread, and he was able to take a series of pictures.

White pelicans are increasingly seen in eastern areas, and they appear to be expanding their range. A few fall migrants move through Wisconsin, usually between October 15 and November 10, but they remain a rare sight.

89

Conjunctions

In November of 1995, Jupiter, Mars, and Venus converged to form an isosceles triangle low in the southwestern sky. For the rest of the month, they changed positions relative to one another in the early evening sky. On the evening of November 19, the three formed a tight circle just two degrees in diameter. The series of rare conjunctions, during which the planets were so close together for so many nights, occurs just once or twice in a decade. The three planets were visible for only about half an hour after sunset, and they rose only ten degrees above the horizon.

A similar triangular conjunction of Mars, Jupiter, and Saturn occurred in the year 6 B.C., and it's widely speculated that what became known as the Star of Bethlehem was in fact this conjunction.

Night Sky

Winter stars take center stage in November's night sky. Orion the Hunter, visible from October to April in our skies, rises in the early evening; by midnight, it is high in the southeastern sky. Its glittering, three-star belt is prominent among the many bright stars of winter. Two stars frame Orion's body at the shoulders and two more at the legs, creating a constellation that's almost as recognizable as the Big

Dipper. Fifteen stars with a magnitude of four or better comprise Orion (with the naked eye, we see stars beginning at magnitude six). Orion is the only constellation that has two first-magnitude stars--Betelgeuse and Rigel. A hazy area appears immediately below the belt. This area, known as the Orion nebula, is in the process of forming hundreds of new stars. Betelgeuse, on the other hand, has nearly blazed its last hurrah--it may go supernova at any time. When it goes, Orion will be short a left shoulder, making the hunt a bit more difficult.

Like the Big Dipper, Orion can be used to quickly locate other prominent stars and constellations. If you follow the line of Orion's belt to the left for about 20 degrees (the distance of two fists held together at arm's length out in front of you) you will find Sirius, the brightest star in the night sky at magnitude -1. If you follow the line of the belt to the right for 20 degrees, you will be looking just below Aldebaran (magnitude 0.9) in Taurus the Bull; go another 20 degrees and you will be in the midst of the Pleiades, the most prominent star cluster in the sky. Pleiades is often referred to as the Seven Sisters, because seven stars are visible to most people with above average eyesight. Using binoculars, you will see several dozen stars; with a telescope, you'll spot over a hundred.

90

Leonid Meteor Shower

Watch in November for the Leonid meteor shower, which produces extraordinary shows every 33 years or so. Check an astronomy magazine for the exact date when the shower will occur. The last spectacular shower happened in 1966, when several thousand meteors were seen per minute. In recent years, though, only 10 per hour have been spotted. Expectations are high for the years 1997 through 1999, but predicting the dazzle factor for these meteor showers is, at best, educated guesswork. The best hours to watch usually occur between two a.m. and dawn. These meteors are very fast and bright, and nearly two-thirds of them leave lingering vapor trails.

There Goes the Sun

By November 29, we will experience just nine hours of daylight. Most of us are now leaving for work in the dark and coming home from work in the dark.

Ice Records

In early 1995, Woody Hagge sent me his 17 year summary of ice cover on Foster Lake in Hazelhurst. In 1991-92, he noted, we "enjoyed" the longest ice cover and shortest open water season since he began keeping records in 1976. That winter provided 172 days of ice cover. The shortest ice duration occurred in the winters of 1990-91 and 1980-81, when we were mercifully treated to only 132 days of ice cover.

The 172-day record is just 10 days short of half a year, providing a statistical explanation for the wonderful underpopulation of the north country (by humans, that is) during the winter.

91

Thanksgiving

Thanksgiving, like many holidays, has an ambiguous past. The traditional story of the holiday's origin is more myth than actual history. A letter from Edward Winslow, written on December 11, 1621, is the apparent source of the Thanksgiving story: "Our harvest being gotten in, our Governour sent foure men on fowling…they foure in one day killed as much fowle…many of the Indians [came] amongst us, and amongst the rest their greatest King Massasoyt, with some nintie men, whom for three dayes we entertained and feasted, and they went out and killed five Deere, which they brought to the Plantation and bestowed on our Governour."

But no national holiday ensued. George Washington declared February 9, 1795, to be a day of Thanksgiving, but this day celebrated the defeat of the Whiskey Rebellion. Sam Adams proposed a permanent Thanksgiving holiday on May 9. Thomas Jefferson said the whole thing was a matter for the church, not for the government. Years later, Abraham Lincoln attempted to proclaim August 6 as a national day of Thanksgiving, but was persuaded by Sara Hale to move the date to a more traditional harvest time. As a result, the last Thursday in November became a holiday. The date had little to do with Pilgrims; instead, the holiday served as a means for Lincoln to build political bridges in a nation divided by war.

Historian Samuel Wilson concludes that "the feast of Thanksgiving celebrated this month is a phenomenon of our time, not theirs [the Pilgrims], a morality tale dealing with values central to modern

American culture--religious freedom, self-reliance, political independence, and racial harmony."

Christmas Presents

As Crhistmas approaches, I'm often asked to recommend natural history books that shed light on the northwoods, so I've listed my current favorites. I'm doing this now in November so you have time to make the purchases if you so desire. I offer these suggestions with two caveats: First, I don't pretend that I've read all the good, available books; secondly, books are a matter of personal taste, and these reflect mine.

I highly recommend any books written by these authors: Aldo Leopold, Sigurd Olson, Edward Abbey, Wendell Berry, Diana Kappel-Smith, Annie Dillard, and Farley Mowat.

Reference books:
Fieldbook of Natural History, by Palmer and Fowler
Mammals of Wisconsin, by Hartley Jackson
The North Woods: A Sierra Club Naturalist's Guide, by Daniel
    & Sullivan
The World of Northern Evergreens, by E.C. Pielou
Northwoods Wildlife: A Watcher's Guide to Habitats, by Janine
    Benyus
*Animal Tracking and Behavior; Amphibians and Reptiles; Bird
    Behavior;* and *Enjoying Wildflowers,* Stokes nature guides
Wisconsin Birdlife, by Sam Robbins
The Birders Handbook, by Ehrlich, Dobkin, and Wheye
The Audubon Society Encyclopedia of North American Birds,
    by John Terres
The Vegetation of Wisconsin, by John Curtis
Amphibians and Reptiles of Wisconsin, by Richard Vogt
Spring Flora of Wisconsin, by Norman Fassett
The Voyageurs, by Grace Lee Nute
Chippewa Customs, by Frances Densmore
American Wildlife and Plants: A Guide to Wildlife Food Habits,
    by Martin, Zim, and Nelson
Autumn Leaves, by Ronald Lanner

It's Raining Frogs and Fishes, by Jerry Dennis
A Field Guide to Mammal Tracking in North America,
    by James Halfpenny

For poetry about the natural world, I suggest Mary Oliver's *American Primitive* and *Dream Work.*

For anthologies, try:
Norton Anthology of Nature Writing, edited by Finch and Elder
This Incomparable Land, edited by Thomas Lyons
Words from the Land, edited by Stephen Trimble
Of Discovery and Destiny, edited by Junkin and Baron

93

> **Late-November Musings**
>
> *The wonder of a single snowflake outweighs the wisdom of a million meteorologists.*
>   —Francis Bacon

For nature quotations, try:
Things Precious and Wild, by John Terres

For general interpretive writing:
Open Spaces, by Jim dale Vickery
Learning Nature by a Country Road, by Tom Anderson
Book of Plough, by Justin Isherwood
North Country Notebook Vol. 1 and 2, by George Vukelich

You might also give a magazine subscription and/or membership to *Audubon, Wisconsin Natural Resources, Birder's World, The Passenger Pigeon, The Nature Conservancy,* or *Natural History.*

There are many other superb writers and books. Authors like Barry Lopez, John Burroughs, John Hay, John McPhee, Wallace Stegner, and Diane Ackerman are all highly respected. The gift of any good book will be appreciated, so don't get hung up on finding "the right one." As Edward Abbey said, "Freedom begins between the ears." There are many paths to that freedom.

If books aren't enough, a *good* pair of binoculars (plan on spending at least $150), a hand lens, a spotting scope, a microscope, or a telescope are essential items for any outdoorsperson. I emphasize quality. You don't want to frustrate someone with poor-quality optics.

94

DECEMBER

The Ojibwe word for December is *manidogizisons*, meaning "the diminutive spirit month." By contrast, January is the big spirit month.

December usually delivers the first major blows of the winter, though November has been known to pack a wallop as well. Fortunately, our woodstoves and insulated homes allow us to withstand December's rigors, and our greatest winter stresses amount to inconveniences. But for northern flora and fauna, winter is THE limiting factor in their survival. Consider the spreads of record temperatures our flora and fauna must adapt to: 112°F in summer and -51°F in winter, a variation of 163°. Since temperature records have been kept, the temperature has fallen to -40°F somewhere in the northwoods during more than half of all winters.

For those who live in upper Michigan's Keweenaw Peninsula, cold is probably less of a concern than snowfall. The area's record snowfall, which occurred in the winter of 1978-79, brought a total of nearly 390 inches! South of the Lake Superior snowbelt, we average around 70 inches--an amount still sufficient to create major adaptation problems for plants and animals.

let's go snowshoeing!

EXTIRPATED

1833

1840

1872

1908

1925

PROTECTED
OR
REINTRODUCED

1957

1993

Come & get it!

DECEMBER 1-15

AeL ©97

December 1 to December 15

Supercooling and Extracellular Freezing

For plants, winter is a time of drought. Water is unavailable in the soil because it takes the the form of ice. Because we have five months of winter, our plant life must be able to withstand conditions rivaling those of a desert for nearly half of the year. Our evergreens have evolved a series of adaptations that allow them the luxury of keeping their needles and photosynthesizing during warm spells in the winter. Their needle-shaped leaves expose little surface area for evaporation compared to a maple or oak leaf. The needles are coated with a waxy finish, which helps retain moisture. Conifers also have recessed stomata, or breathing pores, situated on the underside of their needles, again helping to reduce evaporation.

Beyond these means of holding onto the small amount of water available, all northern trees and shrubs must be able to withstand profound cold. They accomplish this either through supercooling or extracellular freezing. Those that use supercooling are hardy down to -40°F. The liquids in their cells remain liquid at below-freezing temperatures because they provide no minute particles or edges inside the cells, around which ice crystals could form. Like snow and rain, ice crystals require a nucleus such as a dust particle in order to form. However, if the temperature plunges below -40 °F, the cell liquids freeze anyway. In fact, they burst, killing the cells and usually the tree.

> **December Musings**
>
> *After a 10,000-foot fall, snow can land with every crystal, every cornice and gable intact. Snow waltzes down a December sky like a debutante down a Danish staircase. It knows how to act when wearing the crown jewels of meteorology. It enlists all virtue, all elegance, and worth, all beauty and erudition in one flight, one flirtation of air.*
>
> -Justin Isherwood

Look at a range map for trees. You will discover that -40°F is the temperature that separates hardy species such as white pine and hemlock from *very* hardy species such as balsam fir and white spruce. The very hardy trees use extracellular freezing to survive up to the Arctic treeline. Liquid moves from within the cells to spaces *between* the cells. There it freezes, without damaging the cells. Paper birch, quaking aspen, and balsam poplar are the only northern hardwood trees capable of this feat, as are willow and alder shrubs.

The Character of Snow

In early December, 1995, I took a long walk in the woods, traversing a series of bogs and wetlands. The ground was frozen, and the snow was minimal. While I was pleased with the conditions, I'm sure easy walking isn't high on the appreciation list for the small animals that need snow as an insulating and protective cover. Both the depth and character of the snow profoundly affect life at the ground level. The temperature at the groundlayer must be at or above freezing to ensure the survival of many small mammals.

The comfort zone for these mammals is based on the snow's thermal conductivity--the amount of heat that can pass through the snow. Granite and concrete conduct heat exceptionally well, so these materials have a high thermal conductivity. As a result, they aren't favored by contractors as insulating materials. On the other hand, fresh snow conducts heat very poorly, and so has a low thermal conductivity. If only it wouldn't melt, snow would make a great insulating material for buildings. In fact, fresh snow has a lower conductivity than fiberglass insulation. Eight inches of fresh powder snow prevents any temperature change at the groundlayer, no matter how cold the air temperature.

However, snow changes character as it ages. A "destructive metamorphosis" takes place, in which the snowflake crystals compact and are reshaped into rounded ice grains. The result makes good packing snow for pelting enemies, but poor insulating material. So, as snow ages, its insulating properties degrade until a new snow covers the old pack and changes its density and character. Once snow reaches a depth of 20 or more inches, though, the character of the snow ceases to affect the groundlayer temperature, and the small mammals stay protected.

Because small mammals can produce only a limited layer of insulating fat and fur for the winter, the constant fluctuation of temperature values based on snow conditions probably dominates their dinner conversations. And dinner is what they will become if the snow fails to cover them sufficiently.

Slumping

One thing I have always noticed on winter walks is the slumping of snow around tree trunks. Here's why it happens. Fresh snow is nature's best reflector, mirroring back nearly 95 percent of the sunlight that hits its surface. Older snowpacks covered by dust and leaf litter may only reflect 50 percent of the sunlight, so they heat up more quickly. But while snow is a good reflector of shortwave solar radiation, it is an equally good absorber of longwave radiant energy emitted by objects like you, your house, or trees. Trees radiate heat that they have absorbed from the sun, and that heat is absorbed by the snowpack, leaving a melted hollow around the tree trunk.

99

Wintergreen

Wintergreen berries have been ripe since early fall. If there is a lack of early winter snow, animals and humans can partake in some fine trailside munching. There are usually numerous red berries on a plant, and the fruit will persist into spring and summer. Oddly enough, grouse, black bears, and mice are about the only animals that eat the berries according to wildlife books. Deer and grouse eat the leaves. The berries taste very good, and were the source of all wintergreen oil until someone discovered that yellow birch twigs are full of wintergreen, too, and began using the twigs for distilling the oil. Eventually a synthetic substitute was found, and both yellow birch and wintergreen plants were given a reprieve.

The name "wintergreen" has a simple genesis--the waxy, good-tasting leaves remain green throughout the winter. Many other northern groundlayer species are evergreen, too, just like the conifer trees we usually associate with the term. Trailing arbutus, pipsissewa, partridgeberry, wild cranberry, bearberry, creeping snowberry, and bog laurel are examples of groundlayer evergreens.

Highbush Cranberries

Below my house stand several highbush cranberry bushes, which are laden every December with translucent, scarlet fruits that hang in clusters like upside-down umbrellas. Beautifully backlit by the white snow, the fruit usually remains on the branches all winter. It is seldom gleaned by birds or squirrels unless all other food sources fail. These beautiful berries remain untouched because most fall-fruiting shrubs and trees have low-quality fruit, which means the fat (or lipid) content of the fruits is generally less than 10 percent by weight. Migrating birds need high fat content in the fruit or seeds they consume, in order to attain the energy needed to cross large water bodies, buck winds, and dodge predators. A high fat content food source provides roughly twice the energy per unit weight compared to carbohydrates. If a bird wants to fly light with the highest octane fuel, it'll choose a high-quality food source. Species like highbush cranberry, mapleleaved viburnum, mountain-ash, winterberry, and sumac don't make the grade. A study of mapleleaf viburnums showed that more than 70 percent of the fruits remained on the plants as of January 1, even though they had ripened in August. Two-thirds of the missing fruits simply fell off.

100

Since low-quality fruits have a low fat content, the fruits rot very slowly, unlike the fruits of late summer. Lower-fat fruits can remain fresh until late in winter, when all the higher-quality foods have been exploited and the poor-quality fruits are all that's left. In human dietary terms, I suppose highbush cranberries and their poor nutritional mates are the equivalent of white bread, in that they provide lots of volume but little substance. In late winter, the birds and mammals turn to them anyway. The fruits are consumed and dispersed, hopefully far enough away from the parent plant to generate a new seedling in the upcoming spring.

A plant that has chosen the strategy of producing a high-quality fruit must invest a great deal of energy into its creation, then hope the fruit is found and eaten before it rots. If all plants produced high-quality fruits, they would either be eaten or rot well before mid-winter, leaving many animals with little to harvest during the toughest months of the year. Both kinds of fruit production--low quality and high quality--have their pros and cons, but each occupy a necessary niche in the lives of animal species.

Frogs on Ice

Where do the frogs go in winter? Most burrow into the soil or a lake bottom to avoid freezing. The leopard frog simply settles to the bottom and lies exposed on the mud, often becoming a convenient meal for cruising northern pike, walleye, and musky.

All winter long, frogs breathe through pores in their skin. Consider how remarkable a frog really is. It begins life breathing through gills. Then it changes into a lung-breathing animal. In winter, it switches to breathing through its skin.

The wood frog goes to great physiological extremes to survive winter. It buries itself just a few inches down in the soil, where the ground usually freezes. The wood frog itself freezes, often becoming hard as a rock, but when warmed up it can start hopping around like normal. It accomplishes this by packing its cells with glycogen to keep them from freezing. Water that moves between the cells does freeze, but the frog's cell structure is not harmed. This procedure, called extra-cellular freezing, is much the same as the strategy used by trees in northern Canada to survive temperatures of -80°F.

101

When spring comes, the wood frog thaws out, transports the glycogen back to its liver (where it's used for other purposes), and probably yawns and stretches, commenting on the fine dreams it has had for the last five months.

Keep Those Cavities

Below our house sits the bulk of our "land," probably better described as "occasional river bottom." Many old, dead, or dying black ash fall down when the wind blows hard enough, but when they're standing they provide great nesting sites for a lot of animals. In the Upper Midwest, nearly 43 species of birds and 25 species of mammals use tree cavities as nesting or den sites. Twenty-one of those species will only use natural cavities--they accept no substitutes. The cavities also provide important roosting sites that allow many birds and mammals to get out of the cold. That's why we leave those old snags up, even though they don't look very tidy.

Mixing It Up

The mixed foraging flocks of birds (chickadees, nuthatches, grosbeaks, finches, redpolls, and others) that come to our feeders during the fall and winter might seem counterproductive, since the individuals spend a lot of time competing with each other for the seed. But foraging in a mixed-species flock has its advantages. One obvious advantage of feeding in a group is the number of eyes available to watch for predators. If other members are "on watch," each bird can forage at the feeder for a longer time. Detection of the food source is also enhanced by the number of birds searching for nourishment. I'm always amazed at how quickly a variety of birds find my feeder once I've filled it. Whether birds use a communication signal equivalent to the triangular dinner bell I don't know, but it certainly seems as if some bird is ringing out the news.

102

As a rule, mixed-species flocks are nicely balanced when it comes to specialized skills. Chickadees like to glean insects and seeds from outer, higher branches; juncos prefer ground feeding; hairy woodpeckers take to the trunks with their hammer-drills and barbed tongues. Feeding specialization ensures that all the available nooks and crannies of the food resource are exploited, while reducing competition between individuals. Vigorous competition would result in an energy loss that would be difficult to overcome in winter.

A Swimming Snowy Owl

One December a couple in Irma watched a snowy owl sit on the cab of their pickup truck for two hours. On three separate occasions, the owl flew into the couple's pond and took a "swim." I have never heard of owls swimming before, but all birds are capable of floating on the water because of the buoyancy of the air held in their feathers, air sacs associated with their lungs, and air-filled bones. The "how" of swimming makes sense, but why a snowy owl would purposely swim is beyond me, unless it was bathing, an activity that large birds like hawks, crows, and owls have occasionally been observed to do.

Goose Bumps

One of the first things I check when I get up in the morning is our bird feeders. In trees near the feeders, birds are often "fluffed out" in order to protect themselves from the cold. Animals can puff out their hair or feathers at night to trap more air, employing the same principle as fiberglass insulation. Humans try to do the same when chilled, but the muscles at the base of our hairs, which once hoisted fur, instead produce goose bumps. Evolution has robbed us of our fur mantle, but we retain the means of elevating it.

We imitate animals in another way. One year on my birthday, my wife Mary gave me one of those jackets that's really two jackets in one. The outer layer keeps moisture from getting in, but lets body moisture out; the inner fleece lining provides warmth. It's a reasonable replica of the winter fur generated by most animals. The animals' outer coat consists of long, water-shedding guard hairs, while their inner coat is a batting of soft fluff that traps body-warmed air.

103

Snowshoeing Grouse

Grouse grow horny comblike projections on either side of their toes in winter, effectively doubling the surface area of their feet. This "snowshoe" effect allows them to walk on the surface of the snow more easily.

Cold Comfort

I'm often not fully acclimated to the cold until sometime in December. Until then I hover around the woodstoves until I'm nearly baked; then I move away for a while, only to return later, chilled again. Humans have very few physiological adaptations to cold. Our best means of reducing heat loss involves constricting the blood vessels close to our skin surface. Thus we radiate and conduct less body heat to the air by shunting our blood to deeper veins. If our extremities are in danger of freezing, our blood vessels dilate intermittently as we try to bring temporary heat back to freezing areas.

But not all humans are alike. Alaskan Inuit adults use dilation more than constriction in order to weather the cold. Their fingers are usually four to five degrees warmer than those of other test subjects when immersed in ice water. While this increases heat loss, it also provides much better dexterity at low temperatures--a necessary adaptation for an Arctic culture.

If constriction doesn't work, we use muscle activity to produce heat, either through voluntary exercise or by shivering. Vigorous exercise can increase our heat production tenfold, as anyone knows who has slogged through deep snow and has had to peel away layers of clothing to avoid sweating to death.

Humans can increase their tolerance of cold through long-term exposure and conditioning. We've probably all read about individuals who wear T-shirts and walk barefoot in Alaska during the winter. Australian Aborigines sleep virtually naked on the ground at near-freezing temperatures without experiencing any discomfort, while Nepalese mountain people wear thin clothing and no gloves or boots in cold weather. These are exceptions to the rule of being human, though. We're basically tropical animals that get by on our ingenuity, not on our physiological adaptations.

104

Snowshoeing

One Sunday in early December, I went snowshoeing in the Manitowish River Wilderness Area, across the river from my home. The temperature was in the high 30s, and the snow melting from tree branches sounded like a gentle rainstorm in the deep woods. The evergreen trees were laden with snow from a storm that hit several weeks earlier, a storm that began with sleet and then piled snow on top. Northern tree species need supple branches to withstand heavy snow loads; these trees looked as if they were wearing heavy white gowns that bent their branches downward. The brief thaw spelled relief for many trees that probably would have lost numerous limbs with additional snow loads.

As with nearly everything in nature, the loss of tree limbs has a positive side. Downed branches provide new buds for browsing snowshoe hares and deer, and openings in the canopy where May sunlight can reach the forest floor and germinate quiescent seeds.

The swamp forests were thinly iced over. The ice cracked frequently as I walked, so needless to say I saw no wildlife. But I did see extensive deer sign, particularly in one area that contained many cedars and big pines. Deer droppings were abundant, and eight times I found that the scat was stained with blood.

The snow had the texture of a thick cotton candy, compressing easily, and it triggered memories of the brutal snowball battles of my youth. Aldo Leopold wrote of "the elemental sadness" that comes upon all living things after a heavy snow. "Nevertheless," he said, "my pines, each with his burden of snow, are standing ramrod-straight, rank upon rank, and in the dusk beyond I sense the presence of hundreds more. At such times I feel a curious transfusion of courage."

Buying Snowshoes

I highly recommend snowshoeing to any of you who haven't tried it. Snowshoes are the best means of exploring the woods that lie beyond the ski and snowmobile trails. You can find silence and isolation on showshoes--rare commodities given the huge influx of snowmobiles into the northwoods over the last decade. And wildlife signs are often more common away from the well-used trails.

When buying snowshoes, be sure to buy a pair with upturned toes of at least four inches. Without this feature, it's entirely too easy to bury the tips in the snow as you walk, then end up on your face. For this reason, I see little value in the flat, bear paw-style snowshoes--unless you're consistently able to walk on crusted snow or you're walking through heavy brush.

Flying Squirrels

Jim Bell from Minocqua wrote me one December, reporting that six flying squirrels were soaring down from his oak trees nightly to visit his bird feeder, where they dined on sunflower seeds. They typically came in around five p.m. and were quite tame--so much so that Jim could walk right up to them. I know other people in our area who spend as much time watching their bird feeders at night for flying squirrels as they spend watching the feeders for birds during the day. Floodlights apparently don't scare the squirrels away--nor does the presence of someone who sits quietly outside on a deck, watching them come in.

Of course, the northern flying squirrel doesn't really fly. Instead, it glides by extending a loose fold of skin (the patagium) that stretches from the outside of the wrists of its front feet to the ankles of its hind feet. To take off, a flying squirrel must climb a tree to acquire some height, then leap out. It steers by using its feet, and by changing the "airfoil" effect of its patagium. According to the literature, a flying squirrel may glide for distances of 100 to 150 feet!

Truly nocturnal, flying squirrels have large, dark eyes suited for night vision. Omnivorous, they forage on the ground or in the trees for nuts, fruits, mushrooms, insects, and any meat they can find. Their winter diet consists primarily of tree buds. They serve as prey for predators that work dense, forested areas, including martens, fishers, great horned owls, and goshawks.

In excellent habitat such as mature mixed hardwood and conifer stands, three to four flying squirrels may be found per acre, though one or two per acre is most common. In winter, though, they may congregate by the dozen in tree cavities, undoubtedly trying to stay warm.

Beavers

A large beaver lodge protrudes from the western shore of Frog Lake in the Manitowish River Wilderness Area. Inside, the temperature should be about 45°F or higher. As a rule, a black hole at the top of a lodge, like a smoke hole in a wigwam, indicates that the lodge is active. The warmth of the family rises through this air vent and melts away a circle of snow.

Fishers

Fishers were once a very unusual sight in northern Wisconsin, but they have now become relatively common. The DNR reintroduced them in the late 1950s and 1960s, long after they had been extirpated from Wisconsin in 1932. Fisher pelts fetched an incredible $345 apiece in 1920, ensuring their elimination. Trapping protection and reintroduction allowed them to gradually regain a foothold; now they are more common in many areas than red foxes and bobcats. Trapping was reauthorized in 1985, but pelts now bring a mere $35 or so, depending on the year.

Members of the weasel family, fishers are perhaps best known for their ability to predate upon porcupines--a skill that any dog or dog owner can greatly appreciate. A fisher will attack a porky's face until the porcupine is so bewildered that the fisher can flip it over and gain access to the porky's soft underbelly. A porcupine has some 30,000 quills, covering every part of its body except the nose and the belly. Once they penetrate your skin, the quills work their way in at a rate of an inch per day.

Female fishers mate in early spring, within a week after giving birth. Through delayed implantation, females eventually implant their embryos in late January, after carrying them for nine to 10 months. The fertilized eggs free-float in the uterus until an instinctive measure initiates the attachment of the embryos to the uterine wall. Young are born between March 15 and April 15, whereupon the female will mate again within seven -10 days of birthing. Thus female fishers remain effectively pregnant throughout their lives, suggesting that the women's movement has yet to reach the fisher population.

107

Snowshoe Hares

Snowshoe hares finalize their "change of coats" in early December, although the molt begins back in October. First their ears and feet turn white; their backs are the last to undergo the color change. Snowshoes become pure white except for the black tips of their ears.

The hind feet of a snowshoe hare are four to six inches long, and they're attached to a body that's just 15 to 20 inches long. If our feet were proportionate in size to the hare's feet, they would be nearly 30 inches long, making them a size 45. It's little wonder that snowshoe hares have such exceptional ability to maneuver in snow. Thanks to their white camouflage and their winter mobility, hares are one of the few animals who could be called "snow-lovers."

Death in the Winter of 1995-96

The winter of 1995-96 was exceptionally long, cold, and snowy, resulting in the death of an estimated 30 percent of the northern deer population. DNR biologists projected that nearly 150,000 deer died, out of a total northern herd of about half a million. Most of the mortality occurred among fawns and the oldest bucks. Despite the dramatic mortality figures, deer populations remained well over management goals for every management unit in the north as we headed into the fall 1996 deer hunting season. Deer numbers continue at unsustainably high levels.

108

Projections such as the above are extrapolations from what has been seen historically. Two variables may have decreased the actual loss. First, the number of people feeding deer may have significantly increased the survival rate. Secondly, the snow in many areas featured a walkable crust, which allowed deer to access browsing sites outside of the confines of their deer yards.

A Chronology

The controversies surrounding the deer hunting season often stimulate my thoughts on the management, status, and history of other wildlife species. The following is an incomplete, wildlife-specific chronology that illustrates most of our historical mistakes and some of our recent successes. Note that the dates of extirpation from Wisconsin for some species vary within the literature.

1833   buffalo extirpated
1840   trumpeter swan extirpated
1866   elk extirpated
1872   wild turkey extirpated
1878   whooping crane extirpated
1879   carp planted in Wisconsin by sportsmen
1899   passenger pigeon extirpated
1900   beaver reduced to about 500 individuals in Wisconsin
1903   last recorded Eskimo curlew in Wisconsin
1908   cougar extirpated (or 1884, according to another source)
1909   smelt planted in Lake Michigan (1926, according to another source)

1910	woodland caribou extirpated
1921	moose extirpated (1912, according to another source)
1922	wolverine extirpated
1923	first starling observed in Wisconsin
1925	pine marten extirpated (1940, according to another source)
1932	fisher extirpated
1944	ghost shiner extirpated
1949	alewives first seen in lower Michigan
1950	sharp-tailed grouse population nearly gone
1950s	commercial trout fishing ends in Lake Superior and Lake Michigan, due to lamprey eel
1950s	timber wolves thought to be extirpated
1956	reintroduction of fisher begins in Wisconsin
1957	Canada lynx and timber wolf protected by law in Wisconsin
1974	double-crested cormorants in Wisconsin reduced to only six rookeries
1975	pine marten reintroduced in Wisconsin
1987	trumpeter swan recovery program begins in Wisconsin
1993	bald eagle and osprey removed from Wisconsin's threatened species list
1996	18 pairs of trumpeter swans nested in Wisconsin
1997	timber wolf population estimated at around 150, with about 35 packs

109

Ice-Up

For over 40 years, Paul Brenner has kept track of the comings and goings of ice on Maple Lake, near Boulder Junction. In 1990, Maple Lake iced-over on December 1, the second-latest date since Paul began keeping records. The latest ice-up date was December 7, which occurred in 1962. The dubious honor of the earliest ice-up date goes to 1988, when the lake skimmed over on October 30.

Wintering Deer

Few of us think of deer as migrators, but indeed they are. They simply migrate on a smaller scale than birds. Only about 10 percent of the total deer range in the Upper Great Lakes Region will support wintering deer, so some deer must follow a regular migratory path in the late autumn to arrive at their wintering sites. Most deer in northern Wisconsin and Michigan's Upper Peninsula travel 10 miles or less to their wintering areas. But in the central U.P., deer often travel more than 50 miles to find suitable winter cover.

Poor winter habitat tends to concentrate deer in limited locations, which can in turn create a survival bottleneck. Large, uniform stands of lowland conifers provide the best habitat, but not all conifer species offer the same benefits. Dense stands of white cedar, spruce, balsam fir, or hemlock provide better habitat than pines, for instance. The ideal stand provides plentiful food, shelter from the wind and snow, overhead cover for heat retention, and protection from predators. A dense stand of 60-year-old white cedar can reduce the wind flow by 60 to 200 times that of an adjacent, more open upland forest. Dense conifer stands offer the narrowest range of temperatures and the warmest average temperature during cold weather. The trees catch snowfall in their branches, so snow accumulates more slowly on the ground.

Deer survival hinges heavily on the amount of reserve fat the animals carry into the winter, and the rate at which the fat gets burned. By midwinter, deer have reduced their movement by at least 50 percent, in order to conserve energy. They generally have five peak activity times, spaced four to six hours apart--sunrise, midday, sunset, and twice at night. In the coldest part of winter, they reduce their food intake, stop growing, lose weight, drop their heart rates, and become far less active. As the deer weaken over the winter, they also move less at night. Deer commonly lose 10 to 30 percent of their body weight without dying in the winter.

As might be expected, fawns are in the greatest jeopardy during the winter. If they are to survive, they must be born early in the season and they must get optimal nutrition during summer and autumn. Male fawns are born weighing six to seven pounds around Memorial Day; they should weigh 100 pounds by early December (female fawns should weigh 80 to 90 pounds). Fawns consume most of their calories as part of the growth process in the summer; in the autumn, they must change their growth strategy and put those calories into fat reserves and not into growth if they hope to survive a long winter.

Rut-stressed bucks lose 20 to 25 percent of their peak autumn body weight chasing does around--a behavior that is almost suicidal in our northern climate. Still, most manage to survive somehow, though it's not clear how they manage to do this.

Does that have raised fawns late into the fall are usually in poor condition when winter begins, because lactation takes energy--particularly if a doe has given birth to twins or triplets. The does that miss out on mating during the initial rut will come back into estrus in early December, in the hope of "catching their man."

In most years, winter die-offs in Wisconsin are not significant, but in northern Michigan in 1994, an estimated 117,000 deer died. The most critical month is March, when weakened deer are most susceptible to stress. Many records exist recounting times when American Indians and early settlers ran down deer on snowshoes in March, the deer wallowing in deep snow or exhausting themselves by breaking through thin-crusted snow.

111

The Complexity of Winter

We tend to think of winter as a simple group of factors that animals must respond to. We experience winter as cold temperatures, chilling wind, deep snow, shorter days, and less sun. But winter is more complicated than these factors might indicate.

Organisms must respond to additional factors in adapting to the wind, cold, and snow. They must be able to handle the mean temperatures and total accumulation of snow throughout a season, but they must also deal with the *extremes*--the record-setting excesses such as -40°F, blizzard conditions, or 40 inches of snowfall over a weekend.

The timing of the occurrence is also significant. For instance, an early deep freeze is much worse if it comes before the snowfall; or a late-winter storm packs a greater punch because of the weakened condition of winter-ravaged animals.

The duration of an event is equally important. Will it be -30°F for an entire week, or just one day? The extent of the differences between the seasons can severely affect an animal, too. Will it reach

100°F in the summer but go down to -40°F in the winter?

And finally the repeatability of a factor must be considered. One blizzard may not be bad, but frequent blizzards require energy expenditures that many animals can't afford.

In the natural world, as in human society, timing can be everything. Winter survival hinges on a constellation of variables that are impossible to predict and often difficult to weigh. Unfortunately, only spring will open the final curtain and reveal what has survived and what hasn't.

112

December Musings

As I sat there on the rock, I realized that, in spite of the closeness of civilization and the changes that hemmed it in, this remnant of the old wilderness would speak to me of silence and solitude, of belonging and wonder and beauty... I named this place Listening Point because only when one comes to listen, only when one is aware and still, can things be seen and heard. Everyone has a listening point somewhere. It does not have to be in the north or close to the wilderness, but some place of quiet where the universe can be contemplated with awe.

–Sigurd Olson

<u>113</u>

December 16 to December 31

The Cabin Door

Our goal one December morning was to snowshoe to Johnny Ingersoll's cabin, downriver four miles from our home in Manitowish. Overnight three inches of snow had fallen onto the existing two foot snowbase. The sky had cleared, though the morning air glittered as if the tiny snowflakes still drifted down.

On a morning like this, the quiet settles into your bones, as does the cold. We were off quickly, our snowshoes compressing the powder and floating us forward.

Johnny's cabin is little more than a shack, listing to the side, and settled in upon itself like the melting snows it had sloughed off for the last 60 years. We wanted to go there to read again the writing on the doorframe where in the winter of 1935 Johnny and his friends had penciled the

> ### End-of-the-Year Musings
>
> *Winter is a predictable kind of Armageddon, a calamity calmly weathered, an end of a world that they [wildlife] understand and are preparing for; caught between the forces of darkness and light.*
>
> —Diana Kappel-Smith

conditions they had weathered during that season. I'd never asked Johnny why he didn't use paper, but I suspect he simply didn't have any. The cabin, five miles by sedge hummocks and scattered pine islands from town, was too isolated to waste a day tracking down paper.

In his youth, Johnny would never have thought his doorframe accounting would be valued as an historical marker, a vignette of life along the Manitowish River. Now in his eighties, and too unsteady to make the cabin trek again in his lifetime, Johnny considers us amusing for our interest. But his eyes cloud and mist whenever he talks of the cabin. Those doorframe dates aren't abstractions to him. He lived there when his body was muscled and vibrant. Because we respect him, and the river, the dates matter to us, too.

We shoed across the snow-covered river and listened for the current under the ice, but the snow absorbed all sound. My mother always said, as every mother to come will probably say, "Silence is a virtue." That must hold true for the silence of ice and the purity of snow. For five months every year life must survive under the ice in that dark quiet. It is a wonder.

We left the narrow river channel to wallow through the marsh grasses where the snow is always deeper than anywhere else. The old pines that lined the shoreline between the forest and the sloughs were heavy with snow. We stepped up out of the slough and into the pines, a topographical change of no more than several feet. Yet in the northwoods that slight difference provides dry enough conditions for the shallow, wide pine roots which have little regard for spending a lifetime standing in water. Under their umbrella, the snow thinned and we entered the forest.

116

Chickadees and nuthatches worked the seed cones and gleaned the bark furrows of the old pines, chitchatting as they peered and probed. Chickadees enliven winter better than any animal I know. Unlike most animal's fear and distrust of humans, they make you feel welcome in their community. I made a "pishing" sound that mimics the call notes of many birds, and in they came, fluttering around Mary and me from branch to branch, and singing back. They soon tired of my limited conversational skills and moved on. I reminded Mary of the first law of all good naturalists–"Never pish into the wind," I said. She shook her head in mock disgust, and shoed into the pervasive understory of hazel brush.

Hazelnut provides a good mast crop for squirrels, catkins for grouse, and nesting cover for songbirds, but their whiplike stems usually manage to snap back on cold faces or knock hats off all too often for my liking. If you live in pine country, you better get used to hazel though, because it dominates the understory in the fleeting sunlight that drifts through the pine needles. If not for the hazel, the pine forest would be open parkland, easy to walk through, but with little to see.

Deeper into the pines we found piles of cone scales, the "middens" of red squirrels who are fastidious in their eating and waste disposal. These miniature landfills are sprinkled throughout the pines, but usually far enough apart to raise the question of whether another squirrel's territory has been entered or whether individual red squirrels create numerous midden sites.

Mary led the way into a stand of cedar. The deer had browsed the foliage in an obvious line about six feet high–it looked like a woman's high skirt exposing the long legs of the cedar. Where the cedar needles began marked the height to which the deer could reach. The buds of numerous interspersed red maple were also shred from their branches. The ragged tearing of other woody stems all around us were the unmistakable signs of deer browse. Later we were to see sugar maples browsed over for so many consecutive years that they looked more like the arthritic hands of an elderly man than the new growth of a vigorous year. Yet deer have never evolved front teeth on their upper jaw. Why is an evolutionary mystery, though their excessive numbers indicate they manage quite well without them.

117

Deer tracks wound throughout the lowland, some paths traveled so heavily as to be more highways than paths. Smoothed saucer-like depressions marked their evening beds. Coyote tracks overlapped a deer trail neer the edge of the cedar. What must it be like for deer at night when coyotes circle into their yard?

We left the cedars and were soon into a series of leatherleaf bogs dotted with small pine islands. Bogs epitomize the state of "no event" that winter can offer–no movement, no sound, no apparent life of any kind–just a standstill. The bog's black spruce trees looked like scruffy orphans, all bushy hair on the top and a stick below. The tamaracks looked dead to anyone unaware that they shed their needles in mid-October.

There's no better wilderness to be found in this increasingly populated north country than bogs. No better silence too. We could hear our breathing, our heartbeat, and nothing else. No black flies, no mosquitoes. The wind picked up for a moment, and lifted the pines on the boundary of the bog in a softening and steady "thrum," a rhythm of sound as smooth as waves on sand. A winter bog may be the daytime equivalent of looking into the heavens at night and wondering the whys.

The cold began to work down through our clothes, and we struck out hard for the cabin, compassing as we went, hoping to hit just upriver from Johnny's and then follow the river down to the cabin. Familiar landmarks transform in winter. We couldn't trust our memory, so there was an edge of tension to the travel. Doubt always seeps in because there's no such thing as a straight line in the woods, and distances can't be paced off like in a parking lot. There's windfall to go around, alder thickets to thrash through, topography to take and to avoid.

A grouse exploded from an aspen limb right next to Mary and we both jumped as high as is possible when strapped into snowshoes. Grouse are beautiful birds but the damn things can take your heart from calm to a scream in a second. We caught our breath and then noticed the grouse tracks and droppings along several downed trunks. We'd come into an opening with young aspen vying for the front row seat in the canopy. The grouse must have been "budding," nipping off the male buds.

118

At the top of one of the aspens was the dark fat figure of a porcupine, dining on the soft inner cambium of the bark in nature's version of "The Life of Riley." What animal lives a better life than a porky, shambling from tree to tree, climbing to the tops, eating its fill, and watching the world go by?

We worked our way up a short pine ridge, and below us stretched the willow sloughlands that border the Manitowish. The river loops and coils back upon itself again and again, a white corridor through the muted green of the winter conifers and the rusty brown of the alders and willows.

The pine ridge runs south and eventually drops to the water. Johnny's cabin was just down river, and we were relieved to know how near we were. Snowshoeing works the body, and hunger had settled in.

We crossed the river and saw Johnny's cabin shuttered tight and slumping on its foundation. Mary fumbled the key into the lock and we tramped in. We opened the shutters to let in some light, and found some kindling to get the fire going. Soon the little cabin warmed up and we took our coats off and relaxed.

The doorframe beckoned immediately. Johnny's old friend Bill Kruiser had his cabin a mile south on the river, and he too had penciled his history on his doorframe, though in much greater detail than Johnny. When Bill died, the cabin and land was purchased by the DNR, and soon burned down in the debilitating 20th century fear of insurance liability. Bill's door to history was lost. We know this could

happen to Johnny's door too, so we wrote it all down. It wasn't that
much after all–not like we'd remembered it. But it still chronicled in
broad terms one man's response to living out the Depression Era on a
wild river. The doorframe read:

Oct. 1, 1935	We arrived.
Nov. 1	Lawrence left.

This door was hoisted in position Wed. November 27, 1935
   Jack and Chunk, Contractors.

Dec. 1, 1935	River jammed in front of cabin–had a hell of a job crossing.
Dec. 4	Crossed river on ice 1st time.
Dec. 6	Raining today, sleet.
New Year's Eve	Was over to Bill's. Had a quart of spirits.
Jan. 1, 1936	Very mild, 36° above zero.
Jan. 12 (Sunday)	1st snowstorm–all day.
Jan. 15	No clouds in sight–sleighing in the woods.
Jan. 20	Big party last night at Bill's.
Jan. 22	Rip snortin blizzard, -26°.
Jan. 24 (Friday)	-36°
Feb. 5	-42° windy
Feb. 7 (Friday)	-45°–ate supper without lighting lamp, first time
Feb. 8	Southeast blizzard
Feb. 9 (Sunday)	-45°
Feb. 23-25	Warm, melting fast
Feb. 25 (Wednesday)	Easterly blizzard
Mar. 1 (Sunday)	Snowstorm
Mar. 2	Very warm
Mar. 21	Very warm, river soft on edges
Mar. 23 (Monday)	Ice unsafe–saw 1st blackbird
Mar. 26	Snow, cold
Mar. 30-Apr. 3	Helped John cut ice
Mar. 30	-10°, snow
Apr. 6 (Monday)	-8°
Apr. 12 (Easter)	River opened last night, snowshoed to town.

119

Apr. 17	Went to vote on snowshoes
May 2 (Sunday)	Bill, Jack and I traveled to Bud Prey's "River View Estate"–Bacon and eggs!
May 3	2:30 We are checking out–weather very warm.

We thought about how Johnny's almanac compares to the one we keep today. Our records for the first arrival of blackbirds are always around March 23rd, too. It's good to know the red-wings keep their word over so many years.

On this December day in 1994 nearly 60 years later, we needed to check out soon, too. The sun was angling for the horizon in its winter swiftness, and soon the sunlight would stream from the horizon and fire the tree tops. There was time to get home if we moved fast.

We write on the door before we leave, "Dec. 23, 1994. 18°, snowshoeing home to Manitowish on same day. Thanks to Johnny and all who came before him."

Performance Art on a Winter Canvas

Winter may seem "dead" to many observers, but it actually offers unrivaled wildlife observation opportunities, because the snow reveals animal tracks that are usually invisible during the summer. Animals also stand out visually in winter, because the foliage is thinner and the landscape background is a pure white. Inga Brynildson Hagge from Hazelhurst, a good friend and writer, wrote that "nature is a kind of performance artist. With each fresh snow, the old master wipes the canvas bare and begins again."

Where should you look to find tracks and see animals? Try getting away from trails on showshoes if you want to see animals--although many animals do use our trails, particularly in deep snow conditions. Twilight is a great time to see animals, as are warm, thawing days when animals, like humans, are excited to feel the sun. Check out south slopes, springholes, or open water. When it's very cold, animals often stay inactive to conserve energy unless they must search for food. On these days, I suggest that you do the same.

A Dancing World of Rubies

December often unleashes an ice storm, the beauty of which can be stunning. I discovered an 1897 passage written by Mark Twain, which is as eloquent as any about ice storms:

"In time the trunk and every branch and twig are encased in hard, pure ice; so that the tree looks like a skeleton tree made all of glass . . . All are waiting; they know what is coming . . . The sun climbs higher, flooding the tree from its loftiest spread of branches to its lowest, turning it to a glory of white fire; then in a moment comes the great miracle, the miracle without its fellow in the Earth; a gust of wind sets every branch and twig to swaying, and in an instant turns the whole white tree into a spouting and spraying explosion of flashing gems of every conceivable color . . . a dancing and glancing world of rubies, emeralds, diamonds, sapphires, the most radiant spectacle, the divinest, the most exquisite, the most intoxicating vision of fire and color and unimaginable splendor that ever any eye has rested upon in this world, or will ever rest upon outside the gates of heaven."

121

Winter Solstice

The winter solstice usually occurs on December 21 or 22, marking the southernmost rising and setting of the sun during the year as well as the shortest day and longest night of the year at our latitude. At the solstice, we receive just eight hours and 41 minutes of sunlight. Fundamentally, winter solstice means "the sun stands still." The Saxons celebrated the solstice with bonfires meant to urge the sun on in its return to spring. We, too, can celebrate the lengthening days, although the process of recovering daylight is a very slow one until mid-January.

Heavy Snows

While skiing one December in the pine woods across from my home, I was struck by the amount of snow caught in the branches of balsams, and by the way their supple branches bend toward the ground in an effort to shed the snowload. Three weeks earlier, in our first snowstorm of the year, hazelnut shrubs were bent completely over in an arc, their tips touching the ground and held there by the icing up of the snow layer. Winter is a very tough time on trees and shrubs. They must contend with the mechanical forces of snow and ice, the browsing activity of mammals and birds, and they must adapt to cold temperatures intent on bursting their cells.

Over time, spruce and balsam trees evolved their first line of defense against heavy snow and ice storms by selecting a spire-shaped growth form that acts like a steep, pitched roof, allowing the snow to slide off. Still, snow can and does get caught in the foliage. In his book *Life in the Cold,* Peter Marchand notes that the snow retained in a 40-foot-tall balsam can reach an astounding weight of 3,000 kilograms, or 6,600 pounds!

Ice, too, can affect tree growth and survival. Along the surface of the snow, damage from blowing ice particles can pit or wear away the bark on the windward side of a tree. The ice particles can also strip needle foliage, increasing water loss and drying. Or ice storms can increase the weight of branches so dramatically that winds can break off branches altogether--branches that would have supported new growth in the spring. The resulting trees are then often lopsided, leaning toward the heavier foliated side, which increases the chances that they will eventually be downed due to wind or snow.

Plant Defenses

Plants that survive the cold, snow, ice, and winds must still contend with animals like deer, moose, mice, and hares that browse buds and bark. Many plants have evolved means of protecting their overall population from overbrowsing in winter. One indirect survival technique involves compensating for the loss of buds and shoots by producing heavier and longer shoots in the spring. These shoots bear larger leaves that are retained for a longer period by the plant. All of that growth effort is done in an attempt to grow tall enough quickly enough to exceed the reach of the browsing animals come next winter.

Many northern plants employ a direct defense mechanism, too. They produce unpalatable or toxic compounds that deter browsers, sending them elsewhere in the search for a better meal. Juvenile plants usually produce these anti-herbivory compounds; once a plant is tall enough to be safe from a mammal attempting to browse its leader stem, it probably doesn't care if its mature lower branches are nipped.

For example, young paper birches produce an anti-browsing compound called papyriferic acid in concentrations 25 times greater than those found in adult trees. Resin droplets of the compound may actually bead up on the surface of the juvenile twigs.

Experiments in which differently aged willow, aspen, and birch twigs were offered to hungry hares demonstrated that the hares much prefer mature shoots because they don't contain the anti-browsing compounds; hares can apparently detect age differences by scent alone.

The production of these compounds has ramifications beyond simply deterring a few hares. Some researchers believe that the eight- to 11-year population cycle of snowshoe hares is affected by this preferential browsing on mature stems. When the hare population is on the increase, the browsing pressure on trees and shrubs obviously increases. The plants eventually respond by producing juvenile shoots which have very low food value and contain a higher level of anti-herbivory compounds. In effect, before the plants become totally overbrowsed, the plants call a halt to the peaking hare population and help initiate a population reversal. In response to the shortage of high-quality browse, hare reproduction decreases and winter mortality increases. Add to this the pressure exerted on hares by the typically increasing predator population and the net effect is a plummeting hare population.

123

After several years, the plants recover sufficiently. They decrease their production of anti-herbivory compounds, the hare population responds positively and begins to increase, and the cycle starts up again.

Strategies

Consider some of the wintering problems that our wildlife must overcome. A 200-pound deer needs nearly 10 pounds of nutritious, woody browse each day to stay healthy. Shrews, which weigh about one-tenth of an ounce, must eat their body weight in food daily to survive. In a temperature of 23°F, mice lose 3.7 times more energy per minute on the snow surface than they lose in their snow tunnels. While traveling in open meadows, mice can get dangerously cold. To warm up, they burrow into the snow, sometimes taking 20 minutes to regain body heat before they venture out again.

Honeybees are the only insects that maintain an elevated body temperature all winter long; to do this, they must cluster in a colony, packing themselves into a compact ball and maintaining a core temperature of 64°F. The unlucky bees that find themselves on the outside of the cluster still maintain a temperature of 50°F. If they become cold, they rev up their flight muscles to increase heat in the cluster, an activity that generates a 25-fold increase in heat production. They're even smart enough to point their heads toward the core and their backsides outward.

<u>124</u>

Christmas Bird Count

Sponsored by the National Audubon Society, the Christmas Bird Count began in 1900, when 27 birders covered as much of the country as they could. Today, close to 40,000 birders take part in some 1,600 counts, sampling bird populations in every state and Canadian province, and in Central and South America.

In Wisconsin, about 1,300 bird-watchers hit the fields and woods in 80 separate counts. Each count is done within a 15-mile-diameter circle, and all take place during an 18-day period between mid-December and early January. The national data is published in the Audubon Society's journal *American Birds*, and the information is used in an attempt to demonstrate population trends. The Wisconsin data is published in *The Passenger Pigeon*, the journal of the Wisconsin Society of Ornithology.

We northwoods birders have to be content with the approximately 20 species that are present during any given winter. Southern Wisconsin birders commonly tally 80 species on their counts. The difference, of course, is the quality and quantity of our winter.

Tom Nichols has compiled the Christmas Bird Count totals in the Fifield-Park Falls area for more than 30 years. His figures reveal a great variation in numbers for species like redpolls, pine siskins, goldfinches, pine grosbeaks, and crossbills. In 1988, for instance, no redpolls were seen; in 1989, 141 were counted; in 1990, the species again disappeared; but in 1991 the birders saw a total of 352.

The long-term data prevents us from engaging in knee-jerk, fear-driven responses to momentary lows in populations. Redpolls clearly irrupt every few years in the northwoods; during other years, they choose to take their winter vacation elsewhere. On the other hand, the statewide data has shown clear increases or decreases over time, such as the increase in the cardinal population and the decrease in the number of black ducks.

The following is an account of a typical Christmas Count Day in Iron County:

The thermometer, illuminated by my kitchen light, read -12°F. It was 6:30 on the Sunday morning of the 1992 Christmas bird count. I pulled on layers of wool, poured hot tea and toast into my system to act as antifreeze, and headed north for the town of Gurney in north-western Iron County. Here, nine other committed birders (or birders who should have been committed, depending on your perspective) had gathered at the home of Joan Elias and Jim Meeker. I hung around the woodstove for more than my share of the time, but before long the maps were distributed, groups were formed, and we were off to find birds of any kind or number. We drove slowly along snow-covered back roads, stopping near homes and farms where birds might be drawn to feeders. Spotting birds from the back of a car tries my lim-ited skills on the best of days, but a continually frosted window, im-mune to my scraping and scratching, rendered me nearly useless on this occasion.

125

For the birds' part, they felt little compunction to cooperate. Be-low-zero temperatures encourage them to stay at home, fluffed into a ball, instead of engaging in the flitting about or exposed branch-perching we hoped to see.

We stopped at Potato River Falls, hoping to kick up a few birds on the trail or to find a few that were using the open water. There was not a bird to be seen anywhere. The falls rushed, and steam billowed where the relatively warm water made contact with the brittle air. The low-slung sun shone through the steam, backlighting the roiling water. There were no birds, but as is often the case when one ventures out-doors, what we saw exceeded our expectations. In this case, the unexpected beauty of the falls offered a greater gift than the birds we were seeking.

We returned to the road and finally, after we had been skunked for an hour except for the sight of a few ravens, a northern shrike lit on a phone wire while we were scanning a bird feeder outside of a country home. Then, not far down the road, a rough-legged hawk perched over an open field and a pair of pine grosbeaks called from some thin trees along the edge. We thought we were getting hot, but another hour of driving, stopping, and driving revealed only a few chickadees and more ravens.

Upson Falls offered another chance to stretch our legs and survey some open water that might attract birds, so we hiked toward the sound of falling water. The falls was sheeted over with a soft ice, but behind the ice cover we could see water tumbling over rocks. Defying gravity, the ice somehow stayed intact, despite the fact that it had no real foundation. We discovered a patch of Canada yew--a low, shrubby evergreen that is regarded as candy by deer and thus is totally absent from most of its natural range.

The highlight of our journey back came when we spotted a goshawk that was being mobbed by a host of ravens. Here are the bird count totals for the entire group that day:

102 chickadees	5 downy woodpeckers
92 ravens	4 blue jays
76 house sparrows	4 hairy woodpeckers
56 goldfinches	3 crows
50 snow buntings	2 shrikes
17 starlings	1 pileated woodpecker
7 evening grosbeaks	1 eagle
7 rough-legged hawks	1 white-breasted nuthatch
5 pine grosbeaks	1 goshawk
5 goldeneyes	0 partridges in a pear tree

Altogether, we saw 19 species--the same number as the previous year. However, a few species were new to the list and a few that had been seen in the past, like redpolls, did not return.

Tough Billing

I've always been impressed by how remarkably adept birds are at extracting seed kernels from shells. Birds have no teeth, but they've evolved a number of methods for removing seeds. Some birds, like mourning doves, pigeons, and grouse, swallow seeds whole, gorging themselves at the feeder. Gorging reduces the length of time they are vulnerable to predators at feeders, since feeders are often located in areas of marginal cover. Gorgers first hold the seeds in their crop, then transfer the seeds to the gizzard, a muscular portion of the stomach. The gizzard, filled with grit, contracts and grinds the seeds until they open. A sunflower seed is small potatoes for a gizzard. Hickory nuts are easily crushed in turkey gizzards, as are clams and mussels in the stomachs of diving ducks.

Other birds, including chickadees, nuthatches, and woodpeckers, hold the seeds in their feet and strike them with their bills to extract the seed. I've timed this process, and it can take anywhere from 10 to 45 seconds. The kernels are then swallowed, the shell is discarded, and another flight is made to the feeder to procure more seeds.

Finches, like purple finches, evening and pine grosbeaks, dark-eyed juncos, and redpolls, simply crack the seeds between their upper bill (the maxilla) and their lower bill (the mandible). The upper bill is grooved into two ridges, creating a slot for the seeds, while the lower bill is a single ridge with a sharp edge that slices through the seed kernel. Finches use their tongues to position the seed edgewise between the halves of their bill, so it will pop open along its seam. An upward, crushing motion is applied, and the mandible is thrust forward to provide a slicing motion. Then the bill is moved from side to side, in order to separate the husks from the kernels. Some finches can apply 100 pounds of pressure to a seed–a remarkable feat of strength, given that most finches weigh only an ounce or two. The seeds are usually extracted within a few seconds.

127

Pine Grosbeaks

We had a flock of 14 pine grosbeaks at our feeders during the winter of 1995-96. We're seldom visited in winter by these beautiful, rosy-plumed finches. They tend to prefer deciduous trees over conifers, and they are particularly fond of mountain-ash berries and sumac-neither of which are available on our property. Nevertheless, the grosbeaks were quite content to feed on our sunflower seeds. They also eat the seeds of many northern trees, including maple, birch, tamarack, pine, spruce, and fir. A gular pouch allows them to store extra food as they eat.

Pine grosbeaks are the largest of the grosbeaks, ranging from eight to 10 inches long; their typical wingspread is 14 inches. They nest in far northern forests around the world, visiting northern Wisconsin in winter when shortages of seed crops occur in their nesting range. Only twice have possible breeding pairs been seen in Wisconsin during the twentieth century, so pine grosbeaks are truly northern birds.

Bird Economics Equals Big Bucks

A 1995 U.S. Fish and Wildlife Service report concluded that Americans spend more money on bird-watching than they do on sporting events! While even an avid birder like me finds that hard to believe, here are the statistics. Sixty-five million adults watch and feed birds in the United States, spending between $5.2 billion and $9 billion yearly. We spend $2 billion yearly on wild-bird seed alone. According to the USFWS, over 200,000 jobs are supported by bird-watching. By comparison, Americans spend $5.8 billion on movie tickets each year, and $5.9 billion on sporting events.

In areas near major national wildlife refuges, wildlife watchers distribute significant dollars. Bird-watchers at the Chincoteague NWR in Virginia spend nearly $10 million annually while watching shorebirds and waterfowl.

Few bird-watchers are motivated by economics, but the fact that birds can bring a huge cash flow into communities can lead to environmental benefits. For instance, the population decline of popular migratory songbirds like thrushes and warblers, estimated at 2 to 4 percent per year, has long been a concern to conservationists. But now the loss may also be appreciated from another perspective–an economic one. The loss of bird habitat and the resultant population decline should now be factors that concern chambers of commerce as well as the Audubon Society. In the glare of the economic spotlight, we may be more likely to enforce current conservation laws and to pass new ones.

Raptor Invasion Years

The appearance of redpolls at your feeder in any given winter probably indicates a poor seed crop year in Canada. If the small birds are coming south, many of us hope that they will be accompanied by an influx of raptors like goshawks and owls. On the average, an invasion year of northern raptors occurs once every four years. The last invasion year occurred during the winter of 1991-92, which was considered an exceptionally big invasion year. The "big" invasion years occur every 10 years, so the winter of 2001-02 is one to mark in your long-range calendar. You may see species like great gray, snowy, boreal, and hawk owls.

129

Full-Moon Snowshoeing

Mary and I snowshoed one late December night during the full moon. The moon was so bright that I actually needed to wear a long-billed cap to keep the moonlight out of my eyes. The snow on the ground presented a sparkling light show, along with an optical illusion that made the sparkles appear to hover above the snow. In the deeper woods, the big pines blocked most of the light, but pools of light shone wherever there was a small wetland or opening. The effect was similar to a spotlight shining on a stage.

We tried to call in an owl, because we have often heard barred and great horned owls in the area, but the owls showed little interest. The moonlight on the snow created an otherworldly effect, one that we carried with us long after we returned home.

Black Spruce

We cut our Christmas tree every year from state or county forest land, often culling an upland black spruce. Balsam fir and pines get all the good press for being the desired Christmas trees, but black spruce grows full and thick, and it exudes a pitch that can make your hands stick together while smelling great, too. We haven't seen them lose their needles too quickly either, even when we keep our tree up well into January.

Birding: Another Christmas Bird Count

In the U.S., two million hard-core birders are able to identify a hundred or more birds on sight; another five million can recognize 40 or more species, and another 53 million people are considered "casual" birders (according to 1980 statistics). I believe that more folks live in the northwoods or visit here for the inherent beauty of the wildlife, forests, and lakes, and for endeavors such as birding and wildflower seeking, than we suspect.

Three birders and myself scoured a new Christmas count area in western Vilas County during the winter of 1993. We turned up 18 species of birds, including more bald eagles (five) than evening grosbeaks (two), although I suspect that if we had stayed home and watched our feeders, we would have reversed those numbers. Instead we drove and drove, slowly wending our way along every navigable road we could find, and stopping every so often to get out, listen, and look. Black-capped chickadees topped the list--no surprise there. But at the end of the day, we watched more than 30 ravens cross Highway 51 on their way to a communal roost site, bringing the total for the day to 52 ravens, a substantial number that was second only to the chickadees.

For the sake of comparison I called Joan Elias, who coordinates the count for northern Iron County, which is centered in the little town of Gurney. Their group found 20 species, including four goldeneyes and a hooded merganser on the open waters of Lake Superior's Saxon Harbor. Twenty species seems about average, give or take a few, for the northwoods in the winter. The other 140-plus species that nest in the area are happily enjoying piña coladas somewhere south of here.

Nutty Nuthatches

During the 1993 Christmas Bird Count, we counted six red-breasted and six white-breasted nuthatches, nearly all of which were at our feeder during the day. Mary kept an infrequent eye on the birds' comings and goings. Nuthatches, affectionately known as "the upside-down birds," are the only tree trunk-foraging birds that feed while moving down a tree or glean insects while hanging upside-down from branches. They scour trunks and branches for insects and spiders hidden in bark crevices; their unique approach allows them to find insects that are overlooked by "up the trunk" foragers like creepers and woodpeckers.

Nuthatches are the Flying Wallendas of the bird world, capable of hanging upside-down from a swinging branch, running down a swaying rope, and descending trees with short, headfirst hops. They seem to understand that viewing the world from another angle offers a landscape that's different in its occupants and its movements--just as the experienced lake country canoeist knows to continually look behind him, because the way out of an area looks very different from the way in.

Red-breasted nuthatches forage in conifers, examining the seed cones and winding around the twigs in search of seeds or insects. They'll come to backyard feeders filled with suet, nuts, and sunflowers seeds, usually flying away with the seed and wedging it into a bark crevice in order to hammer it open.

White-breasted nuthatches, which always remind me of someone wearing a natty tuxedo, forage mostly in deciduous trees. Like red-breasted nuthatches, they can be quite tame and eat from your hand at your feeder. Both species often stockpile food in bark crevices or other dry places for later use. And both offer "songs" that won't make the bird-watcher's hit parade--single notes in repetition, often delivered with a nasal twang and sounding like *yank, yank, yank.*

Nuthatches fill an ecological niche, assuming the role of free spirits that choose to see the world from a different perspective. By doing so, they reduce competition for a resource that is in limited supply. Perhaps they realize that there's more to this world than meets the eye if one only takes the risk of looking from another vantage point.

The SCREW Factors

During an Audubon Society Christmas Bird Count on December 30, 1995, we found 23 species of birds--the highest total in the three years we had conducted the count. Nevertheless, 23 species is a mighty small number compared to counts done in central and southern Wisconsin, which typically yield 60 or more species. In our area it's not only possible but usually the norm to search for hours while only seeing a bird or two--unless you are watching backyard feeders.

131

The reason so few birds challenge a northwoods winter boils down to the "SCREW" factors, a term coined by winter ecologist and tracker James Halfpenny. SCREW is the acronym for snow, cold, radiation, energy, and wind--the forces of winter that make survival difficult to impossible for most organisms.

While we humans have developed an artificial paper currency to drive our economy, energy is the currency of life in a northwoods winter. The SCREW factors conspire to throw the energy balance into the deficit column. Without a societal safety net or savings and loan institutions, spending too much energy spells death for an organism.

132

Each SCREW factor drains away vital life forces. Snow can reduce access to food and make travel a major energy drain. Cold forces increased metabolic rates, which consume energy and deplete fat reserves. Radiation of heat from the body to the winter snow or atmosphere requires burning more fuel to compensate for the loss. Less available energy means an organism has less ability to find food, to defend itself, and to overcome illness or injury. Wind increases cold and loss of energy. Even if the organism survives, reproduction may fail the following spring, due to the winter stress triggered by these factors.

Adaptations to the SCREW factors have evolved over thousands of years, although the specific purpose of an adaptation may be unclear. Were the long legs of the moose meant to carry the animal through deep winter snow, or were they designed to help it wade in the deep water of summer wetlands? It's difficult to be certain.

Many responses to winter are possible. The season can be avoided entirely through migration, or through laying eggs and then dying. Alternately, winter can be tolerated through activity or inactivity. Some animals stay through the winter, but migrate vertically. A frog, an insect, or a turtle may bury itself in the soil or mud of a lake, or may hide in the cracks of tree bark.

Animals may assume inactivity by going into hibernation or torpor (a short, light period of dormancy). Bears remain in torpor all winter, but mammals like badgers, chipmunks, or skunks may go into torpor for short periods.

Some animals lower their body temperatures, thereby lowering their metabolic rates and conserving energy without actually going into torpor. Moose lower their body temperatures in winter but remain active. Still other animals remain active, but do so from beneath the snow, including mice, voles, and shrews.

Big Bodies Versus Little Bodies

Body size has a lot to do with an animal's ability to tolerate the winter. It is very difficult for a small animal to maintain its body heat through a severe winter. An animal must be able to produce a great deal of heat, and it must also be able to hold on to that heat. Heat is lost along the surface area of the organism. Ideally, the ratio between the capacity to lose heat and the capacity to produce heat should be as small as possible. Compared to small animals, large animals have a high heat-producing capacity in relation to their body surfaces, so they have a significant advantage in coping with the rigors of a northern winter.

133

Imagine two animals, one larger than the other, but each in the shape of a perfect cube (just to make the math easy). The smaller animal is one inch on a side, while the larger animal is two inches on a side. Volume represents the capacity to produce heat, while the surface area represents the capacity to lose heat. The volume of the small animal (the heat producing capacity) is determined by cubing the length of one side. One inch cubed is one cubic inch. The surface area (the heatloss capacity) of the animal is determined by taking the length times the width of one face and multiplying by six (the number of faces in the cube). The area is six square inches (1 x 1 x 6). The ratio of the surface area to the volume is 6 to 1, or just plain 6--quite a high ratio.

The volume of the larger animal is 8 cubic inches (2 x 2 x 2), while its surface area is 24 square inches (2 x 2 x 6). The ratio of the surface area to the volume is 24 to 8, or just 3. A still-larger animal, say three inches on a side, has a volume of 27 cubic inches and a surface area of 54 square inches. Its surface-to-volume ratio is 54 to 27, or just 2. Thus an animal with a large body has a much greater ability to produce and conserve heat than a smaller animal.

Now you know why very few small organisms are found above the snow, and why very few small birds remain here for the winter. Their internal furnaces just can't keep up with the heat loss from their bodies. Of course, exceptions are the rule in the natural world, so chickadees that weigh one-third of an ounce can manage to survive a northern winter. The price is heavy, though. Nearly 80 percent of the year's young won't survive to see spring. Bears, the bulkiest mammals we have, would seem able to survive the SCREW factors by virtue of body size alone, but instead they go into torpor and become inactive for five months. Go figure.

The speed at which an organism cools off or heats up is called the temperature transient. Small organisms have a short transient--they heat up or cool down in a hurry. Large organisms have a long transient. If you were to place a hummingbird and an owl in your freezer, the hummingbird would freeze more rapidly. The hummingbird would also warm up more quickly on a summer morning.

A Morphological Index

A bear going into torpor for the winter is not quite the exception to the size rule that it may appear to be. Other variables must be factored in, too, like how well an animal can maneuver on top of the snow and the animal's chest height. The amount of weight each foot places on the snow is called "foot load," and it's determined roughly by dividing one-fourth of the total weight of the animal by the surface area of each foot. Animals with low body weights and big feet will have low foot loads. A bear has big feet, but its enormous weight cannot be supported by them, so it struggles to move through deep snow. The Canada lynx and the snowshoe hare have the lowest foot loads, so they can move effortlessly over most snow surfaces.

A tall chest height helps further reduce the energy needed to wade through deep snow. A moose stands on long, thin legs that usually permit it to keep its body out of the snow, thus reducing the energy it needs to get around. A bear, with its short legs, would move like a small bulldozer through deep winter snows, losing enormous amounts of energy as it tries to find food.

A winter "morphological index," developed by researchers E.S. Telfer and J.P. Kelsall, combines both chest height and foot load into one value. Caribou score the highest overall rating in the index, with a value of 154. Thus they are best-adapted physiologically to withstand a northern winter. Moose are next at 140, then wolves and wolverines at 135. White-tailed deer are rated at 112, while pronghorn antelopes bring up the bottom at 81.

The next time you're outside this winter, consider the extraordinary lengths every organism must go to in order to survive winter in the northwoods. While the species numbers may be way down, the numbers on our "appreciation index" should be way up.

Rare Woodpecker

Naturalist and friend Peter Dring called in December of 1995 with news of a sighting in the Three Lakes area of a black-backed three-toed woodpecker, an uncommon northern woodpecker with a solid black back and barred sides. Known to breed only in Douglas, Price, and Iron counties within Wisconsin, the black-backed is found most often in tamarack bogs and recently burned-over jack pine stands. Winter may be the best time to see a black-backed, as they occasionally feed at feeders or in parks during the cold months. If you wish to search for one in a tamarack bog, winter offers better footing and the absence of biting insects.

135

Robins?!

Jim and Sue Coffman from Eagle River wrote to report that they saw a robin in their yard on November 27, 1994. Our moderate winter weather must have induced it to stay well past a robin's normal checkout time, which is mid-October. Robins have been counted in Oneida and Ashland counties during the Christmas Bird Count, so we might assume that if enough fruit remains on trees and the weather is kind, a few robins may stay into December before taking their southern sojourn.

Tracking Skills

One December I attended a tracking skills workshop at Treehaven Field Center in Tomahawk, conducted by Dr. James Halfpenny, who is a world-renowned tracker and the author of *A Field Guide to Mammal Tracking in North America* and *Winter: An Ecological Handbook.* As generally happens when I attend workshops led by such true experts, I found out how abysmal my knowledge of the field was, and how rich and complex the subject is for those who have made it their specialty.

Halfpenny goes into the field with calipers hooked up to a laptop computer. He takes at least 11 different measurements of every print he wishes to record, along with data concerning the animal's gait, the habitat, the ground surface, the location, and the season. Each measurement is automatically fed into data banks he maintains on every species, enabling him to determine the statistical probability that the print was left by a given species by comparing it to thousands of other prints he has recorded over the last 20 years. These days, Halfpenny spends a good deal of his time in court, where he is called upon to try to prove or disprove the existence of some rare animal in an area where commercial development has been proposed, or where state or federal agencies need to document the presence of a species.

His tracking book is the best I've seen on the subject. I'm now trying to put into practice some of the things I learned from Halfpenny during that weekend, but practice is the key, and no amount of book learning can compensate for a lack of field time.

136

By the way, if I've not mentioned Treehaven before, it's a beautiful facility built on 1,200 acres. It offers programs galore on various natural history and resource education topics. Call (715) 453-1811 for a schedule of winter programs.

Crossbills

Crossbills were very common during the winter of 1996-97. Carol Bohn from Lac du Flambeau brought us a red crossbill to identify that had been killed by a car. A few days later Ada Karow, also from Lac du Flambeau, called me with a sighting of a dozen or more red crossbills feeding in the trees and on the ground near her home. A birding friend from Eagle River was the first to call several weeks earlier to say he had many red crossbills in his area.

If you're unfamiliar with crossbills (we have two species: white-winged and red crossbills), you needn't feel alone. Crossbills seldom come to feeders, so to see them you must get out among cone-laden conifers which are the favorite dinner ground for crossbills. They do eat deciduous buds and seeds at times, too, and are particularly fond of road salt. Thus they have a bad habit of ending up as roadkill.

Both crossbills are the epitome of an irruptive species. They are virtually impossible to predict as to where and when they may show up. They're irruptive not only in various years, but in various seasons, and within seasons. Crossbills may be seen one day gleaning seeds from a conifer stand, and then never return. Their irregularity is their trademark. Several years may go by when no crossbills are recorded in the state, and then there comes a year like 1977 when half of the state's 72 Christmas Birds Counts noted white-winged crossbills in their count areas.

Crossbills do indeed have crossed bills, and individuals are considered "left-handed" or "right-handed" in opening cones based on which way the mandibles cross. The mandibles are inserted into the cone to pry it apart, and then the crossbill uses its tongue to extract the seeds.

Like redpolls, crossbills have an "esophageal diverticulum," sort of a pocket about halfway down their neck which is used to store seeds for later eating. The birds can eat from this cupboard later from the relative greater safety of a more sheltered perch.

The white-wingeds have a very pretty song. It's a series of lengthy trills that occur at different pitches with musical warbles occasionally mixed in. If you have a bird tape, the song may be worth listening to. The call note, a series of harsh *chet* notes, is also helpful to learn.

137

Look for crossbills in flocks of a dozen to 50 or more, though they occasionally mix with other winter finches like evening and pine grosbeaks and pine siskins. They are often very tame if approached slowly; they may allow you to stand among them while they feed.

Orphaned Bear Cubs

What happens over the winter to bear cubs who were orphaned during the autumn bear season? Bruce Bacon, the wildlife manager at the Mercer DNR, says that the cubs which reach 40 pounds in weight by denning time ordinarily survive. In a normal year, most cubs reach 40 pounds by September 1st, and many are 50 or more pounds by the fall. In studies of eartagged orphaned cubs, those that went into the winter well fed 40 pounds or more being the key measure—did reasonably well, though their survival is still a little lower than similar-sized cubs denning with their mothers.

Sow bears typically mate for the first time when three years old, and the average number of cubs in Wisconsin is about 2.5, one of the highest rates in the nation. The sows mate every other year, the yearling cubs denning with the sow in the off years.

It is illegal to kill a sow with cubs during the bear season, so most families are protected, though a few sows are taken if they become separated from the cubs. Many yearling females are harvested, but that is well before their breeding age.

Rare Bird Alerts

If you want to know where rare birds are currently being sighted in the Upper Midwest, here are the phone numbers to call:

For Wisconsin statewide, (414) 352-3857

For the Madison area, (608) 255-2476

For Michigan statewide, (616) 471-4919

For the Sault Ste. Marie area, (705) 256-2790

For Minnesota statewide, (612) 780-8890

For the Duluth area, (218) 525-5952

138

If you want to get a look at your first great gray owl or hawk owl or boreal owl, call these numbers and follow the directions to the reported sites. Sault Ste. Marie and Duluth are arguably the two best places in North America for sighting Arctic owls in the winter.

Ice Cover

Woody Hagge from Hazelhurst sent me his statistics for ice cover on Foster Lake, numbers he has kept for over 20 years. Open water for 1996 lasted 199 days, 20 days less than the average, and 39 days less than his record of 238 days of open water in 1981. Winter 1996-97 was the longest by far for ice cover. The ice lasted 178 days, a full 46 days longer than the mild winters of 1980-81 and 1990-91.

Wintering Birds - Where Do They Spend their Christmas?

While we may wish for more birds to show up at our feeders, most had the good sense to head south long ago. If you've ever wondered where some of "our" birds lead their winter life of leisure, here's a sampling of some of my favorite birds:

whip-poor-will	Gulf Coast, South Carolina to Central America, Panama, Costa Rica
nighthawk	northern South America to central Argentina
Eastern kingbird	Colombia to northern Chile and Argentina
American kestrel	southern Texas to Panama

cliff swallow	Paraguay and central Brazil to southern Argentina
red-eyed vireo	western Amazonia
gray catbird	Gulf Coast to Panama
hermit thrush	southern U.S. to Bahamas, Guatemala, and El Salvador
veery	northern Colombia east to Guyana and south to Brazil
winter wren	southern U.S.
Eastern wood-pewee	Colombia and Venezuela south to Peru and Brazil
blackburnian warbler	Costa Rica south to Peru and Bolivia
black-throated green warbler	Bahamas, Cuba, Jamaica, and Panama
yellow-headed blackbird	southwestern border of U.S. to southern Mexico
northern oriole	central Mexico to northeastern South America
scarlet tanager	Panama and Colombia to Bolivia

139

End-of-the-Year Musings

In human history, we have learned (I hope) that the conqueror role is eventually self-defeating. Why? Because it is implicit in such a role that the conqueror knows, ex cathedra, just what makes the community clock tick, and just what and who is valuable, and what and who is worthless, in community life. It always turns out that he knows neither, and this is why his conquests eventually defeat themselves . . .

The ordinary citizen assumes that science knows what makes the community clock tick; the scientist is equally sure that he does not. He knows that the biotic mechanism is so complex that its workings may never be fully understood.

–Aldo Leopold

140

JANUARY

The Ojibwe word for January is *gitcimanido'gizis*. *Gitci* means "big," *manido* means "spirit," and *gizis* means "month." Perhaps, in part, the Ojibwes meant to indicate that this month is the time when Manido has the greatest effect on the land and water. January, the coldest month in Wisconsin, provides the cruelest hammer blows of winter. We can expect below-zero low temperatures during about half of our January days in the northwoods, while 26 or more days will generate high temperatures below 32°F.

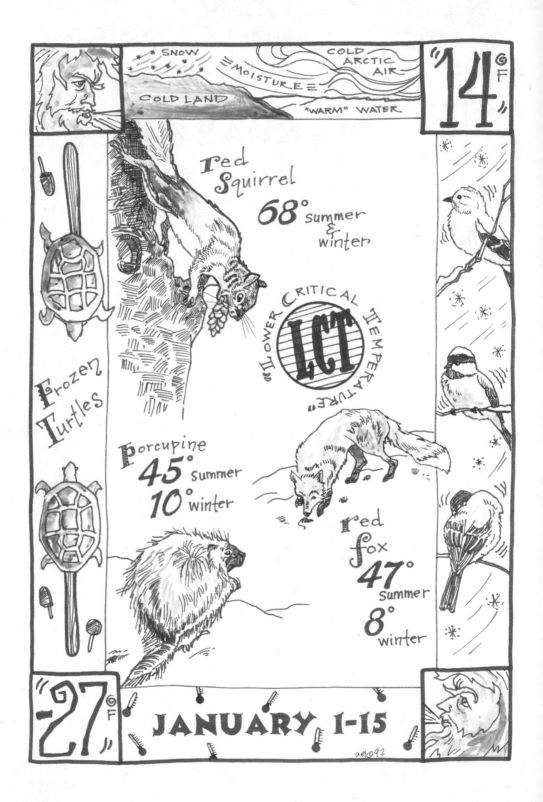

SNOW

COLD ARCTIC AIR

MOISTURE

COLD LAND

"WARM" WATER

"14°F

red Squirrel
68° summer & winter

"Lower Critical Temperature" LCT

Frozen Turtles

Porcupine
45° summer
10° winter

red fox
47° summer
8° winter

-27°F

JANUARY 1-15

ael©97

January 1 to January 15

Snow Math

It takes more than one million snow flakes to cover a two-square-foot area with 10 inches of snow.

Frozen Turtles

January Musings

The months of the year, from January up to June, are a geometric progression in the abundance of distractions.

–Aldo Leopold

Young painted turtles may currently be wintering over in their nests. An average clutch of seven to nine eggs generally hatches around the end of August, but later-hatching clutches may remain in the nest until the following spring. While this strategy helps avoid predation until spring, it also exposes the turtles to temperatures that often drop to 18°F in their three-inch-deep nest cavity. Come April, they will nonetheless emerge. How do the hatchlings survive the subfreezing temperatures? The answer is rather amazing. Two Canadian researchers found that the hatchlings' body fluids freeze at 26°F, and they can survive in this frozen state for at least 11 days. When the hatchlings freeze, ice grows inward toward their body core, shutting off blood circulation to their legs and periphery, until only the heart-brain corridor is open. Eventually, that corridor is frozen, too. In this state, the hatchlings experience no muscle movement, no breathing, no heartbeat, no blood flow, and virtually no brain activity. Yet when thawed, they rapidly return to normal activity.

They accomplish this seeming miracle because the fluids that freeze are extracellular, meaning that they are located between the body cells. If fluids within the cells froze, the ice crystals would damage the cells beyond repair, killing the turtle.

Only 53 percent of the hatchlings' total body water actually freezes at 26°F. Some water remains within the cells, and this must remain liquid. A special protein is produced to stimulate the formation of tiny ice crystals within the cells. The protein acts to keep the ice crystals so small that they don't damage fragile tissues.

Oddly, only the hatchlings have this ability to freeze. Adult turtles cannot withstand freezing. Still, their winter survival is no less extraordinary than the survival of their hatchlings. The adults have evolved to spend their winters at the bottom of lakes and rivers–sometimes resting on the bottom sediments, sometimes burying themselves in the mud. Turtles must breathe air, so how do the adults manage to survive? Remarkably, painted turtles have developed the greatest tolerance for oxygen deprivation of any vertebrate animal. They can live in 37°F water that contains no oxygen whatsoever for more than 150 days! By comparison, humans will sustain major brain damage after just a few minutes without oxygen.

Some gas exchange may occur in hibernating painted turtles, much like the ability of frogs to breathe through their skin underwater. But if the water contains no oxygen, gas exchange won't help. Oxygen deprivation will trigger metabolic arrest in painted turtles, resulting in a tenfold drop in their metabolic rate. This gives them much more time in which to use the limited body fuels they have stored for the winter.

In the future, lessons learned from painted turtles could have major implications for humans. The capacity of the hatchlings to survive freezing and the adults' ability to withstand a total lack of oxygen are unknown in any warm-blooded animals. No mammalian organs have ever been restored after freezing, although transplant organs can be put on ice for several hours before they degenerate irreversibly. With continued study, the riddles of the common painted turtle's tolerance for freezing and oxygen deprivation may provide advanced medical technology with critical tools to enhance human survival.

Out Cold, Too

Painted turtle hatchlings aren't the only species capable of surviving freezing. Other cold-blooded animals like garter snakes, box turtles, some lizards, and land-hibernating frogs (wood frogs, eastern gray tree frogs, spring peepers, and chorus frogs) can also endure freezing. However, the extent of their ability to survive freezing varies widely among the species.

144

Cold Weather Survival: Balancing the Winter Equation

Mary and I, bundled up like a pair of polar bears, were out walking once on a typical, -20°F evening in January. The intensity of the cold made us marvel at how the animals of the northwoods manage to survive. Each species has its own bag of survival tricks. The bottom line, however, is that each has evolved a series of physical and behavioral traits enabling it to balance an extremely important equation: HEAT IN = HEAT OUT. Incoming heat is produced by metabolizing food or fat, and by absorbing energy from external sources like the sun.

145

Energy balancing acts much like our human need to maintain a positive checkbook balance in order to economically survive. If we spend too much money and need to borrow some, we visit the bank or ask a friend. If an animal spends more energy than it receives, it must borrow from fat stores which it accumulated over the summer and fall. If we borrow too much from our economic stores, the bank calls the note due and we're forced into bankruptcy. If an animal borrows too much from its physical stores, it usually dies.

Outgoing heat is generated primarily when one of three things happens–conduction, convection, and latent heat exchange. Conduction takes place when, for example, heat is exchanged between the skin and the air or water. Convection occurs when heat is transferred from one point to another, courtesy of air or water movement. For instance, wind speed acts to increase convection. Latent heat exchange happens when heat is carried away by converting water into vapor through perspiration or respiration. With every breath, we remove heat through evaporation from our lungs.

Each of these four processes may dominate the heat loss equation in different situations. For instance, conductive loss is far worse at night for a deer when it sleeps on the snow. Evaporative loss is likely worst during the day when an animal must move around to find food, and thus breathes out moisture and heat at a much higher rate. Convection is usually worst during the day when an animal like a chickadee comes to your feeder and must expose itself to the wind in order to feed–at night the chickadee hopefully can find a tree cavity in which to get out of the wind. Radiation is usually worst at night when the temperatures are lowest.

The trick for any animal is maintaining a constant metabolic rate while the temperature plummets. One way animals achieve this involves decreasing conductivity by layering on more fur or feathers. Birds like redpolls and goldfinches may increase their total feather layer by 50 percent in winter. They also fluff out their feathers (called piloerection) while roosting, thus reducing their heat loss by 30 to 50 percent. Mammals may also decrease their conductivity by adding fur, which acts as insulation.

Communal Living

Reducing conduction is seldom enough to survive extreme cold, so animals also reduce the amount of surface area they expose to the cold, through a series of behaviors like huddling together in communal nests, curling up, or retracting their extremities. Huddling reduces the exposed surface area by one-third. Many noncolonial species like meadow voles and deer mice make communal nests in the winter in order to conserve heat. A beaver lodge is a communal nest on a large scale, and the inside of a lodge may be 60 degrees warmer than the outside temperature. Communal nests also reduce latent heat loss due to evaporation. If you've ever been in a cow barn in the winter, you know how humid a communal area can become. That humidity helps retain heat.

There are disadvantages to communal living, however. Predators that find a communal nest eat from a full cupboard. Diseases and parasites can travel more readily from one individual to another–and with all those mouths to feed, competition for food increases. But all these are secondary to the highest priority, staying warm.

Lower Critical Temperatures

There are limits to how much an animal can modify its environment or reduce its conductivity. Every animal is subject to what is called a "lower critical temperature," or LCT. The animal's LCT is the point at which its metabolic rate (heat in) must be jacked up in order to offset the amount of heat being lost. The LCT varies from species to species, and from season to season. Porcupines have an LCT in summer of 45°F, but their LCT is reduced to 10°F during the winter. Red fox

LCTs are nearly identical to those for porcupines: 47°F in summer and 8°F in winter. Both accomplish their winter acclimation primarily by increasing the thickness of their fur. An Arctic fox is the supreme example of such an adaptation, dropping its LCT to -40°F in winter. It can rest comfortably at this brutal temperature, without changing its behavior or physiology.

Red squirrels have no such luck. Their fur is too short to make a difference, so their LCT remains 68°F in both summer and winter. They must stay warm by thoroughly insulating their nests, and by eating a great deal in order to keep their internal furnace stoked. The latter is evidenced by their abundant midden piles in the winter and their continual presence in bird feeders.

147

Get Yourself Some Brown Fat

Mammals contend with temperatures below their LCTs in one additional manner through "nonshivering thermogenesis." This is a means by which they can increase their heat production without having to increase their muscular activity through shivering, a neat trick similar to getting more heat out of your woodstove from the same amount of wood. This trick is accomplished largely by increasing the brown fat deposits near vital organs during the winter. Brown fat produces more heat when "burned" than white fat. In fact, it's so energy-efficient that the temperature measured just over deposits of brown fat may be warmer than inner body core temperatures.

But even nonshivering thermogenesis has its limits. When a mammal is unable to keep up with the cold through all other means, it must begin shivering. Shivering is a last resort for mammals, but even the efficiency of shivering is increased during the winter months in order to ensure survival.

Birds have the hardest go of it. They are less able to reduce exposed surface area; they seldom use huddling or communal nests; and they can only add so much fat or feathers before they impair their flight. Generally, birds are able to add just enough fat to get them through one long, cold winter night. The next day, they must venture out to seek more fuel.

Shivering Birds

Birds seldom modify the environment in order to conserve heat. Grouse may dive into the snowpack for up to three days, taking advantage of the insulating value of snow. They can reduce their heat loss by up to 45 percent while they stay in their snow burrows. But most birds are only able to seek shelter in dense vegetation or tree cavities, a tactic that is moderately effective at best. Unlike mammals, birds do not produce brown fat, so they aren't capable of nonshivering thermogenesis.

What they must resort to is nearly continuous shivering. Studies of birds like ravens and crows show that even larger birds must shiver continuously in winter to stay warm, unless they are generating heat through flight. In experimental conditions, goldfinches can produce heat at a rate 5.5 times their normal rate by shivering; this enables them to stay warm for six to eight hours at temperatures below -74°F!

Chickadees employ one other trick to reduce heat loss. They allow their body temperatures to drop gradually during inactive periods, until they enter a regulated condition of hypothermia. In this condition, they shiver just enough to maintain their cooled-down state. Chickadees seem to realize that the less the temperature variance between their bodies and the air, the less heat they will lose. A chickadee's body temperature may drop by 18 to 22 degrees, providing a 20 percent energy savings.

Considering the problems posed by a five-month-long season with extreme temperatures that often reach -40°F, I find it remarkable that so many mammals, insects, fish, and birds can survive the rigors of the northwoods winter. I just wish mosquitoes weren't quite so good at it.

The Bear Facts

Bears don't actually hibernate. Instead, they go into a physical state called torpor, from which they are easily awakened and can become immediately active. While in torpor, bears don't urinate or defecate. If you're not impressed, try this yourself for five months. Bears actually reprocess urea from their urine into muscle tissue, so they literally gain muscle mass during the winter. The human mind reels when it considers the possibilities of an exercise gym that operates on this principle.

Urea recycling allows the kidneys to virtually shut down–an essential process, because the loss of water through urine would cause dehydration. Though water is still lost through breathing and evaporation, bears compensate by metabolizing a mixture of fat and protein.

Space scientists are trying to replicate the urea recycling process. If they're successful, they might ultimately be able to place space travelers in suspended animation during flights that take many light years. Shutting down the waste cycle in humans is a prerequisite for such travel.

By mid-January, sows usually give birth to several cubs; most of their nursing takes place while Mom is "asleep." Cubs weigh a mere seven to 12 ounces, and are six to eight inches long at birth.

149

To say that bears are in torpor means that their body temperatures don't drop down to near freezing as temperatures do for "true" hibernators. Whoever measured the body temperature of a hibernating bear and discovered that its temperature remains near 86°F must have been a brave soul. Sneaking into a bear den, inserting a thermometer where one must in a bear, and then discovering that bears sleep lightly takes courage beyond what I possess. (Actually, the researchers drug the mother in order to take measurements and check her health, but they may still crawl partially into the den first in order to reach her.)

Life Under the Ice

Under the winter ice, fish are effectively sealed off from their replenishing oxygen supply. Without the mixing of air and water by waves, and with photosynthesis at a minimum, very little oxygen is introduced into the water. What do the fish do to survive under all that ice and snow? Probably the most important thing they do is they slow down. They moderate their eating, growth, movement, and reproductive patterns. With less to eat and a limited oxygen supply, fish adapt to a more leisurely pace, employing a "Life of Riley" approach.

As the winter progresses, oxygen first disappears from the bottom of lakes, because that's where decomposition takes place. Bacteria take in oxygen as they do their work of decomposing leaves and other organic material in the sediment. The fish adapt to less oxygen near the bottom by moving up in the water column.

Lakes that are very small or very shallow, or lakes with very high decomposition rates, may simply run out of oxygen. This phenomenon, known as "winterkill," may kill all of the fish in the lake.

Black Water

A newly fallen powder snow reflects back so much incoming solar radiation that 95 percent of the light fails to penetrate the first three inches of snow. This explains why you can get snow blindness from a winter landscape. It's almost like looking right at the sun.

Older, crystalline snow allows six times as much light to pass through it as newly fallen snow, but the amount of light that gets through is still so small that the net effect is similar. The high reflectance of snow, its "albedo," is an important factor in darkening the waters of a snow-covered winter lake. Little light is available for photosynthesis, so oxygen in the water can become drastically depleted. Other factors enter into the oxygen equation, too, like the shape of the lake basin and the amount of decaying organic matter it contains. All of this adds up to a dicey existence for aquatic organisms in northern winters.

If there is no snow covering the ice, then the quality of the ice determines the transmittance of light. Six inches of clear ice (often called "black ice") transmits 84 percent of the light, while six inches of cloudy ice transmits just 22 percent of the light, absorbing the rest in the texture of the ice itself.

Ice and snow also stop the normal exchange that takes place between a lake and the atmosphere. The heat, oxygen, and nutrients stored over the autumn have to suffice through the long winter. Lakes are effectively "locked up" for the ice season.

Some heat radiates from the bottom sediments and rises to the surface. This helps stratify, or layer, the temperatures in a winter lake. The coldest water (at about 33°F) sits near the surface, while the warmest water (around 38°F) rests at the bottom. This is, of course, the opposite of conditions that prevail during the summer, when the coldest water is found at the bottom. Imagine being a fish and having your world turned upside-down during the five months of ice cover.

Snow cover and ice thickness on lakes also vary according to the size of the lake. Because the wind blows more powerfully across large lakes, the snow gets packed or blown away, creating a propor-

150

tionately thicker ice layer than is found on smaller lakes. On smaller lakes, the wind doesn't affect the snow to such an extent. The snow is often composed of layers of snow and slush, insulating the ice and forming a comparatively thin ice layer. Thinner ice is quite common on small, north country lakes in times of heavy snowfall.

One winter I skied across part of the Turtle Flambeau Flowage, a 14,000-acre impoundment in Iron County. The conditions were ideal for skiing. A hard-packed, thin layer of snow covered the ice, although the wind in my face was brutal. Several otter holes were evident, each situated around a stump that projected above the surface. I wondered how the otters were able to surface through the ice at the stumps, but the answer became obvious as I thought about it. The dark surface of the stump absorbs sunlight, causing it to warm up, and the water current hits the stump. The two factors reduce ice buildup, keeping the hole open.

151

Some northwoods streams are very slow to ice over–in fact, some never ice over. These waters make ideal sites for otters, mink, and other mammals. I've crossed the Little Turtle River near Mercer while skiing the Mecca Trail, and it nearly always remains open. Portions of the Manitowish River, especially areas where Highway 51 crosses the river, have never frozen during the winters I've lived here.

Lake Effect Snows

Lake effect snows occur when cold, dry Arctic air crosses the "warm" water of Lake Superior (or any of the Great Lakes) and picks up moisture. The moisture turns to snow as it again passes over the cold land. In northern Wisconsin, this occurs as the moist air flows over the highlands of the Penokee Mountain range.

One of the more remarkable snow effects occurs on Birch Hill, which is situated between Ashland and Hurley in north central Wisconsin. Here, you might experience a cloudy but snowless day at the base of the hill, but find yourself caught in a bona fide blizzard at the top. I've experienced the change while driving on U.S. Highway 2 more times than I wish to recall. While the hill is a rise of only 400 feet or so, its height is sufficient to trigger the snowfall. Because 30 to 50 percent of the big lake normally remains open throughout the winter, the snowbelt area gets hit long and often.

Lake effect snows seldom reach my home, which is located some 60 miles south of Lake Superior. About halfway between Hurley and Manitowish is the Northern Highlands Divide, separating the watersheds of our area. Waters south of the divide flow into the Gulf of Mexico by way of the Mississippi River; waters north of the divide flow into Lake Superior and subsequently into the Atlantic Ocean. This divide also effectively serves as the cutoff for the Lake Superior snowbelt, so many northwoods residents don't experience lake effect snows.

For those of you who think you get too much snow where you are, the record annual snowfall in the snowbelt of Michigan's Upper Peninsula is over 390 inches.

152

What Makes a Species?

One January, a Minocqua couple called to say that an "Oregon" junco had come to their feeder. I had to look up the Oregon junco in my bird book, because I couldn't recall what they look like. I discovered that both Oregon juncos and "slate-colored" juncos are now lumped together into one species, known as the dark-eyed junco. Still, the dark-hooded, rusty-sided western version (the new depiction of the former Oregon junco) appears quite different from the slate-colored bird that is most common in our area. The Oregon junco is now considered a "race," no longer a separate species.

Determining what does or doesn't constitute a single species is an evolving process–pun intended. Back in 1973, taxonomists lumped all the juncos together, because the birds interbreed where their ranges overlap. But interbreeding is not a definitive criterion when identifying a species. For example, dark-eyed juncos interbreed with white-throated sparrows, and while they form a hybrid, the two species are still considered separate.

The definition of a species is an interbreeding group of birds, other animals, or plants that in natural conditions does not interbreed significantly enough with another group to break down species identity. Wild birds like the junco and the white-throated sparrow rarely interbreed and produce hybrids. Even when they do, each species maintains its identity through its own defining calls, songs, behaviors, and physical characteristics, although what one calls the hybrid is a bit of a mystery.

As a rule, birds mate only with their own species because they respond to specific behaviors of the opposite sex. Each species produces a series of signals and displays during its courtship period, to which only the female or male is responsive. This constellation of behaviors is so specific that species living adjacent to each other might just as well live a thousand miles apart. The species simply don't respond to one another. Even if similarities exist in their courtship patterns, readiness to breed may not occur at the same time or in the same habitat, so time and place are factors as well.

Taxonomists are often characterized as "lumpers" or "splitters," and each camp has its dogma. In the future, you can expect to see new species split off from what was previously considered one species; you can also expect to see different species lumped into one. The changes will depend on whether splitters or lumpers rise to power. One way or another, the process makes you buy a new field guide every few years, in order to keep up with the changes.

153

Speciation aside, in the winter dark-eyed juncos are rare in the northwoods, uncommon in central Wisconsin, and common in southern Wisconsin. Summer nesting ranges are just the opposite, although nesting is rare anywhere in Wisconsin except in the northwoods.

Birds to Watch for in January

For those of you who watch birds in the northwoods throughout the winter and want to know what you are likely to see, the following is a general list. However, I offer no money-back guarantees.

American crow
American goldfinch
bald eagle
barred owl
black-capped chickadee
blue jay
brown creeper
common raven
common redpoll
downy woodpecker
evening grosbeak

gray jay
great horned owl
hairy woodpecker
house finch
mourning dove
northern goshawk
northern shrike
pileated woodpecker
pine grosbeak
pine siskin
purple finch

red- and white-winged crossbills   ruffed grouse
red-breasted nuthatch   snow bunting
rock dove   white-breasted nuthatch
rough-legged hawk

1996 Christmas Bird Count

We conducted the annual Audubon-sponsored Manitowish Waters Christmas Bird Count on December 29th. Twelve different households counted the birds that came to their feeders, while four of us drove slowly around assigned areas within our count circle searching for birds along roadsides and sometimes snowshoeing back in the woods to search for birds that prefer deep woods habitats. Frankly, it's always amazing to me how many hours I can search the winter woods for birds and find barely a handful. Most of our birds seem to spend their daylight hours at backyard bird feeders where the living is obviously easier. So, the drivers among our group spend most of their time driving up to people's houses and then spying with binoculars from their cars on active bird feeders, sort of like a bird stakeout. I'm always nervous some angry homeowner will come stomping out his door with malice on his mind for the snoop with the binoculars, or call the police and I'll have to explain that I'm counting chickadees.

Anyway, the collective group identified 23 species of birds, the most unusual of which was a lonely mallard on the Trout River and two separate sightings of tree sparrows. Conspicuous by their absence were common redpolls, snow buntings, and northern shrikes.

Winter Fawn

A Manitowish Waters couple sent me pictures of a spotted fawn eating whole corn from their feeder on December 5. It continued to visit throughout the winter, coming day and night. While cautious, it fed even when bucks were at the feeder. Fawns usually lose their spots by the time they're four months old, so this fawn may have been born in August. If so, it was quite a rarity.

A Whale of a Tradition

A few years back my wife Mary, my daughter Callie, and I concluded that we didn't have enough traditions in our family, so we decided we would snowshoe every New Year's Day into an old-growth forest, making an attempt to feel the spirit of ancient trees. One winter we hiked into the Star Lake/Plum Lake Natural Area. There was only an inch or two of snow cover that winter, so we walked easily without our snowshoes through the big hemlocks, maples, and yellow birches. When we stopped and ate by Star Lake, the deep rumblings and groanings of the ice sounded like whale songs. We had heard ice crack and boom on previous occasions, but this sound was more unearthly. Perhaps lakefront owners hear these songs all the time, but for us they were a remarkable chorus.

155

Here Comes the Sun

The days are gradually lengthening. January 1 provides eight hours and 45 minutes of daylight; by January 13, we'll savor nine full hours of daylight (7:38 a.m. to 4:38 p.m.).

While December 21 is the shortest day of the year, the latest sunrise actually occurs on January 3. By January 31, the sun will peek over the horizon at 7:21 a.m., gaining a momentum of sorts. By the end of February, those of us in northern Wisconsin will be able to rise at 6:38 a.m. with sunlight streaming through our windows.

Sightings

Lu Karl was driving home on Hwy. K on January 6th, 1997 when he came around a corner and startled 10 adult eagles who were feasting on a recent roadkill deer. Lu said it was very impressive to see 10 eagles launch all at once along a roadway, and that several flew up just over the top of his car. Some adult eagles seem to remain in the northwoods every winter, as long as there's some open water to fish from, and opportunities for finding carrion.

That same winter, Bob Kovar saw a robin eating the fruits of a flowering crab tree in Manitowish Waters on January 5th. And Betty Wishman, who lives on Fence Lake, called with a sighting of a northern flicker on January 4th. I must admit I was very surprised at Betty's sighting at first until I looked at the range maps and some Christmas Bird Count data, and northern flickers do winter in central Wisconsin and are occasionally counted in northern counties on the Christmas Bird Count. It's the first winter flicker I have ever heard of in this area.

156

January Musings

There is but one requisite of a fire, that it should burn. For myself I like best to woo it with pine, both as kindling and log-wood. Pine burns brighter and hotter, and needs less kindling than any other wood. It has the sweetest odor and sizzles con-tentedly. What good is a cat that does not purr, a chestnut that will not pop, or a log that cannot sing?

—Donald Culross Peattie

January 16 to January 31

Snow Ecology: Deep is Good

Snow has a dramatic effect on the ecology of our northern forests. Deep snow protects plants from dry winter winds and protects roots from frost. It also insulates hibernat-

ing insects like bumblebees and caterpillars; amphibians like wood frogs, toads, and spring peepers; and snakes. A deep snow blanket keeps temperatures from fluctuating, preventing cycles of freezing and thawing in the snowpack. Small animals have a difficult time adapting to these ecological swings.

Deep snows provide the nighttime quilt under which grouse may bury themselves. If temperatures remain too cold, they may stay covered during the day. A shallow snow cover, or

Late-January Musings

Winter is no mere negation, no mere absence of summer; it is another and a positive presence, and between its ebbing and the slow, cautious in-flow of our northern spring there is a phase of earth emptiness, half real, perhaps, and half subjective.
–Henry Beston

crusted snow, could induce an Excedrin headache for a grouse that misjudged the snow quality and/or depth.

Snow provides warmth and concealment for small mammals such as voles and mice, which are prized by a legion of predators. Owls hunt them by sight and sound, while foxes try to find them by scent. Four to six inches of snow are ordinarily enough to shield them from easy predation. However, more snow is certainly preferable for rodents, because more snow means more insulation from cold.

One winter snow study found that, with two feet of new snow on the ground and an air temperature of 9°F, the temperature at the top of the snow surface was 11°F. Eight inches into the snow, the temperature jumped to 25°F. At the soil surface, the temperature rose again to 34°F Four inches into the soil, the temperature climbed to

36°F. This variance spells the difference between life and death for thinly furred rodents.

Snow quality, based on the density of the snowpack and its moisture content, can offset these numbers. A dry powder snow insulates exceptionally well (90 percent of a powder snow is air). A wet, heavy snow, on the other hand, can do more harm than good because it contains a high percentage of water.

Northwoods vegetation has adapted to a heavy snow cover. Snow protects dormant plants from freezing temperatures and drying winds. A professor of mine used to say that white pines don't grow well in southern Wisconsin because the weather is too cold there. As counterintuitive as that sounds, it makes sense. The early snows in the northwoods insulate our soil from the cold, whereas the snows often come relatively late down south, allowing frost to penetrate the soil more deeply and reducing the amount of water available to the roots. Most of our wildflowers and shrubs are low to the ground, in order to take advantage of the snow's protection.

Snowshoe hares must love winter. They depend on deep snow to slow down pursuing predators, while their huge, snowshoelike feet carry them over the snow to safety. Heavy snows also break branches and bend them down to hare-level, making tender shoots more accessible in spring. You can sometimes see the hares' browse marks 15 feet up in a tree. If you didn't know how snow bends branches, you might imagine that a population of giant, leaping rabbits had invaded the north country.

Come spring, deep melting snows perform one last service, replenishing the groundwater reserves and the water levels in lakes and streams.

But Sometimes Less Is More

There's always a flip side to life. Predator species probably cheer for a thin snow layer. They lose far less energy when they're not forced to wallow through deep snow. Foxes, coyotes, wolves, and martens ordinarily have to stay on trails or travel across the compacted snow that covers lakes, because the energy lost by floundering through deep snow seldom justifies the potential gain. Red foxes can bound through six inches of snow, but deeper snows usually restrict them to trails.

Larger herbivores like deer appreciate minimal snow cover, too. Deer can easily access woody browse in shallow snow without an excessive loss of energy. In such conditions, they can avoid the need to yard up and the possibility of starvation that accompanies overbrowsing in a limited area.

Birds are also among the creatures that are delighted with minimal snow. Heavy snow generally covers cones, buds, insect eggs, seeds of low shrubs, and other food sources.

Even the fish appreciate light snow cover, because it allows sunlight to penetrate the ice layer more extensively, which in turn triggers photosynthesis and the creation of life-giving oxygen.

As with most environmental change, the cost-benefit ratio of snow depth doesn't exactly tip; instead it merely swings, offering advantages to some, disadvantages to others.

161

Slush

One mid-January I skied on the part of the Willow Flowage where the Willow River begins to open up. The flowage covers over 7,300 acres and contains 70 miles of shoreline, so although I skied on the ice for half an hour, I saw very little of this beautiful area.

Curiously, the snow in many spots was a thin blanket over a deep layer of icy slush that readily bonded to my skis. A skier has limited ability to glide when the skis are encased in pounds of slush, so the going was tough. The slush was formed by a recent deep snow, which had weighed down the ice to such an extent that lake water had emerged through cracks in the ice. The water then formed a slush layer between the snow and the ice. If the snow layer is heavy enough, the surface of the ice can even be pushed an inch below the water surface!

Walking on such a lake can be more than alarming if you don't know that two feet of solid ice still lies beneath the slush. To make matters more interesting, the top layer of the slush sometimes freezes; a snowfall may then cover it up, resulting in a four-layer composite of snow, frozen slush, thawed slush, and solid ice. Breaking through the frozen slush layer can easily be misconstrued as breaking through the real ice, amplifying one's heartbeat to a drumroll.

Deer Browse and Old Growth

Mary and I frequently snowshoe in the Sylvania Wilderness Area. Sylvania contains 21,000 acres of crystal-clear lakes and old-growth forest, and it's located just over the Wisconsin border in Michigan's Upper Peninsula. During one snowshoe exploration, two things stood out amidst the overall beauty: the amount of deer browse, and the silence of the deep woods. The deer browse was so extensive that Mary and I both got excited when we saw a maple seedling that still had some buds on it. In fact, that was an unusual find. Sugar maple seedlings often blanket the understory of old-growth forests, and their winter buds provide good deer browse. In the area we visited, the seedling maples were crooked and gnarled, like the hands of an elderly man who has performed hard, physical labor all his life. Sugar maple seedlings can tolerate browsing for many years while awaiting an opening in the canopy, but even they have their limits. We found many seedlings that had succumbed to the long wait.

However, we found no hemlock seedlings in the area. Young hemlocks can withstand browsing for a few years. They are often found with a bushy skirt of branches and needles positioned several feet above the ground; a skinny leader branch rises an additional six to eight feet, just out of the reach of the deer. The bushy skirt prospers, because it is covered by snow throughout the winter. On our hike, though, we found no evidence whatsoever of hemlock reproduction. Perhaps the seedlings were the victims of an overpopulation of deer, though the reproduction of hemlock usually relies on a series of relatively complex factors.

Winter Silence

Silence soothes some and drives others to escape. For Mary and me, total silence provides not only an emotional peace, but an intellectual pleasure derived from knowing we have found a spot that is momentarily apart from the myriad influences of other humans.

"That's no big deal," some might say. "You can find silence anywhere." Not so. There is no place left on Earth that is free from the noise of helicopters and airplanes. Noise pollution is a worldwide problem. Those who record nature sounds report that they are hard-pressed to find areas free of human sound. A few years ago, Cornell University wanted to hold a seminar on nature sound recording, but the college couldn't find a site within the entire eastern United States that offered sufficient silence.

Many people enjoy the northwoods partly because of the sounds generated in a natural forest, or because the forest offers respite from urban noise. Bird songs, wind in pines, waves on shoreline sand, coyote howls, spring peeper choruses, rushing rivers--these are sounds we still hunger for. Author Peter Steinhart 'notes in one of his essays that, in the past, "Those were the meters to which our hearts and minds were calibrated."

163

The animals of the northwoods are still calibrated in this manner. They speak with voices far more complex than we generally recognize. A killdeer makes one call when it's courting; another call when nest building; another when attempting to distract something that is threatening its chicks; and yet another when calling to its young. White-crowned sparrows that lived on three sides of a university in California were recorded using three distinct variations of a "dialect." Every individual chipping sparrow sings a slightly different song. Marsh wrens may sing 200 different songs in an hour.

If we slow down recordings of bird songs, we begin to hear some of the details that the birds themselves hear. When a winter wren's song is slowed down, we hear single, distinguishable notes, making the song become all the more complex and melodious.

Remarkably, some animals appear to adapt their sounds to fit the terrain. For instance, bird calls in close, dense areas are generally high-pitched--presumably because the songs don't need to carry for a long distance. On the other hand, bird songs in wide-open areas are usually low-pitched, allowing them to carry farther. White-crowned sparrows within a specific habitat will even alter the pitch of their calls so they can be heard within the available audio spectrum.

Humans generate so much noise that the messages of the natural world often cannot reach our brain for purposes of interpretation. Steinhart writes: "Few of us know the voices of...even backyard bird song. In part that is because we don't listen. In part it is because, even if we do listen, our neighborhoods are so rattled with sounds of automobiles and airplanes, leaf-blowers, and amplified music that we can't hear crickets or mockingbirds. We roll up our windows and turn up the stereo, borrowing noise to screen out noise. We are the only creature that tries not to hear."

What our noise does to the rest of the natural world is unclear. A rumbling semitrailer or a pack of snowmobiles can be heard from 10 miles away at night. Would an owl that nests near a snowmobile trail be driven from its habitat because the noise disturbs its hunting? What happens to those animals that rely on their acute sense of hearing to avoid predation? Hopefully, research is currently under way that will help us address such concerns.

164

Majority for Silence

After listening to the maddening noise of snowmobiles for many years, I now propose that a new organization be formed in every town, in order to combat the incessant discord. By popular vote (meaning Mary and me), we suggest the name "The Majority for Silence" for the new organization.

What will this organization do? I see it as an organized means of promoting increased appreciation for silent sports, and as a way of getting a grip on "wreckcreation"--the sports that insist on the use of fast, noisy machinery when "seeing" the northwoods. Political organizing is not my forte, but I know that silence allows me to experience beauty, while noise drives me away in anger. I also know that many others feel the same way.

Maybe we can become a voice that is heard over the din. Hopefully someone will step forward one day soon and lead the efforts of such an organization.

Humans in the Cold

When you exercise outdoors, cold temperatures and dry air substantially increase your need for food and water. Human metabolic rates may be forced to increase by 20 percent in order to keep up with the cold, requiring a corresponding 20 percent increase in calorie intake. If you're exercising heavily outdoors, be sure to also drink three or four quarts of water per day, because your lungs expire a tremendous amount of moisture.

Delayed Implantation

Delayed implantation occurs in many northwoods mammals, including black bears, martens, fishers, weasels, and otters. Why it occurs in some animals but not in other, closely related animals of the same species is a puzzle. Delayed implantation allows females to remain light and swift through the summer and fall, when food is most readily available. A female bear is in her den by the time the embryo implants. Thanks to delayed implantation, the sow may be able to self-abort if her body tells her she doesn't have sufficient food reserves to carry the baby.

165

Brown Creepers

Mary and I frequently ski and hike through the Manitowish River Wilderness Area, exploring areas we aren't familiar with. During one weekend journey, the shallow snow cover was barely sufficient to cover the marsh grasses; even in the uplands, we had to ski over the stems of invading sweet fern and various brambles. Eventually, the old trails became so overgrown with rank vegetation that we took off our skis and walked.

Although we saw few wildlife signs, we did observe our first brown creeper of the winter. Creepers are often difficult to see, because their brown and white plumage serves as excellent camouflage. The little bird's habit of flattening itself against a tree trunk and remaining motionless for minutes when in danger compounds the difficulty of observing it. Brown creepers seldom come to feeders except to obtain suet, apparently preferring the more rigorous life of foraging tree trunks for insects. They usually begin at the bottom of a tree, spiraling their way slowly upward; then they drop to the base of the next tree, repeating the performance. Their long tails provide a brace, much like the long tail of a woodpecker.

Creepers disdain the flashy colors and songs of most of their brethren, instead seeking unobtrusiveness. Their preference for older, deciduous trees in lowland areas prevents easy sightings by bird-watchers--in contrast to other birds like goldfinches, which regularly visit our feeders and seem to demand our attention.

Pileated Woodpeckers

An old, large white spruce once stood next to our house. For several years, a pileated woodpecker hammered away on the base of the tree in the winter. When we cut it down one summer so we could build an addition onto our house, scores of carpenter ants spilled out. Sensibly, they headed straight for our house. How does one stop a stampede of carpenter ants?

Unfortunately, I failed to slow the ants down, and the value of the work that had been performed by the pileated in preceding years became graphically evident. Pileated woodpeckers do humans and many other animals a huge service in the winter by excavating large nesting cavities in trees and eating insects. The birds function like a natural "insecticide" by eating adult insects and larvae before they can mate in the spring. The old saying goes something like this: "Eat one in winter, kill a hundred in May."

Nearly 30 northwoods birds nest in tree cavities, so the pileated is also the building contractor for numerous species that happily move into their newly excavated homes in the spring. In the overall ecology of the north, the pileated may be our most important bird species, and an added bonus is its beauty. The pileated's red crown is strikingly handsome.

166

Goldfinches

The star of the northern winter bird world is often the American goldfinch. We usually see dozens at our feeder every day, and others who feed birds enjoy similar populations. Goldfinches love the seeds from composite flowers like thistles, dandelions, and sunflowers. These plants grow in full sun environments and pioneer open ground like gardens, so they have been dismissed by some as "weeds."

From the same perspective, the goldfinch might be regarded as a feathered weed. Its population today is far higher than it was in settlement times, when heavy forest cover dominated our area. Forest clearing opened new habitats for the goldfinch; it has responded by extending its range and vastly increasing its numbers.

The introduction of European "weeds" like bull thistle and Canada thistle helped accelerate the goldfinch expansion, and the explosion in home bird feeding further contributed to its population growth. Goldfinches seem to particularly savor the small, black-oil sunflower seed, which is easy to handle and crack open. One author has referred to our nation's well-stocked feeders as "the avian answer to fast food"--an accurate analogy. Certainly the goldfinch's high numbers, evidenced by the National Audubon Christmas Bird Counts throughout the Midwest, indicate that they've adapted splendidly to the drive-through feeding concept.

Outside of the breeding season, goldfinches socialize happily. Flocks of up to several hundred are not unusual. Their winter plumage is far less brilliant than the "wild canary" look assumed by the male when he wears his spring mating finery. If you wish to distinguish the young from the old, juveniles have wing bars and upper parts tinged with a cinnamon buff.

167

Goldfinches can also be identified by their characteristic, undulating flight, which results from a few rapid wingbeats upward, followed by a pause and descent, then another upward burst. Birder and author Jerome Jackson describes a flock of goldfinches in flight as "a bouncing black-and-yellow ball." He wonderfully sums up the pleasure of winter goldfinches by saying: "People who attract goldfinches to their feeders have the Midas touch."

Lichens

January is a good time to notice the many forms of lichens growing on tree trunks and branches. Some 20,000 species of lichens have been identified; they grow in virtually every habitat on Earth, including Antarctic rocks. The only habitat lichens refuse to colonize are areas that suffer from significant air pollution.

Lichens are actually two plants--fungi and algae--that act as partners in a relationship that forms one new entity, a lichen. Two theories attempt to explain the relationship of the two plants. The most popular theory describes the relationship as a mutualistic union--a partnership from which both sides benefit. The algae provides nutrients through photosynthesis, while the fungi provides water and protection from extreme weather. A contrasting view holds that the fungi parasitize the algae, taking the nutrients and giving nothing in return--a kind of marriage not unknown in human circles.

An old adage claims that lichens grow only on the north side of trees, so if you're lost, you can look for lichens to guide your way. Perhaps it's true that, overall, a larger concentration of lichens grow on the north sides of trees. But I doubt that anyone has undertaken a comprehensive survey, and in fact most trees support lichens on all sides. You're better off remembering your compass.

Sightings

While the January woods may seem lifeless, much is going on. Beavers begin breeding in late January and mate into the latter part of February. Their gestation period is 120 days. Red foxes, monogamous for life, also begin breeding in January, experiencing a gestation period of 53 days. Coyotes and bobcats are sniffing the air in anticipation of their early to mid-February breeding season. White-tailed bucks commonly lose their antlers in January.

Great horned owls, our earliest avian nesters, have been voicing their somber, six-note call for months in order to establish territories; they are now ready to begin nesting, and they will soon begin to lay eggs. An average clutch consists of two to three eggs, requiring about 30 days to hatch. Great horned owls don't build nests; instead, they take over the nests of crows, ravens, or hawks, or nest on artificial platforms. The young will hatch in March--blind, featherless, and helpless.

Spell-Checking Bird Names

One of the most useful features of a computer is the spell checker. Whenever a word isn't recognized, the computer provides an array of options intended to suggest the correct word. However, computer programmers apparently are not birders. Courtesy of *Winging It*, the newsletter of the American Birding Association, here are some names that spell checkers have suggested for birds:

The Bird's Real Name	*The Computer Version*
willet	wallet or wiglct
parasitic jaeger	parasitic jogger

The Bird's Real Name	*The Computer Version*
Heermann's gull	hormone gull
glaucous gull	glucose gull
ancient murrelet	ancient moralist
dark-eyed junco	dark-eyed junkie

Size Rules: Bergmann and Allen

Bergmann and Allen may sound like a comedy team, but they are in fact ecologists. In the December section of this book, I wrote that having a large body is an advantage for an animal in the north country, because large bodies can hold on to heat much longer than small bodies. Bergmann and Allen have coined two rules that further govern the relationship of size to climate.

169

Bergmann's rule states that, within a species, the geographic races will be larger in the cooler parts of the species' range. Thus white-tailed deer in the northern parts of their range (from the northwoods into southern Canada) are significantly larger than white-tails in the southern portions of their range (all the way into Mexico and Florida).

When you think about it, this makes sense. A large body in a warm climate loses heat too slowly. As a result, nearly every animal that lives in the tropical regions of North and South America is relatively small when compared to equivalent animals that live in temperate climates. Don't ask me, however, why this rule doesn't seem to apply to the warm regions of Africa.

Allen's rule states that the extremities of an animal, including ears, tails, and bills, will be shorter in the cooler parts of a species' range, because extremities radiate heat. Thus deer in southern areas have proportionately larger ears in order to remove heat, and northern deer have shorter ears in order to retain heat.

The Exceptions: Small Can Survive

If you're a small organism like an insect in the northwoods, how then do you cope with winter? Insects--and small organisms in general--face some insurmountable physical barriers. Few tiny organisms have the capacity to migrate for long distances. Few can generate any heat whatsoever. Few can grow more fur or feathers, so they have little ability to self-insulate. And because all face the great risk of losing heat to the winter air, few small organisms have the option of remaining active as adults in winter.

One survival strategy employed by small organisms involves avoiding exposure to the cold air. They may hide under the snow, in bark crevices, in the soil, in the water, under downed timber, or elsewhere. The challenge is finding a microhabitat that's warm enough to let them avoid freezing. When the organisms find such a site, they adjust their biochemistry so their bodies can drop to a near-freezing temperature. Then they simply shut down their metabolisms.

Snowfleas, which are seen by many of us on the snow surface during warm winter days, employ a variation on this strategy. When it's cold, they hide in the insulation of the snow cover. On warmer days, they emerge to soak up the sunshine.

170

Chickadees, Nuthatches, and Redpolls: How Do They Survive?

Small birds and mammals are big enough to withstand the winter, but only through specialized adaptations. They have evolved to survive the northern cold by allowing the temperature of their extremities to fall almost to the point of freezing–well below their inner temperature. Even with this ability, they often lack sufficient energy reserves, so these small animals took the next adaptive step–they evolved the ability to adjust their internal core temperature, a process called heterothermy. For several hours to a day or more, they can lower their internal body temperature to reduce the amount of energy consumed. They maintain a high internal temperature if the external temperature is warmer, but drop into brief states of inactive torpor when it's very cold. This is essentially a compromise between being fully active like a deer and going into hibernation like a woodchuck. A chickadee, for instance, can lower its internal body temperature by 20 degrees or more at night in order to conserve fuel. By contrast, we humans suffer dramatically if our core temperature rises or falls even a few degrees.

Slumping and Puddling

I'm often asked why snow slumps around trees, and how puddles can form between the ice and snow on a lake or river. Both phenomena are due to the fact that, while snow reflects nearly all shortwave radiation from the sun, it acts like a black box when it comes to longwave radiation, absorbing nearly all of it. However, some shortwave radiation manages to pass through the snowpack--enough to be absorbed by dark objects like tree trunks and rocks within the snowpack. These objects warm up, emitting longwave radiation that is readily absorbed by the snowpack. The heat from the longwave radiation makes the snow soft around the objects and initiates the melting process. We notice this most often as snow that slumps around trees, but people in rocky mountainous areas may fall into these soft spots around rocks. They're called "elephant traps" in those regions.

171

Puddling on lakes may occur when shortwave radiation passes through the snow and is absorbed by the ice. The temperature of the ice increases, and it begins to emit longwave radiation back into the snow. The snow then absorbs the heat from the longwave radiation and melts at the interface of the ice, forming a puddle under the snow.

The Desktop Planetarium

If you look to the east in the early evening, you'll see numerous first-magnitude stars, including Rigel, Capella, Aldebaran, and Betelgeuse.

I'm an amateur stargazer, but my skills have progressed since I bought a computer program called "Voyageur, the Interactive Desktop Planetarium." The program allows me to view the night sky as it appears specifically in our area at the moment I wish to go outside. I can print out the skyviews I want to explore and, with the aid of a headlamp and a clipboard, I can identify stars and planets in the field by using the needed references. I can now easily identify virtually every star on any given night. Remembering them is, of course, another matter.

Fishers–Devil in Disguise?

Fishers have become the scapegoat for virtually any species decline in the Northwoods, and are an item of hot debate. Here are a few facts about fishers that may temper and/or inflame some of the hot air.

1- Fishers were re-introduced into the Nicolet National Forest from 1956-63, and then into the Chequamegon National Forest in 1966-67. By 1975, the statewide population was estimated at 1,000-1,500. It then spiraled to 6,000 in 1991, and is estimated in 1996 to be 11,000, or about one per square mile in prime habitats.

172

2- Fishers are exceptional predators, but also regularly eat fruits, berries, nuts, mushrooms, and a significant amount of carrion, particularly deer roadkills and wounded deer during hunting season. They are about as picky of eaters as black bears, which means they'll eat whatever the moment offers.

3- Fishers are not the reason for the decline in ruffed grouse in the early 1990s. One study showed grouse represented about four percent of the early winter diet of fishers. Goshawks and great horned owls have a much greater impact on grouse.

4- Fishers do eat suet from backyard bird feeders, and housecats that wander around in backyards.

5- Fishers may be a major predator on birds of prey, like red-shouldered hawks. Eighteen of 19 red-shouldered hawk nests in the Nicolet National Forest were raided by fishers a few years ago. Fishers may also raid nests of broad-winged and sharp-shinned hawks, as well as barred owls and saw-whet owls.

6- Depending on who you talk to, fisher numbers are still going up, or they are declining. Time will tell. In the meantime, fishers are now one of the most common mammals in the northwoods, as they were prior to their extirpation from Wisconsin in 1932.

Bending Boughs

A major ice storm hit the Lakeland area in November of 1996 and downed thousands of trees. As significant as the damage was, more remarkable were the number of trees that came through the ice storm just fine. The question in a circumstance like this is always why does one tree survive when another doesn't? Well, there probably are several reasons. One would be the age and size of the tree. Smaller, immature trees usually fare much better than mature, large trees. Usually young trees are thinner and more pointed than older trees which have large spreading crowns. More snow and ice can obviously collect on wider and denser limbs than on thinner limbs, causing more damage.

The suppleness of the limbs is another factor. The more supple the limb, the less damage from the weight of ice or snow. I've often wondered why tamaracks lose their needles in the fall, and I think it is because tamarack branches are quite brittle. Do an experiment sometime and simply try to break off an equal-sized winter limb from a tamarack and a spruce or balsam fir. The fir and spruce bend while tamarack snaps off. It appears tamarack must shed its needles in the fall or run the risk of having its limbs stripped from the tree due to accumulating snow loads.

173

Finally, the shape of the tree may be the most important variable in what survives an ice storm, and what collapses. Spruce and fir, and to some extent pine, are shaped like cones. Each year they produce a new whorl of three to six branches that grow horizontally like spokes from the hub of a wheel. Each branch is flexible, and has the added advantage of being supported by last year's branch growing just under it. When the tree collects snow, the branches bend and support one another like a collapsing umbrella or a tepee. As the branches bend down farther, the snow and ice tends to slide right off as the "pitch of the roof" is increased. The design of these conifers is quite different from that of an ash or maple or oak, all of which have minimal flexibility and little supporting framework.

Wintering Hawks

Jack Bull from Winchester called me on one late January afternoon with his wife Barbara's sighting of an unidentified hawk. Given that he didn't have many physical details of Barbara's sighting, he wondered what species of hawks overwinter in the northwoods, and thus might be possible as the mystery bird. Hawks that nest here in the summer include sharp-shinned, Cooper's, northern harrier, northern goshawk, broad-winged, red-shouldered, and red-tailed hawks, as well as American kestrels and merlins from the falcon family. All migrate south except the northern goshawk, but it nests so uncommonly in the northwoods that it is seldom seen. Red-taileds winter in southern Wisconsin down to Panama. Broad-wingeds winter from Guatemala to southern Brazil. Cooper's winter mostly in Central America. Harriers winter in the southern U.S. and head as far south as Venezuela and Barbados, while sharp-shinneds winter from southern Wisconsin south to central Panama and the Greater Antilles. Red-shouldereds range from southern Wisconsin into Mexico during the winter. Merlins winter mostly in the southern U.S. down into northern South America, while kestrels winter from lower Wisconsin south into Panama.

So what is the hawk that Jack and his wife likely saw? With no information other than it was a hawk, I would guess it was a rough-legged hawk or goshawk. Rough-leggeds nest north of the tree line in Canada and Alaska, but they migrate south into our area in the winter. They're a bird of open country, however, and are more plentiful in Northwoods areas with farm fields, like Ashland or Sault Ste. Marie. Jack and Barbara feed scrap meat to animals all winter long, so it may be possible a rough-legged or goshawk stopped by for a free meal. With all the snow we have, and the density of forest cover, we offer little quality winter feeding for hawks, who with little effort, can find the living much easier in southern Wisconsin and points south. Sightings of hawks around here are a fairly rare winter occurrence and worth noting.

174

Real Frozen Tundra–Permafrost

The frozen tundra of Lambeau Field!! How many times do we hear that negative phrase trumpeted every year about the playing field of the Green Bay Packers? Well, I'd rather play on frozen grass any day than on an indoor carpet laid over concrete. But grass takes money to maintain while Astroturf merely injures inordinate numbers of players.

Now that I have that off my chest, all this racket about frozen tundra has led me to research what the real stuff amounts to. Next time you attend a game at Lambeau, take this fact sheet on permafrost along to impress your bleacher mates:

• Permafrost underlies about one-quarter of the earth's land surface. It underlies all of Greenland, much of northern Scandinavia, half of the former Soviet Union, 80 percent of Alaska, and nearly half of Canada. But…no permafrost has been located under Green Bay to date.

• The more intense the cold, the thicker the permafrost. Thompson, a town in northern Manitoba, has a mean annual air temperature of 24°F and permafrost 50 feet deep. Barrow, Alaska, with a mean annual temperature of 10°F has permafrost 1,300 feet thick. And in scenic Verkhoyansk, Siberia, where the record low is -96°F, the permafrost extends down in one place 4,800 feet! That would really be a tough place to play football.

• Permafrost preserves permanently. Entire mammoths have been preserved perfectly in permafrost. The most famous adult mammoth was found in 1900 in northeastern Siberia and had been buried for about 40,000 years. Although wolves had eaten part of the body of the animal once it was exposed, the mammoth still had 33 pounds of food in its stomach. Stomach analysis of another mammoth discovered near to the first mammoth showed it had been browsing buttercups just before its death. Gilbert Brown, the Packer's resident mammoth of a defensive nose guard, and of Gilbert-burger fame, should be apprised of this.

• Permafrost can preserve life too. Ten-thousand-year-old lupine seeds found in 1954 in an ancient lemming burrow were kept by a scientist for 12 years before the seeds were placed on wet filter paper in a petri dish where six seeds germinated within 48 hours. One plant, upon reaching 11 months of age, and after 10,000 years of dormancy, then bloomed. This could give new futuristic meaning to playing on the frozen tundra when the phrase is heard, "He really planted that guy with that hard hit!"

• And for a permafrost paradox—most of the circumpolar tundra region receives less annual precipitation, about eight inches, than the Mojave Desert. Greenland receives less than one inch of precipitation per year, most of which falls as snow. Yet the tundra landscape is a maze of perhaps millions of rivers and lakes (no one has tried counting them all).

175

Staying Warm at a Packer Game:
Human Adaptations to Cold

So besides drinking oneself into total oblivion so as to not feel anything whatsoever, how do human beings adapt to cold weather? Well, it turns out, not very well. We're really a tropical animal whose brain has permitted us to extend our range well beyond our biological limits. We have virtually no physiological adaptations to low temperatures. To conserve heat, the best we can do to reduce our heat loss is constrict the blood vessels near the skin surface when we get cold. Blood is then shunted through deeper veins, which reduces heat loss from radiation and conduction from the skin. We can reduce the temperature of our appendages significantly without danger, but we're still nowhere near as good at it as winter-adapted animals.

176

> ## Late-January Musings
> *Deer spend four months of the year eating cereal and the other eight months eating the box.*
> –Source Unknown

To produce additional heat in winter, we have to either increase our muscle activity or start shivering. Vigorous exercise can increase the heat production of our skeletal muscles tenfold, while shivering can raise our metabolic rate fivefold. Still, we're physiologically ill-suited to living in the cold. The best way to deal with the cold, as often expressed by the Inuit, is to "take care not to be cold."

FEBRUARY

The Ojibwe name for February is *onabinigizis*, meaning "snow-crusted month." February thaws commonly form a crust layer on top of the snow. The upside of the crust is that it creates the first off-track, ski-skating opportunities of the winter. For lighter animals with large, padded feet, such as snowshoe hares, the crust offers unlimited highway "pavement" and easy travel. The downside is that crusted snow cuts the ankles of sharp-hooved deer and moose with every step they take, thus confining them to well-trodden areas.

If spring seems eons away, remember that on February 7 we will experience 10 hours of daylight (7:13 a.m. to 5:13 p.m.); by February 17, our day will last 10 1/2 hours (6:58 to 5:28). On February 27, the sun will grace us for a full 11 hours (6:41 to 5:43). Those who are overly optimistic begin to think spring is on the way and get out their seed catalogs. Guess again.

February 1 to February 14

February—Winter in Decline?

I tend to think of winter as "declining" once we get through January, but a look at our weather records from 1996 reveals the truth.

On 1/29/96, we began the coldest week of weather I have ever experienced. The lows at my house were as follows:

1/29: -32°F	2/1: -48°F
1/30: -30°F	2/2: -45°F
1/31: -46°F	2/3: -50°F
	2/4: -46°F

And then we hit a heat wave on 2/5 and only experienced -24°. So February can still pack a punch. For that matter, so can March—we had -38° on March 7th in 1996. I realize the 1996 winter was exceptionally cold and snowy, and may be seen as an aberration, but the temperatures recorded are ample warning to discipline your mind against spring fever—it's most likely a long way off.

> **February Musings**
>
> *I look up to see the full moon looming large and yellow over the horizon. It is a commanding presence...If I can find the stillness inside me, the silence of the evening slips over my imagination. I become aware of the vast distances of space, the undeflected flight of ancient starlight, and the freshness and improbability of earthly life.*
>
> –Peter Steinhart

Irruptive Birds

Dozens of pine siskins and evening grosbeaks and lesser numbers of goldfinches, pine grosbeaks, and purple finches gorged at our feeder during the winter of 1990, but in 1991 only a few species visited our feeder—and then only a few individuals of each species. Judging by other reports I received that winter, my feeder wasn't the only one with a vacancy sign out front. What went on? Why were the birds here one year and gone the next? The answer is simple and unsatisfying. Winter bird populations are irregular and unpredictable. Robust or limited natural food sources play a large role in determining where the birds winter-over. Surprisingly, though, these food peaks and valleys don't always coincide with the presence of particular species, so they don't provide the definitive answer. The irruptive species of birds vary from year to year on a large geographic scale—northern Wisconsin versus southern Wisconsin for instance—and also on a microscale—your backyard versus my backyard just down the road. Frankly, when asked where the birds are and why they're not present at a particular place, the only answer is often a shrug of the shoulders.

180

Owl and Hawk Irruptions

Great gray and hawk owls have been reported during a number of winters near Fifield, just south of Park Falls. A hawk owl spent a month or more during the winter of 1992 perched in a stand of aspen along Highway 13 near Glidden. Observing the hawk owl was as easy as driving up to the spot, pulling onto the shoulder of the road, and scoping it across a hundred feet of snowy opening.

Both great grays and hawk owls are rare visitors this far south. Snowy owls though are more common. During the winter of 1992-93, snowy owls migrated south in a "winter invasion" of the Midwest. Fourteen snowies were spotted in Indiana—very far south indeed for these Arctic birds.

That same fall, 30 snowy owls were banded at Hawk Ridge in Duluth, but only two of the birds were adults. The numbers indicated a very successful summer for reproduction, followed by a poor winter for food in the far north. Lemmings are the snowies' main prey, and lemmings follow a four-year population cycle. Not surprisingly, snowy owl invasions have occurred on a regular four-year cycle since at least 1882, and one researcher says the cycle extends all the way back to 1833. When the lemmings are down, the banding stations usually see no young snowies and very few immatures the following autumn. Either the young are unable to survive or they aren't produced to begin with. The 1992-93 Hawk Ridge banding was the highest count in the previous 10 years.

The Goshawk Cycle

Goshawks follow an eight- to 10-year population cycle that is thought to be connected to grouse and hare populations. When grouse and hare numbers crash, goshawk sightings in the northwoods increase, as the goshawks are forced southward to find prey. Hawk Ridge sighted 250 adults in the fall of 1992–a high number when compared to 30 sighted in 1989 and 150 reported in 1990. Peak years occurred in 1972 and 1982; the record count came in 1982, when 1,400 were spotted. A typical noninvasion year yields 60 to 80 goshawks.

The Snowshoe Hare Cycle

181

The eight- to 11-year snowshoe hare cycle ranges from high densities of one to four hares per acre to lows of one hare per 200 acres—after which the cycle begins anew. The most important factor in the rise and fall of the population is the survival rate of juvenile hares, a factor that most believe is influenced by the populations of predators like hawks, owls, and foxes. However, in one study of the causes of mortality among snowshoe hares, researchers glued tiny radio transmitters to 254 newborn leverets, then followed their movements. Remarkably, they found evidence that more than 85 percent of the leveret deaths were due to squirrel predation! The researchers located nearly half of the carcasses in trees or in red squirrel middens. Only 5 percent of the leverets were killed by great horned owls, goshawks, or red-tailed hawks, which are the traditional scapegoats.

More Cycles: Grouse and Others

The nine- to 11-year population cycle of grouse, a favorite prey species of goshawks, appears to parallel the snowshoe hare cycle. I've read at least 12 different theories that attempt to explain the cyclic fluctuations of grouse. These theories attribute fluctuations to causes such as internal parasites like roundworms; toxins in aspen buds that are generated every 10 years or so; decreases in plant cover; and increases in prey species like goshawks.

Because a key ecological concept holds that everything is connected to everything else, one must ask what else is affected by a given cycle. For example, the periodic movement of evening grosbeaks into our area is usually linked with the failure of northern seed crops of spruce, pine, and other conifers that occurs every two years. But some bird researchers claim the 10-year cycle that so many large birds seem to follow also affects evening grosbeaks, as well as pheasants, partridges, and blue jays.. It's a complex challenge, not only to find the linkages between species, but to demonstrate their role in the population cycles of each individual species.

Great Gray Owls

The following information comes from Tom Nichols, a bird researcher in the Park Falls area: "A great gray owl was seen [in 1994] for the first time in the 29-year history of the Fifield-Park Falls Audubon Christmas Bird Count. This magnificent bird was seen along Highway 70 east of Fifield. The great gray owl is our largest, gray, round-headed, hornless owl, with a very large facial disk, yellow eyes, and long tail. It is distinguished from our more commonly found barred owl by its bright yellow eyes (barred owls have dark eyes), unbarred breast, conspicuous white throat markings, and definitive concentric rings on its facial disc. It's usually quite tame and frequently hunts in daylight. It often hunts meadow mice in open fields using fence posts, low trees, shrubbery, and woods edges as lookouts."

Only two nests of great grays have been found in Wisconsin in the twentieth century, according to records through 1989. One nest was found in Douglas County, and another in Ashland County near Clam Lake. Winter sightings remain rare in Wisconsin, but a few birds have been tallied nearly every winter since the invasion year of 1968-69, when seven were seen. The winter of 1996-97 was a major invasion year for great grays—at least 40 were seen in Wisconsin.

Wintering Bald Eagles

Adult bald eagles usually migrate only as far south as they need to go to find open water. During a mild winter some may remain in the northwoods, working the open rivers. Within the entire Upper Midwest, the best and most consistent place to view wintering eagles is found in central and southern Wisconsin, along the Wisconsin and Mississippi rivers.

One winter my family and I drove down to southern Wisconsin to view the eagles. We stopped first at a bridge on Highway 21 located at the base of the Petenwell Flowage, along the Wisconsin River. Built in 1950, the Petenwell Dam created a 14-mile-long flowage containing 36 square miles of open water—the second-largest inland "lake" in Wisconsin. The eagles feed below the dam in the morning; in the afternoon, they roost in the large trees along the river's shoreline. We saw 16 bald eagles at one time on both sides of the river. One tree alone hosted six eagles perched on its branches.

The power company maintains a two-story viewing platform just below the dam, but we saw only two eagles from that spot in the late morning. Early mornings are best, because the eagles feed when the water is released through the dam at around 7 a.m.

From Petenwell, we drove to the Necedah National Wildlife Refuge, where we had reserved a blind that was built specifically for eagle viewing. We were excited because 10 bald and three golden eagles had been feeding on roadkill deer carcasses that were set out near the blind for their winter dining. Although many people mistake immature bald eagles for goldens, golden eagles are actually quite rare in Wisconsin, and we hoped to see a few.

However, as luck would have it—and as we deserved, because we didn't arrive until nearly noon—the eagles were nowhere to be seen. I nevertheless recommend visiting the blind at Necedah, and getting there at daybreak. Call the refuge for reservation details at (608) 565-2551.

We then traveled on to Sauk City on the Wisconsin River, where the Ferry Bluff Eagle Council maintains an overlook with a spotting scope. Up to 60 eagles commonly overwinter in the area, feeding below a dam located just upriver from Sauk City. The fish get stunned or killed as they come through the turbines, and the eagles, never dainty in their culinary practices, seem quite pleased to pick off the easy meals.

I appreciated Sauk City's willingness to promote its wildlife. We ate in the Eagle Cafe; the local winery produces Eagle Wine; and the town promotes ecotourism in other ways as well.

Bald eagles begin returning northward in late February, so if you have an inclination to see them on their wintering grounds, do so soon.

183

Feeding Popcorn

Betty Munson from Woodruff and Dorothy Grapentine from Mercer haven't seen a bird yet that doesn't love popped popcorn. The same holds true for squirrels and chipmunks, which seem to think of themselves as birds. Dorothy pops five quarts of popcorn every morning, as well as preparing her own special entree for her backyard visitors. The entree consists of stale bread, peanut butter, cornmeal, and corn oil. She even provides fresh water by using a water heater in a pail to prevent ice from forming.

184

Groundhogs in February?

Groundhog's Day will come and go for another year, and one thing's for certain: the prognostications of Mr. or Ms. Woodchuck (groundhogs and woodchucks are the same animal) will contain not one whit of truth. No sane woodchuck in the northwoods is yet out of hibernation, and the snow and ice are typically here to stay until April, whether the skies of early February are clear or cloudy. As is often the case, though, a custom that seems odd today was once firmly rooted in the seasonal observations of the past. Fred Greeley, Professor Emeritus of Wildlife Ecology from the University of Massachusetts and a summer resident at Camp Wipigaki in Lac du Flambeau since 1922, filled me in on the historical background of Groundhog's Day.

Groundhog's Day has its roots in the Roman Feast of Light, which later became Candlemas. The Roman/Christian celebration of the end of winter's darkness and the revived light of spring was also wrapped up in this religious occasion. Somehow, weather forecasting became tied in, as evidenced by this old rhyme:

> If Candlemas Day be fair and clear
> There'll be five winters in the year.
> If Candlemas Day be dry and fair
> the half of winter's to come and mair.
> If Candlemas Day be wet and foule
> the half o' winter's gone at Yule.

According to a German tradition, if a badger saw the sun shining on Candlemas Day, it would draw back into its hole; if it found snow, it would go walking abroad. German settlers in Pennsylvania Dutch country are credited with keeping the observance alive.

Woodchucks may be awake in Punxatawney, Pennsylvania, but to the hibernating woodchuck in the northwoods, whose heartbeat in winter is down to four beats a minute and whose body temperature is a frigid 38°F, Groundhog's Day is at best a dim dream in a dark, cold, five-month drowse.

The Porcupine in the Outhouse   185

During a February field trip to the Mercer School Forest that I took with a high school biology class, several students opened the door to an abandoned outhouse. Inside, they found a porcupine chewing away on the wooden seat. It eventually sauntered out the door; the students respectfully scattered, then watched as it climbed 15 feet up a nearby balsam fir to take stock of the intruders. Winter feeding means eating bark for porcupines, so we looked high into other trees to see whether they had been dined upon. Many of them had been. A small number of firs and aspens were chewed barkless for expanses of 10 feet.

The students wondered what a porcupine might find desirable about an outhouse seat. The answer is salt. Porkies have an insatiable desire for salt, as anyone who has lost a canoe paddle, leather clothing, an ax handle, or even car tires (loaded with spring road salt) to a porkie can attest. Wooden outhouse seats impregnated with years of human sweat offers dietary cuisine of the highest order to porcupines.

But another question remains. Why do porcupines have such a profound need for salt, particularly when the human contact often necessary to obtain it places them in life-threatening situations? Oddly enough, tree defenses turn out to be the cause of the porcupines' insatiable quest for salt; as you might expect, the story's not a simple one. We think of trees as defenseless against the onslaught of foragers that eat their fruits, leaves, buds, and inner bark, but that's simply not true. Trees have evolved a number of weapons that defend them against potential defoliation—armaments that include poor nutrient content, unpalatable food additives, and indigestible roughage.

A Salty Story

The salt story begins in the spring, when porcupines abruptly switch their diet from tree bark, which contains only 2 to 3 percent crude protein, to new leaves and buds, which may contain 20 percent crude protein. Porkies particularly like to forage on the buds and leaves of sugar maple, the leaves of ash, and the catkins of quaking aspen. However, as summer comes on, these trees defend themselves by producing and accumulating tannins in their leaves. Tannins inhibit the porcupines' digestive processes, forcing them to find other food sources.

186 Typically, the porkies then turn to the leaves of basswood, bigtooth aspen, and quaking aspen. But the crude protein content of these leaves drops by half in the summer, forcing the porkies to eat more, and they gain weight. In this light, a porcupine's bulky body may be seen as necessary, because it must find a great deal of food in order to extract sufficient nutrients.

The salt part of the story begins here. The trees exhibit a highly effective line of defense against leaf-eaters like porcupines. Their leaves contain a highly imbalanced mineral ratio, providing almost 300 parts of potassium for every part of sodium. Meanwhile, porcupines require an even ratio of both sodium and potassium. When they eat the leaves, the mineral imbalance is transferred to their digestive systems, which must somehow get rid of the tremendous excess of potassium, as too much potassium disrupts muscle and nerve functions.

The porcupine's kidneys remove the surplus potassium, but some of the sodium is inadvertently swept away as well; now the porcupine needs a different food source or a sodium supplement. Because natural supplies of sodium are scarce, sodium-laced human implements and artifacts receive a degree of homage well beyond what we might imagine they deserve. Porkies sometimes go to extreme lengths in their search for salt, even eating old camp pots; they apparently seek the salt imbedded in the aluminum. Or, as happened in our school forest, they may commit the socially stigmatizing sin of chewing on outhouse seats.

The Acid Test

The need for salt is easily understood. But trees employ yet another line of defense against porcupines by producing organic acids in their fruits and leaves. Highly acidic foods are avoided by porcupines because the acids apparently inhibit the kidney's ability to remove potassium from the blood. But porcupines have an innate ability to sense the acid content of foods, and thus to avoid them. One researcher observed a family of porcupines feeding in an apple orchard. The porkies nearly stripped the apples clean from four trees but left the rest of the orchard untouched. When analyzed, the rejected apples contained 11 times more acid than those eaten, though their protein and sugar content was the same. The low-acid apples tasted mealy and bland to the researcher. They were the sort of apples humans tend to appreciate least, but they were the kindest to the digestive systems of porcupines.

187

Dying of Starvation on a Full Stomach

In winter, as porcupines change their diet to inner bark, they must yet overcome another line of defense of trees, a combination in the inner bark of a very low concentration of nitrogen and high levels of indigestible roughage. Nitrogen builds proteins, but because so much of the inner bark roughage takes a long time to digest, the porkies try to compensate for the low nitrogen levels by eating more bark. Their stomachs end up full, but they may still be physiologically starving. One researcher who spent seven years studying porcupines in the Catskill Mountains of New York, observed his study group lose an average 17 percent of their body weight over one winter, although literally full of food. One male in his study froze to death in March after losing one-third of his weight, though an autopsy revealed a full digestive tract.

So a strategic battle goes on between trees and porcupines all year around, each responding to the other's tactics, and in the end finding themselves in an even fight in which neither gains the upper hand.

I'm sure our husky will in the near future attempt to upset that balance by having a porcupine snack, and instead come away with a mouthful of quills. Interestingly, the researcher discussed above discovered that quills are antibiotic. He was led to this discovery when, attempting to capture a porcupine, a quill was driven deep into his upper forearm and completely beneath the skin. Two days later, after some intense pain, it emerged from his lower forearm completely intact without leaving a trail of infection behind it. He made an extract of the quills, tested it against bacteria, and found it slowed bacterial growth. The researcher believes the antibiotic quality protects the porcupine against itself, in case its own quills are driven into its body from a fall. Porkies do fall from trees when branches break or they slip.

188   Browsing in February

February is the time of year when the winter survival of browsing animals begins to become dicey. Woody shrubs provide little nutrition compared to summer greens, and the high cellulose content of the shrubs means the animals must spend more time and energy on digestion. If winter browsing has been heavy in an area, older twigs must be consumed, and these have much lower food value. An 18-month-old willow twig contains 50 percent less crude protein than a six-month-old twig. To compensate for this nutrient-poor diet, deer and moose have to metabolize their stored fat and protein, causing continual weight loss until spring.

One way to reduce weight loss is to reduce movement. Deer and moose innately realize this, so they decrease their foraging activity in cold weather. In order to survive, they need to turn their internal furnaces way down. If the furnaces don't need much stoking, then there's less need for fuel.

The deer population remains high in the northwoods—over 20 per square mile on the average. While high numbers are wonderful for the eye and the hunter, they take an enormous toll on the plant species that the deer prefer to browse. Hemlock, cedar, and Canada yew populations are struggling to reproduce in the northwoods, due in significant part to overbrowsing.

The Heart of the Matter

Historically, Valentine's Day has nothing to do with the natural world, but the subject provides an easy tie-in for a look at the hearts of birds. An avian heart is about 40 percent larger than the heart of a similarly sized mammal, but it beats less rapidly. The reason? Birds must have ample energy and power as well as maximum efficiency in order to survive long migratory flights. The heart's large size delivers the extra power, while the slow heartbeat provides the efficiency needed to ensure a maximum ratio of thrust to calorie loss.

Still, a bird's heart beats rapidly. Larger birds like the mourning dove have a heart rate of 135 beats per minute, while the hearts of small birds like the hummingbird hammer away at 615 beats a minute. Maximum rates for songbirds can reach 1,000 beats per minute when they are under stress. By contrast, human hearts average 72 beats per minute.

189

Shrews keep pace with the birds. Although they live under the warming cover of snow in the winter, they still need to eat three times their weight in food per day—equivalent to human consumption of a young moose each day. All of their food intake is dedicated to the task of keeping their hearts beating at a rate of 600 times per minute and their respiration racing along at 300 breaths per minute. How does the small print on the TV commercials go? Do not try this in your own home.

Is It a Mouse, a Shrew, or a Vole?

Because shrews are about as well-known to the public as various species of zooplankton, here's your handy-dandy guide to identifying all those micey-looking critters out there:

Shrews have pointy noses, and their ears are not visible.

Voles have large ears and short tails.

Mice have large ears and long tails.

Moles have pink "tentacles" on their noses and massive front feet.

Regulating Glow

Animals employ a variety of behaviors to reduce radiant heat loss in winter. They may huddle together; they may use shelters like tree cavities or leaf nests; or they may withdraw a leg or bill, tucking it under their feathers or fur.

One of the most interesting adaptations that birds have evolved to prevent heat loss through their uninsulated legs involves "centering" their blood flow. Their heat-carrying veins and arteries are not located near the skin surface, where warmth would fairly leap out into the winter sky; instead, the arteries that carry blood to the extremities are right next to the veins that carry the blood back into their body core. As the warm blood flowing out passes the blood heading inward through the veins, heat is exchanged, keeping the extremities sufficiently warm. Thus the temperature of a gull's skin layer in cold weather may approach zero, but the leg won't freeze. Human appendages would probably freeze if they were exposed like a gull's, because our strategy involves restricting the flow of blood to our toes and fingers—hence the blue/white color of cold toes. Birds choose to regulate glow, rather than restricting flow.

190

Frog Thaws

February is just as likely to offer a 45°F thaw as it is to produce an Arctic blast. When thaws occur, some animals start moving around. A friend wrote to tell me that she had seen an adult leopard frog swimming in the stream that runs alongside the fish hatchery in Woodruff during one February thaw. That's not too unusual. If the rivers open up, frogs and turtles that are buried in the sediments will often "wake up" and start moving.

Tapping Trees

Red squirrels "tap" maple sap from sugar maple trees by piercing the bark with a single puncture bite. They wait for the sap to dry on the tree, which allows the water to evaporate and increases the sugar content, before feeding on it. It's impossible to know, but perhaps American Indians learned to tap maple trees by watching red squirrels.

Who's the Hardiest?

I appreciate the hardiness of our northern trees. For trees like balsam fir, white and black spruce, jack pine, tamarack, aspen, and white birch, which extend way up into Canada, -40°F is only moderately cold. For others, like white and red pine, red oak, the maples, hemlock, white cedar, basswood, and the cherry trees, -40°F probably triggers panic attacks.

In fact, the dividing line between who's tough and who's *really* tough occurs at -40°F. Trees that can survive down to this temperature have the ability to supercool the liquids within them. This is done by limiting the presence of particles inside their cells around which ice crystals can form. If temperatures fall below -40°F, the cell liquids freeze anyway, and the cells themselves die.

191

The super hardy trees that simply smile at -40°F have developed extracellular freezing. This means that much of their cellular fluid oozes out from the cells, freezing in an area between cells where the ice crystals can do no damage. The southernmost range of these trees is generally central Wisconsin. In some ways, extended hot weather is more of a threat to them than extended cold.

Moose Lake

My wife Mary, a friend, and I snowshoed to the Moose Lake Hemlocks State Natural Area in Iron County, a 40-acre stand of old-growth hemlocks and yellow birch. To get there, we compassed through a tamarack/black spruce bog, eventually reaching an upland from which we could see a dark forest ahead. The oldest of these hemlocks have been around for 275 years, and their dense canopy cast a deep shadow throughout the stand. The snow was significantly less deep under the hemlocks, and the silence was complete.

It is difficult to describe the difference between being in an old forest and being in a young forest. I can only suggest that there is a wisdom to be found in such a place. Here, a living history can be imagined, although its text cannot be read. In such a place, I can almost see original American Indian culture, almost hear French voyageur voices, almost feel what the land once was.

Icefalls

One late February, Mary, our oldest daughter Eowyn, and I snowshoed along the shoreline of Lake Superior and into the woods to Rainbow Falls, which is located near Black River Harbor, Michigan. The falls tumbled a long ways in a cascade of ice, but one chute of water spilled from behind the ice, leading us to a series of open holes that rushed sweetly between the sheets of river ice. An otter slide started above the falls, slipping alongside the ice cascade and into a pool below. Deer trails led everywhere from the big hemlocks to the open water, and the deer had browsed heavily on saplings within their winter reach. A number of stems too tall for a deer's full stretch were snapped and hanging down, the buds nipped once they were within the reach of the deer.

192

The lake ice extended as far as the eye could see, and beautiful ice formations were built up in places offshore. But the wind off the lake kept us in the trees, where the sting on the face was diminished. The rugged terrain offered some uphill challenges for snowshoe travelers, but the beauty of the ravines running to the river made the work worthwhile.

Winter Skies

Many people notice that stars seem to shine more brightly in the winter. It's not true. While the winter night sky appears to be the brightest of all skies, the illusion is due to the fact that we can see more bright stars at this time of year. Six constellations—Orion, Gemini, Auriga, Taurus, Canis Major, and Canis Minor—dominate the winter sky. They contain 17 of the 33 brightest stars visible in the United States, all clustered in just one-tenth of the sky. Together, these constellations illuminate the evening skies only from mid-December to late March, and they seem all the brighter because few planets can be seen in February.

If you need further convincing, scientists have actually tested air clarity during the various seasons. They have found no differences in the transparency of seasonal evening skies.

Sun Dogs

In February, Mary and I often see what are called "sun dogs," comprised of two short rainbow arcs on either side of the sun. Some folks call them "sunbows." What causes them? When they appear, the sun is shining through a thin cloud of ice crystals, creating an optical effect similar to the small, scattered rainbows produced by the crystals we hang in our windows. Sun dogs appear most commonly when a low sun shines through feathery cirrus clouds. The ice crystals in the clouds are always hexagonal (six-sided), so they act like glass prisms. Sun dogs can create a complete halo of light around the sun or partial arcs, and they are actually far more common than rainbows.

193

The Ebbing Winter

The sun continues its ascent in the sky, rising 25 degrees south of east and setting 25 degrees south of west on February 2. By February 23, it will rise 15 degrees south of east and set 15 degrees south of west. On March 20, the vernal equinox, the sun will travel directly along the equator, then begin rising and setting *north* of east and west. So, as hard as it may be to believe at this time of year, winter is on the ebb.

Moongazing

A walk in a winter woods lit by a full moon is worth the potential discomfort of cold. Author Peter Steinhart has written: "We may rise on moonlit nights to find the confusions of the city melted away, and an older and simpler nature open to us. Moonlight may restore in us a stillness we have lost. It may join our hearts and minds before the great riddles and vast silences, and lead us to an older sense of peace and joy."

MidWinter

My good friend Woody Hagge has watched the ice come and go at Foster Lake near Hazelhurst for the last 19 years. He reports that February 5 denotes "midwinter," the average halfway point between ice-up and ice-out.

The Origins of Place-Names

Learning about the place-names of our small northern towns often provides historical insights. Loggers left behind the richest legacy of names in our area, although the French voyageurs and American Indians provided inspiration for many names as well. Many place-names revolved around the river drives that were performed by the loggers. Big Bateau Lake and Little Bateau Lake in Vilas County were named after the boats used to transport the loggers across rapids. Dam Lake in Vilas County was the site of a logging dam that held back the river water, building up a "head" until the spring drive began. Big Bull Rapids on the South Fork of the Flambeau originates from the loggers' favorite adjective for a powerful rapids, which they described as a "bull" rapids.

194

Names originated from all aspects of logging. Logging tools were immortalized in names like Bootjack Lake in Oneida County; Grindstone Lake in Sawyer County; Two Axe Lake in Sawyer County; and Jammerhill Road in Bayfield County. Still other names commemorated specific lumbermen, who ranged from the lower-strata workers to the big bosses. These include Harshaw (named after a sawmill worker) in Oneida County; Herbster (a camp cook) in Bayfield County; and Weyerhauser (the timber baron) in Rusk County.

Railroad lines used for hauling logs provided the inspiration for many other place-names, among them the Tank Lakes (sites of water tanks for steam locomotives) in Vilas, Oneida, and Bayfield Counties; Spur Lakes (near short, temporary rail lines running into timber stands) in Price and Oneida Counties; Iron County's Turntable Creek (named after a section of rails mounted on a platform that could be rotated in order to turn a locomotive around); and a series of roads that were built on old railroad grades, like Trestle Road in Forest County and Thornapple Grade Road in Sawyer County. Siphon Creek and Siphon Springs in Vilas County are the namesakes of sites where water was siphoned out directly for the steam locomotives.

A few place-names combined water drives with rail logging. The Hoist Lakes in Oneida and Bayfield Counties were sites where logs were floated across a lake to a hoist that would lift them onto railroad cars. Tug Lake in Lincoln County got its name from a steam tug used to move logs across the lake to the hoisting site.

Sightings

Coyotes and bobcats begin mating in February. The female coyote's gestation period lasts about 60 days, so the pups will be born in April. A typical litter is comprised of six young, evenly divided by sex.

Bobcats usually mate later in February; the female gives birth to one to four young after a 62-day gestation period. The young may stay with the female until the following January or February, when they're three-quarters grown. Thus the young from last year should now be dispersing, prepared to go it alone.

A late February thaw often brings out the romantic tendencies in animals like skunks, squirrels, and raccoons, which commonly begin mating at about this time.

Eagles begin returning to their nesting territories in mid-February, mating in early to mid-March.

195

February Musings

Go to the winter woods; listen there, look, watch, and the "dead months" will give you a subtler secret than any you have yet found in the forest.

–Fiona Macleod

February 15 to February 28

A Voyage into Starvation

Winter presents its inconveniences for modern humankind, but these are nothing like the hardships the French experienced during their explorations of the northwoods. From *Up Country: Voices from the Midwestern Wilderness* comes this passage, excerpted from the journal of Pierre Esprit Radisson and written in the winter of 1658-59:

> ### Late-February Musings
>
> *Cold is why Finns, who are exceptionally brilliant on the subject, invented the sauna instead of the cotton gin. It was the cheapest flight to the Amazon they could find, relieving not only the cold but Calvinism.*
>
> –Justin Isherwood

"We come to a lake [Lac Court Oreille in Sawyer County, Wisconsin] ... We stay 14 days in this place, most miserable like a graveyard, for there falls so much snow and frost with such a thick mist that all the snow sticks to the trees—pines, cedars, and thorns. There is darkness upon the earth, as if the sun is eclipsed. The trees ares so laden with snow that it falls as if sifted. On the ground the snow is not able to bear us, although we make snowshoes six feet long and a foot and a half wide. Often, trying to turn ourselves, we fall over and over again in the snow. If alone, we have trouble rising. By the noise we make, the beasts hear us from a great way off.

"So famine is among many who did not provide for themselves beforehand...Those who have any life search for roots. This is done with great difficulty, the earth being frozen two or three feet deep, with snow five or six feet above it. Our greatest subsistence is the rind tree [bittersweet] which grows like ivy about the trees...

"In the first two week we eat our dogs. We go back over our steps to find bones and carcasses of beasts we have killed before... We reduce to powder the bones-remains of crows and dogs…We take the animal skins from shoes, clothes and leggings, most of the skins from our lodges, even beaver skins where the children beshat more than a hundred times. We burn the hairs off the skins with coals. The rest goes down our throats…

"Finally we become the very image of death. We often mistake ourselves, living for dead and dead for living. We lack strength to pull the dead out of lodges, and when we do, it is to put them four paces away in the snow. Here are more than 500 dead—men, women and children…

198

"In the end, the wrath of God begins to appease itself…Here come wind and rain, that put new life in us. This weather continues for three days. The forest clears. The snow hardens, and we no longer need snowshoes. Those with strings left in their bows take courage to use them. The small deer are caught in the crusted snow, as if by stakes. Now it is easy for us to take them and cut their throats with our knives."

This account offers a perspective from which we can view our modern winter problems—the car won't start, the snowplow pushed snow into our driveway, and so forth. Perhaps it can remind us to take them for what they are—minor nuisances.

Cabin Fever

Cabin fever often rises to new heights around this time of year. If you can't stop thinking about South Seas Islands, here are some thoughts that might help you make it through until spring:

•**At least you have food in your cupboards.** Deer are entering their period of greatest stress, and their cupboards are looking mighty bare. Competition between individuals in a deer yard does not recognize the democratic principles of equality. Dominant bucks eat first, followed by prime does, older does, yearlings, and fawns. While cruel by human standards, this caste system fosters herd "fitness." If you're expendable, you will be expended. Those with the greatest strength will live to pass on their genes.

•**At least when spring does arrive, you'll get to enjoy it.** One of my brothers-in-law lives in Houston, the other in Dallas. They never get to feel the extraordinary surge of life that April presents those of us who live in the northwoods. Of course, they are quick to point out that they are happy to trade the long winter for a muted spring season.

•**At least the noise of snowmobiles will soon end.** Living next to a snowmobile trail, as I do, is like having a neighbor who uses his chainsaw from dawn until 2 a.m. Or it's like having a mosquito take up lodging in your eardrum. Or maybe it's like going to an isolated beach, only to have a dozen teenagers drive up and play their boomboxes at maximum volume on top of their cars. Whatever happened to the peace and quiet of the northwoods?

•**At least you get to go to the bathroom.** If you're a hibernating black bear, you spend five months "holding it in." Well, not really. Bears reprocess their urea into muscle tissue, actually building muscle mass without the drudgery of exercise or the pain of listening to the music that accompanies aerobics. Mother bears even eat the defecations of their recently born cubs, reprocessing them into usable nutrients. Basically, bears are state-of-the-art sanitary sewage districts.

199

•**At least we don't have to shut down our growth processes and effectively sacrifice five months of our lives while we await the end of winter.** If hardwood trees, frogs, snakes, and insects could be active enough to sniff the wind for the arrival of spring, I'm sure they would be. We, on the other hand, have a choice between living in a state of quasi-hibernation inside our homes, cars, and worksites or exploring the world as it has been given us, challenging our minds and hearts to grow despite the apparent dormancy around us. If you choose the latter option, cabin fever subsides as you are discovering the pleasure of the present rather than waiting for the future.

•**Despite the cold, dampness, and mud, late February, March, and April may be the best time to enjoy the woods.** There are no mosquitoes around, and fewer people are in the woods than at any other time of year. If you listen closely, you'll hear the rising note of spring playing in the wind.

Spring Inside in February

If the lack of outdoor greenery is getting you down, cut some woody stems from various deciduous trees and shrubs, like leatherwood, tamarack, alder, willow, or hazelnut. Put the stems in a vase of water. Within a week, leaves will begin to appear. It's very pleasant to have something wild growing in February, even if it's growing in a jar.

Candlelight Skiing

My good friend Steve Stevenoski and I participated in a candle-light ski tour along the Statehouse Lake Trail in Manitowish Waters. It took place in late February of 1994, and I'm sure the date was cho-sen in the expectation that the temperatures would be relatively mod-erate so late in the winter. Such was not the case. We left at 7:30 p.m. with the temperature at -10°F and dropping; when we arrived at the trailhead, about 75 people were gathered around a bonfire. The trail loop we were taking was lined with candles, making an excep-tionally pretty sight. The wind had snuffed out many of the candles by the time we traversed the loop, and we were challenged to feel our way along the trail in sections that were completely dark. Fortu-nately, there were no hills.

Plenty of rosy cheeks and noses surrounded the fire that night. In case you ever wondered, that rosy blush is due to hemoglobin. He-moglobin carries the oxygen in our blood, and it flows into areas like our noses. On such a frigid night, it's generally so cold around one's nose that the hemoglobin molecule can't open up and release the oxy-gen. As a result, the oxygen-deprived tissues of the nose take on the bluish color of the hemoglobin itself. Once we go indoors, stand around a fire, or exercise enough to heat up, the hemogobin releases the oxy-gen. Because blood rich in oxygen is red, our cheeks and noses return to their normal red coloration.

Alder, the Miscreant

One February I tried to snowshoe into an area of the Manitowish River Wilderness I had never visited. I found that I could walk through the shallow snow in my boots as easily as I could by laboring with the snowshoes. I was elated that I could remove the snowshoes, because I hiked into a large swamp so thick with alder stems that I really had to struggle to get through in just my boots. Trying to make progress in showshoes would have been masochistic.

If you've not had the pleasure of wrestling your way through an alder stand, count your lucky stars. Alder has a camaraderie with its alder friends that leads to the continual embracing of neighbors—an intertwinement that only my wife, a weaver by trade, can appreciate.

The stems are usally five to 10 feet tall, and they splay in every conceivable direction. I am seldom thankful for the fact that I wear glasses, but on this day they saved me from several eye pokings by the few errant branches that weren't busy entangling me at every other bodily vantage point. While I could wax at length regarding alder, I've found another author, Ted Kerasote, who has scaled heights of alder hatred that I have yet to reach in an article in *Audubon* magazine. Here's a sampling of his thoughts:

"One could get lost in alder, the black sheep, the miscreant, the apostate of the birch family that has plagued the human race since Olympian times."

201

I like the statement, but it gets better. In reference to Sitka alder on the Alaska coast, Kerasote says, "This bantam-weight tree (large malignant bush might be more appropriate) so infested the watercourses and lowlands of the Great Land that many a strong-willed pioneer fled with demented howls after trying to battle its green wall of perversity."

In reference to European alder: "It takes on every crippled bend of water. Its trunk becomes warped, it juts out over the riffles in tortured angles, it twists and rises in agony toward the sky, dragging in confusion the trunks and the branches of its neighbors. It becomes the stuff of nightmares, of haunted forests, black knights, trolls."

Wow! And I thought I had it bad.

But just like any other species, alder has its ecological value. Its overhanging branches shade and cool many a trout stream that would otherwise heat up and lose its population of the cold-loving trout. Alder helps anchor shorelines by growing in black muck, and it's much favored by woodcocks and snipe, which probe the mire with their long, flexible beaks in pursuit of creepy crawlies hidden in the ooze. The entangling branches of alder serve as the perfect, forked foundation for the nests of many songbirds. They enjoy not only the housing, but the protection afforded by the often impregnable branches.

My final advice to myself on the subject of alder swamps? Go around the damn swamp next time. There are a few places upon which we just weren't meant to tread.

Chickadee Social Agendas

I've watched the comings and goings of black-capped chickadees at our feeders for years, but until I came across an article on their wintering social structure, I had never really understood the strict social hierarchy that chickadees employ.

In winter, chickadees are nonmigratory. They are either "regulars" within a particular flock or "floaters" that move among three or four flocks. This is a dramatic change from their strategy during the spring and summer breeding season, when they form territorial, monogamous pairs. At the end of the summer, the older birds leave their individual territories to join with others in flocks, which occupy and defend a much larger flock territory. The newly fledged young become the floaters, joining established flocks as the lowest members of the social register.

202

Every chickadee flock has a clear pecking order, somewhat noticeable to those of us who casually watch them in winter, but actually measurable to researchers who band the individuals and note their interactions. When a dominant chickadee arrives at a feeder, a less dominant member of the flock will either take off or be chased away. If the two birds arrive simultaneously, the dominant one will eat first and leave before the other dares take a seed.

Because each flock has its own territory, it's fair to assume that the flock coming to your feeder does so every day, to the exclusion of any other chickadees. Flocks are usually comprised of six to 14 regulars. Whatever the number, a flock almost always contains an even number of birds with an even sex ratio, because the flock members pair up. Thus a flock of 12 regulars most likely includes six pairs of chickadees, and the pairs will probably maintain their bonds in the spring.

However, each flock contains a number of young, unbred floaters that range among several flocks. Here's where the unexpected happens. If the dominant alpha male of a flock is killed by a sharp-shinned hawk or a housecat (the two greatest threats to chickadees), the second-in-rank beta male doesn't take over as you might expect. Instead, the highest-ranked floater typically becomes the dominant male of the entire flock, in a true rags-to-riches turn of events. If the alpha female vanishes, her place is similarly taken by the highest-ranked female floater. The new "queen" assumes her role immediately, as if she were born to it. Each newly crowned floater will eventually breed with the mate of the bird it replaced, also inheriting its territory.

But, because nothing is ever simple, floaters don't fill every vacancy. Floaters move in only when high-ranking members die. They apparently understand that only the top two or three pairs in a flock will obtain a territory in the spring anyway. So the widowed, lower-ranked regulars remain mateless for the rest of the winter.

Why bother to be a lower-ranked, adult pair within the flock if you probably won't get a territory in the spring and you can't move up in the hierarchy? There is in fact one other way to move up the ladder. If both members of a top-ranked pair disappear, then the lower members all move up a notch, enhancing their shot at a breeding territory in the spring.

It all sounds a bit like the strange world of WBA boxing rankings to me, but no matter. The elaborate social hierarchy and the rules are designed for one purpose—successful nesting in the spring.

203

The "Soo"

I drove to Sault Ste. Marie in February of 1995, in order to be a part of a weekend owling adventure sponsored by the Whitefish Point Bird Observatory in Michigan. I was lured by the winter record invasion numbers of 1991-92, when 35 great gray owls were seen in one day by one researcher; seven hawk owls were observed on another day.

Because 1995 was not an invasion year, the owl numbers were expected to be way down—and so they were. Invasions occur on an average of once every four years. Nevertheless, we saw three snowy owls. Two of them sat on separate telephone poles and gave us lengthy looks. These two were salt-and-pepper colored, indicating that they were youngsters. The third was pure white; it sat on the roof of a small shed, its pure color disclosing its greater maturity.

The highlight of the trip was not an owl, but a dark-phase gyrfalcon that regularly hangs out on the window ledges of a beautiful old stone-work electrical generating plant in the city. I had never seen a gyrfalcon before, so this was a "lifer" for me. We were provided with spectacular views of the gyrfalcon in flight; at one point, it chased a flock of common mergansers down the St. Mary's River, then returned to fly directly over our heads.

Gyrfalcons are the most northerly of North America's hawks and the largest of all falcons. They nest on cliffs in the Arctic tundra, generally moving only as far south as the tree line during the winter. In Wisconsin, we usually see one or two a winter, and that's it. The total estimated number of individuals in North America is just 5,000.

Gyrfalcons are as fast as any bird known. Only a gyrfalcon can overtake waterfowl like pintails or wigeons in full flight. Peregrine falcons achieve phenomenal speeds during their dives, but they can't match the gyrfalcon for straight-ahead speed. I was impressed with the gyrfalcon's barrel-like build, and the heavy chest that belied its speed.

204

We also saw six rough-legged hawks—one in light phase, four normal, and one in dark phase. Rough-leggeds are one of the easiest hawks to identify. Look for the bold, black patch underneath, at the crook or "elbow" of their wings. They feed over open fields, looking for mice, so don't expect to see them in forested country. The Soo area is quite attractive to wintering hawks and owls, because its surprisingly large expanses of open fields provide ideal rodent hunting grounds.

We saw several oddities, too. These sightings were all the more strange because the Soo was serving us intense cold and killer winds over the weekend. We spotted two robins and four horned larks on the Canadian side of the Soo. Typically, both species opt for views of winter that take them far south of Lake Superior. However, horned larks are noted for their exceptionally early "spring" migrations northward; they often show up in northern counties in early February. They have been found incubating eggs while their nests were still surrounded by snow, so perhaps they were moving north because the winter had been rather mild until this particular week.

We missed the harlequin ducks that commonly feed in fast water on the Canadian side of the border, near a hydroelectric power plant. The wind coming off the lake at the power plant was approximately the speed of the Starship Enterprise in warp drive, so we felt fortunate to simply get back alive. Once we were well out along the channel, looking for the harlequins, one of my fellow birders asked me, "Should I die now, or wait until we almost get back?" It was COLD.

Hawk Owls

I traveled to the Glidden area in February of 1992 to get my first-ever sighting of a hawk owl. The owl had reputedly been sitting for several weeks in a popple tree just off Highway 13. He or she—the sexes are indistinguishable, although the female is larger—didn't disappoint me. It was perched exactly where advertised, quietly scanning the road and the adjoining fields from its popple limb while I scanned it with my spotting scope.

The hawk owl is so named because its appearance, flight, and habits resemble those of some smaller hawks. It jerks its tail up and down, hunts during the day, and often hovers over prey like a kestrel. Its face is bordered by heavy, black "sideburns" that were very visible in my scope.

It felt quite odd to be sitting in my car on a major state highway next to a snowmobile trail, watching a rare northern Canadian owl. The setting didn't seem to fit at all, but from the owl's point of view the variety of rodent hunting opportunities along both a road and a snowmobile trail probably made it a great spot.

Eagles and Osprey

Ron Eckstein, DNR wildlife manager in Rhinelander, and Dave Evans, freelance bird bander, have banded over 3,000 eagles in the last two decades. The data they've provided has launched Wisconsin into a national leadership role in eagle research. As of 1996, Wisconsin hosted nearly 590 breeding pairs of eagles, a number best put in perspective by comparing it with the 1975 total of about 120 pairs. Because it counts only breeding pairs, this population figure does not include all other nonbreeders—a group made up of one- to four-year-old eagles. Thus we might safely estimate the total number of individual eagles to be 1,400 or more.

The Lakeland area contains the greatest concentrations of eagles in the state. Since 1975, Wisconsin has traded or sold nearly 200 eaglets to other states, including Indiana, Arkansas, Tennessee, and New York, where they are used in reintroduction programs.

By this time of year, most adult eagles have returned to their nesting territories. Big white pines seem to draw eagles in to nest. In fact, over 75 percent of all eagle nests are found in white pines. In early

March, the adults will repair their nests and mate. Eggs are generally laid during the third and fourth weeks of March. By May 1, after a 30-day incubation period, the chicks will hatch. Fledging is another three months down the line.

Contaminant monitoring, conducted by using the bald eagle as a "biosentinel," occurred throughout northern Wisconsin in the early 1990s. Over 100 eagle nestlings were sampled for contaminants. Direct observation of nests using remote video cameras was also part of the study. Nearly 3,500 hours of tape were recorded, documenting incubation behaviors, adult/nestling behaviors, prey delivery rates, size and type of prey, and causes of nest failure.

Historically, nest success rates on Lake Superior have been significantly lower than those on inland lakes. The videotapes helped explain why the productivity has been so low. Biologists learned that the breeding adults on inland lakes brought twice as much food to the nest as eagles on Lake Superior. To make matters worse for eagles on the big lake, the Lake Superior pairs spent more time seeking food away from the nest than adults on inland lakes, leaving their chicks open to predation and exposure. These factors, combined with higher contaminant levels in Lake Superior and the close correlation between cold weather and poor nest success, may explain the limited reproduction of eagles on the world's largest lake.

Eckstein also bands many of the osprey in our area. The number of active osprey nests in 1996 totaled around 395. Again, this total can be best appreciated by comparing it with the 1975 total of about 90 active nests. Two-thirds of the active nests are found on artificial platforms, leaving one to wonder what the population would be if the DNR had not implemented an aggressive platform program.

The Return of Color

Pine grosbeaks sometimes flock to our feeders in February. Their red shading supplements the reddish hues of the purple finches and redpolls already using the feeders, bringing welcome color to the white snowscape. If you toss in the blue of the blue jays, the yellow of the evening grosbeaks and the female pine grosbeaks, and the black and white of the chickadees and the hairy woodpeckers, the February canvas greatly brightens.

Gray Jays

Dave Picard, a friend and DNR creel census taker, watched a pair of gray jays on Palmer Lake one February 25th. The birds were carrying what appeared to be nesting material back and forth into a lowland balsam stand. It seemed too early for any bird species to be building a nest, but I looked it up in *Wisconsin Birdlife* by Samuel Robbins (a mere $75, but worth it) and found that gray jays do begin nest building in February. Robbins cites a 1937 record in Sawyer County of gray jays (formerly known as Canada jays) building a nest in late February, seven feet up in a balsam. Another record indicates that three eggs were hatched in a Price County nest on March 30, 1941. The gray jay's incubation period is 16 to 18 days and the young fledge in another 15 days, so the gray jay may be the earliest passerine to nest, hatch, and fledge in our area. By comparison, the earliest nesting date recorded for black-capped chickadees is April 15, and they seldom lay their eggs until May.

207

Great Gray Owls

During February of 1996, I traveled north of Duluth in search of great gray owls. The winter of 1995-96 was an invasion year for great grays, and numerous sightings had been reported in northeastern Minnesota. Laura Erickson, a top birder and author, guided me on my owl search through the Sax-Zim Bog, a wetland complex within an area that encompasses about 150 square miles.

Temperatures hit -35°F that morning. We began the day by visiting a retired couple that had called Laura to report the sighting of a boreal owl at their bird feeder. Unfortunately, we arrived 20 minutes too late. The boreal owl had been sitting for an hour atop the old Christmas tree they had put out near their deck, but it was now gone. We waited an hour for it to reappear. We were sure it was nearby, because the birds at the feeder suddenly took off and never returned, indicating the presence of a predator, but we couldn't locate it.

Boreal owls are just 10 inches long, and they are supposed to be strictly nocturnal, roosting in dense cover during the day. They are true Canadians, nesting only rarely in far northern Minnesota and high in the Rocky Mountains. Every winter a few wander down into the U.S., presumably seeking a better prey base, but for birders they rank as the least accessible of all North American owls. To think that these folks had simply watched one from their dining room table while eating breakfast!

We eventually headed north for the bog. Birding in such a large area, and one that receives as much snow as northern Minnesota, meant spending a lot of time slowly driving along back roads, scanning trees and hoping to spot an owl. The car kept us warm while we cruised numerous gravel roads at top speeds of 30 miles per hour. We saw virtually nothing for several hours, but our persist-ence and Laura's knowledge of the area paid off at about 1 p.m., when we pulled up beside a great gray that was perched low in an aspen. It flew to the next tree down the road, giving us a good look at its five-foot wingspan. We pulled up to it again; this time it stayed put, allowing us exceptional close-ups through our binoculars. We watched for over 10 minutes as the great gray did little more than swivel its head smoothly in a 270-degree rotation, scanning for prey. Arctic owls are typically "tame" in this manner. They are apparently so inexperienced with human beings that they don't perceive danger.

Although the dimensions of a great gray seem immense, they are more feathers than bulk. Snowy owls and great horned owls outweigh them. Great horneds, probably the fiercest avian predators, regularly prey upon their larger cousins. One study turned up 13 radio-marked great grays that died in the talons of great horned owls.

The great gray is unmistakably identifiable due to its impressive size, its rounded head without ear tufts, and the white "bow tie" under its chin. The prominent circles on the facial disc lend the bird a solemnity that is particularly distinctive, as is its deep booming call—a *whoo-hooo-hooo* that thrums low and slow.

Within the next hour, we discovered two more great grays in trees along the roads, both calmly surveying the landscape and taking no notice of us. Laura had predicted that we would see at least six great grays and a hawk owl. While we didn't meet her expectations, mine were more than met. I'd never seen one in the wild, and to see three in one day was quite a blessing.

208

Ice Caves

One February I traveled to view the remarkable Lake Superior ice caves near Cornucopia in Bayfield County. To call them "caves" is a bit of a misnomer. The ice formations really occur along sheer sandstone cliff faces in Squaw Bay, which are occasionally hollowed into caves by wave action. Most of what one sees are the extraordinary ice floes down the faces of these cliffs–ice floes that seem to utterly defy the laws of gravity, hanging in the air despite weights that must exceed thousands of pounds. The formations often resemble an iced version of a lava flow, but sometimes the ice takes on intricate, inexplicable shapes that stir the imagination like cloud formations in summer.

209

Now and again, singular small formations of ice are tinted by colors like robin's egg blue, which appear in a splash as if the Ice Gods simply decided to throw dramatic tints around. I called the Apostle Islands National Lakeshore office, asking staff members to explain why the blue occurs, but no one knew for sure. They speculate that the phenomenon has something do with mineralization, or that it may be due to pure water freezing at a particularly rapid rate.

The ice formations represent some of nature's best, although slowest, performance art. I visited the site with Jeff and Rosie Richter. Jeff works as a professional photographer in our area. He has photographed the caves on numerous occasions over the years, and each time he was treated with different formations. The ice variations depend on the temperature, and on storms that may occur prior to a visit.

Getting to the caves requires a 3/4-mile hike along the icy shoreline of Lake Superior. A well-worn path leads the way. On weekends, you can just follow other folks—the site attracts 100 or more people on a good day. The road to Lake Superior is unmarked, but if you go approximately 3.5 miles north on Highway 13 from Cornucopia, you'll see it on your left.

Ravens Roosting

We remained at the ice caves until well past sunset so that Jeff could take advantage of better light for shooting photos. As the dusk deepened, dozens of ravens flew directly up the shoreline in a ragged procession, undoubtedly heading for their nighttime roost. Why and where ravens roost communally at night is unclear. Roosts may be located near an abundance of food. Some roosts appear to be comprised of flocks of sexually immature ravens that join together at night.

Roosts are generally assumed to help prevent predation, in accordance with the old safety in numbers theory. They also help in spotting food like carrion, and in sharing the resource. The same roost may be used for decades, although ravens have also been known to change their roosts annually or even more frequently. Roosts are of great importance to the birds—ravens have been tracked flying 23 miles to a roost site at night. Generally, only a dozen or so roost together, but they may congregate in numbers up to 200.

210

Roosting is literally defined as resting or sleeping. Birds do sleep, of course, typically with their heads and necks on their backs and their bills buried in their shoulder feathers. Ground-roosting birds like ducks rest on their feet and belly, but songbirds most often stand or sit down on a branch, locking their toes around the perch. Perching birds have flexor tendons in their leg muscles; some think these tendons automatically tighten and lock the birds' claws in place, so they can sleep without fear of falling from the tree. One study of European birds concluded that birds that are very active in the daytime sleep soundly at night, their deepest slumber occurring for half an hour to three hours after they fall asleep.

Island Lake Hemlocks

One February Mary and I snowshoed in an area called the Island Lake Hemlocks, located in central Iron County. The stand currently comprises 120 acres of mature hemlock-hardwoods, including a beautiful, virgin island tract of 10 acres or so. The site has been identified for potential designation as a state natural area, but it's currently enmeshed in the step by step process of receiving approval from the state Natural Areas Preservation Council and the state's DNR board.

Over the years I've written many times about old-growth stands. Mary and I seek them out whenever we hear of them, and winter snowshoeing on such sites is particularly pleasurable. Our voices automatically hush amongst such large trees—I suspect because of some internal understanding we have of the age and experience these trees possess.

A short, well-marked loop trail leads into the stand. I encourage you to visit the site now, while the snow's still good, or to bide your time until late spring, when the dirt road is most passable.

The only discouraging part of our exploration was an adjoining clear-cut. There are good clear-cuts and there are bad ones. Because of its proximity to an old- growth stand, this one is a bad one. The likelihood that the old and tall trees will be blown down in a storm is greatly increased, and the probability that destructive, edge species animals will penetrate to the center of the stand has also skyrocketed due to the clear-cut.

211

Opportunistic Ermines

For three days, Stephanie and Richard Wells of Eagle River had an ermine eating from their suet feeder. On the second day, Richard watched the ermine carrying something in its mouth and moved in to get a closer look. The ermine noticed his movement, dropped its catch, and froze. Richard was able to identify the "catch." It was a mouse caught in a trap that the ermine had stolen from their garage. Stephanie had wondered where the traps were going.

Otter Slides

Mary and I snowshoed in the Star Lake-Plum Lake State Natural Area in the Northern Highlands State Forest one late February weekend. The site is one of the largest remaining stands of climax forest left in Wisconsin. It's quite pristine, and the snow was the white ink pad upon which a host of animals had left their prints. Neither Mary nor I are experts at reading prints, but one set of "prints" we couldn't mistake were the slides of a number of otters that had been traveling between iced-over Star Lake and free-flowing Plum Creek. The slides were smooth, half-rounded troughs around eight inches wide. They were sometimes broken up by footprints or body thrusts that jumbled the otherwise perfectly tubular path. Otters frequently travel overland, and they may travel several miles between waterways, bounding and sliding at speeds that one naturalist clocked at 15 to 18 miles per hour.

Deer paths crossed our trail frequently, and the browsed stubs of sugar maple illustrated their preferred diet. Surprisingly, many young hemlocks were browsed lightly or not at all, and the number of hemlock saplings that rose above the reach of the deer was heartening.

Life Down Under

Under lake ice, the gyrations of air temperatures in late February and March have little impact. Temperatures at the bottom of lakes usually remain a stable 39°F, while the upper waters at the ice surface are nearly always 32°F. Still, I've seen a number of streams open when the weather warms a bit, and then close up when the cold returns. Two friends and I hiked along Moose Lake and Moose Creek north of Mercer in search of wolf tracks one late February. We didn't find any wolves, but we did otter scat all along on the shoreline of the creek.

212

I've seen numerous otter trails, often back in the woods away from water, and I've observed holes in lake ice that appear to be maintained by otter. I've wondered how the otter find these holes since they really can't cut a hole on their own. I once watched otter break very thin ice on the Manitowish River with their heads and then bite the ice to enlarge the holes. I've wondered too how once they dive under the ice, they find their way back to the holes. Wouldn't it be extremely easy to chase a fish and get turned around under the ice and not know where the hole was?

Well, obviously otter are a lot smarter than me, because I would drown on my first foray. A study in Alberta, Canada, found that otters almost invariably used old beaver lodges to enter the water. Sometimes, the otter even ripped apart beaver dams in order to lower the water level beneath the ice, and create a corridor of travel to food resources. The researchers found that otter were so depend-ent on beaver that their northern limit coincided with that of the beavers even though good habitat was available further north.

I hadn't considered abandoned beaver lodges as otter entrance points, but it certainly makes sense. I wonder if otters ever enter active beaver lodges to try and force the residents out so they can gain access to the lake waters?

We did see an active beaver lodge on Little Moose Lake, which is connected to Moose Lake by Moose Creek. We had some fairly easy walking along the creek banks, a favor given us we suspected by the beaver who had probably inundated the area in previous years and made a meadow out of what should have been tag alder heaven.

Our most interesting observation on the hike may have been the fresh eagle tracks we found along the shoreline of Moose Lake. I'd never seen the snowtrack of an eagle, but there it was as plain as day, as well as its wing imprint in the snow from where it took off.

Bear Birth

213

Bear cubs are born between mid-January and mid-February. As half-pound, hairless, sightless, and toothless little bundles, the helpless cubs are only able to suckle milk. A sow's milk contains 33 percent milkfat, compared to three percent in a human mother's milk, so the cubs benefit from a rich initial diet. By the time the cubs and Mom emerge in April, the cubs weigh five pounds. The adult female gives birth every other year, keeping the cubs with her through their first winter. Females reach sexual maturity at the age of four to five years.

Wildlife Rehabilitation

In the winter of 1992, Mary and I went to a Northwoods Wildlife Center banquet in Mercer. Jackie and Dave DeBauche, who perform most of the rehabilitative work for the NWC in Minocqua, told us they had just released a bobcat that had been considered dead after it was hit by a vehicle. The bobcat had suffered a severe concussion and was unconscious when it was brought to the center, but food and rest made it healthy enough to resume its predatory role in the northwoods.

The DeBauches had also cared for an alpha female wolf from a Douglas County pack, which was brought to them with a severe case of mange. The wolf died despite their efforts, but apparently the cause of death was not the mange. The necropsy revealed a porcupine quill in the wolf's lung, which had allowed the lung to fill with fluid and caused eventual heart failure.

In winter, the Northwoods Wildlife Center is open to visitors from 10 a.m. to 2 p.m., Monday through Saturday. The work done there is worth seeing and supporting.

Timber Wolves

Eastern timber wolves mate from late February into March. The dominant pair within the pack is usually the only pair that breeds. After a 63-day gestation period, a litter averaging five to six pups may be born in late April or May, usually in a dug-out cavity. Two packs are currently established in western Oneida County–the Little Rice River Pack and the Boot Jack Pack.

214

Red Squirrels

Blue jays, evening grosbeaks, chickadees, redpolls, and finches usually compete for seed at our feeders. But the most dominant competitors are the red squirrels that nimbly tightrope along branches and launch themselves through the air in long leaps between trees. Their energy and agility are a constant source of amazement to me, even though we're not really trying to attract them to our feeders.

Red squirrels often chase one another through the black ash trees below our house in late February. The chases signify more than simple play. The male is usually chasing the female—a fact easy to infer because the female stops briefly, allows the male to mount her, and runs off seconds later. This goes on for several minutes until they part ways. I assume that mating has occurred during one of these brief encounters.

Weasel Attack

Irene Hobein from Hazelhurst wrote to me, describing a remarkable attack she and her son Joe witnessed in their backyard. Joe had put out a live trap in order to remove a few squirrels that were robbing their bird feeders. Before long, they heard "an awful shrieking . . . a weasel had attacked the squirrel locked in the cage. He circled the cage, biting and screaming. Then he tossed the cage over and over till the door popped open. He grabbed the squirrel and went into the woods. Never had we seen a more vicious attack."

Thaws

Mary, Callie, and I took advantage of a typical late February thaw and the subsequent freeze to hike on a frozen snowmobile trail. We left the trail to hike into the woods at one point where the snow was either eight inches deep or totally gone, depending on how much sun had reached the area. We stopped on one south-facing slope along the shore of a wilderness lake. The ground was clear of snow and the sun warm on our faces, so we reveled in springlike sensations. We were living well for a February 20th in the northwoods.

Late-winter thaws regenerate human spirits, but they can have adverse affects on vegetation. A false spring followed by severe cold can damage trees by freezing cells that have "de-hardened" due to the warm weather. Plants achieve their resistance to cold through a gradual hardening process that takes place in autumn, allowing them to tolerate cold temperatures in winter that they cannot tolerate at other times of year. Hardening appears to be a three-step process, although not many northwoods plants reach the third stage. The third stage conditions the buds of certain northern trees, including white spruce and jack pine, giving them the ability to resist temperatures all the way down to -112°F! Resistance to freezing appears to be lost quickly in spring, so brief thaws in February can undo metabolic changes that took an entire autumn to accomplish.

215

Wood Supply

This is the time of year to be cutting firewood, because wood cut in winter has the lowest moisture content. Spring may be great in virtually all respects, but it's the worst time of year for cutting firewood. As an example, yellow birch doubles its moisture content in May. Wet wood can contain up to 65 percent water, and if you've ever tried to burn such "green" wood, you know how much heat is wasted while the water evaporates from the wood. One author suggests that the term "seasoned wood" may have more to do with cutting the wood in the right season than with allowing it a season to dry.

Even "dry" firewood contains 15 to 30 percent water, although it will lose about 1,000 pounds of water per average cord as it seasons. The term "cord" probably originated from the practice of measuring a stack of wood with a specific length of rope, or cord. According to one author, stones were also sold by the cord in eighteenth-century England. A cord of split wood has more actual volume than a cord of round logs. The volume of a cord can vary from 58 to 100 cubic feet, although the math tells us it's supposed to come out to 128 cubic feet (four feet by four feet by eight feet).

The refinement of the woodstove and the use of insulation have been quite a blessing for our forest lands and ourselves. An average farmhouse with two fireplaces in colonial New England used 20 to 30 cords of wood per year but still remained chilly. An open fireplace has an efficiency rating of just 10 percent, meaning that 90 percent of the heat goes up the chimney. Thomas Jefferson's Monticello estate used 50 cords of wood annually; during one February, his kitchen fireplace alone burned a cord every five days.

216

> ## Late-February Musings
>
> *When you live up in the North Country in winter, you just naturally keep track of things, because you could wind up freezing your buns if you don't.*
> —George Vukelich

Leaping Caesars

Leap year comes upon us every four years. We must compensate for the fact a year actually lasts 365-1/4 days, as the Earth shows no respect for even numbers in its voyage around the sun. Julius Caesar instituted this calendar reform back in 46 B.C. He also decided that July, named in his honor, must contain an extra day so that his fame could be adequately celebrated. In essence, he stole a day from February to accomplish the task. Caesar Augustus soon followed suit, feeling that August must be longer in order to fully exalt him. He took another day from February so the common people had time to express their reverence—an act I'm sure was highly appreciated by the average peasant. Because February had been trimmed, the additional leap year day was eventually and appropriately added to this month.

Full Moon

The full moon in February is called by the Potawatomi "The Baby Bear Moon." The spring equinox will soon arrive, and the first robin will be back.

Hang in there.

218

Selected Bibliography

Ackerman, D. 1990. *A Natural History of the Senses*. Vintage Books, New York.

Anderson, T. 1989. *Learning Nature by a Country Road*. Voyageur Press, Stillwater, MN.

Bates, J. 1995. *Trailside Botany*. Pfeifer-Hamilton, Duluth, MN.

Bates, J. 1997. *Seasonal Guide to the Natural Year; Minnesota, Michigan, and Wisconsin*. Fulcrum Publishing, Golden, CO.

Bates, J. 1997. *A Northwoods Companion: Spring and Summer*. Manitowish River Press, Manitowish, WI.

Benyus, J. 1989. *Northwoods Wildlife*. NorthWord Press Inc., Minocqua, WI.

Berry, W. 1964. *Collected Poems*. North Point Press, San Francisco.

Curtis, J. 1959. *Vegetation of Wisconsin*. University of Wisconsin Press, Madison, WI.

Daniel, G., and Sullivan, J. 1981. *A Sierra Club Naturalist's Guide to the North Woods of Michigan, Wisconsin, and Minnesota*. Sierra Club Books, San Francisco.

Densmore, F. 1974. *How Indians Use Wild Plants for Food, Medicine and Crafts*. Dover Publishers, New York.

Densmore, F. 1979. *Chippewa Customs*. Minnesota Historical Society Press, St. Paul, MN.

Dickinson, T. 1983. *Night Watch*. Camden House Publishing, Camden East, Ontario

Dunn, G. 1996. *Insects of the Great Lakes Region*. The University of Michigan Press, Ann Arbor, MI.

Dunne, P., Sibley, D., Sutton, C. 1988. *Hawks in Flight*. Houghton Mifflin Co., Boston.

Eastman, J. 1992. *The Book of Forest and Thicket*. Stackpole Books, Harrisburg, PA.

Eastman, J. 1995. *The Book of Swamp and Bog*. Stackpole Books, Harrisburg, PA.

Ehrlich, P., Dobkin, D., Wheye, D. 1988. *The Birder's Handbook.* Simon and Schuster, New York.

Erickson, L. 1994. *For the Birds.* Pfeifer-Hamilton, Duluth, MN.

Halfpenny, J. 1986. *A Field Guide to Mammal Tracking in North America.* Johnson Books, Boulder, CO.

Halfpenny, J., and Ozanne, R. 1989. *Winter, An Ecological Handbook.* Johnson Books, Boulder, CO.

Henderson, C. 1995. *Wild About Birds.* State of Minnesota, Department of Natural Resources, St. Paul, MN.

Hubbell, S. 1993. B*roadsides from the Other Orders.* Random House, New York.

Jackson, H. 1961. *Wisconsin Mammals.* University of Wisconsin Press, Madison, WI.

Kappel-Smith, D. 1979. *Wintering.* Little, Brown and Co., Boston.

Kricher, J., and Morrison, G. 1988. *A Field Guide to Eastern Forests.* Houghton Mifflin, Boston.

Lanner, R. 1990. *Autumn Leaves.* NorthWord Press, Minocqua, WI.

Leopold, A. 1949. *A Sand County Almanac.* Oxford University Press, New York.

Lyons, J., and Jordan, S. 1989. *Walking the Wetlands.* John Wiley and Sons, New York.

Marchand, P. 1987. *Life in the Cold.* University Press of New England, Hanover and London.

Martin, A., Zim, H., and Nelson, A. 1951. *American Wildlife and Plants.* Dover Publications, New York.

Oliver, M. 1978. *American Primitive.* Little, Brown and Co., Boston.

Oliver, M. 1992. *New and Selected Poems.* Beacon Press, Boston.

Palmer, E., and Fowler, H. 1949. *Fieldbook of Natural History.* McGraw-Hill Book Co., New York.

Peattie, D. 1948. *A Natural History of Trees.* Houghton Mifflin, Boston.

Peterson, L. 1977. *A Field Guide to Edible Wild Plants.* Houghton Mifflin, Boston.

Pielou, E. 1988. *The World of Northern Evergreens.* Comstock Publishing Associates, Ithaca, NY.

Robbins, S. 1991. *Wisconsin Birdlife.* University of Wisconsin Press, Madison, WI.

Rupp, R. 1990. *Red Oaks and Black Birches.* Garden Way Publishing, Pownal, VT.

Seno, W. Ed. 1985. *Up Country.* Round River Publishing Co., Madison, WI.

Stegner, W. 1986. *The Sense of Place.* Wisconsin Humanities Committee, Madison, WI.

Stokes, D. and L. 1976. *A Guide to Nature in Winter.* Little, Brown and Co. Boston.

Terres, J. 1991. *Things Precious and Wild.* Fulcrum Publishing, Golden, CO.

Verch, D. 1988. *Chequamegon Bay Birds.* Dick Verch, Ashland, WI.

Vogt, R. 1981. *Natural History of Amphibians and Reptiles of Wisconsin.* Milwaukee Public Museum, Milwaukee, WI.

Voss, E. 1972. *Michigan Flora, Vol. 1.* Cranbrook Institute of Science and University of Michigan Herbarium, Bloomfield Hills, MI.

Voss, E. 1985. *Michigan Flora, Vol. 2.* Cranbrook Institute of Science and University of Michigan Herbarium, Ann Arbor, MI.

Voss, E. 1997. *Michigan Flora, Vol. 3.* Cranbrook Institute of Science and University of Michigan Herbarium, Ann Arbor, MI.

Vukelich, G. 1992. *North Country Notebook, Vol. 2.* North Country Press, Madison, WI.

222

Index

Also by John Bates:

Trailside Botany
©1995, Pfeifer-Hamilton

Trailside Botany is concise and presents that blend of science and history often lacking in other guides.
> —Howard Meyerson, Grand Rapids, MI Press

I found it fascinating...Bates crafts his language to reflect the beauty he sees in each plant... Trailside Botany is as lively and diverse as a patch of woods.
> —Tom Hastings, The Minnesota Volunteer

Trailside Botany is a perfect addition to any hiker's backpack...a natural for everyone who loves the outdoors.
> —The Nature Conservancy, Minnesota Chapter

A Seasonal Guide to the Natural Year: Minnesota, Michigan, and Wisconsin
© 1997, Fulcrum Publishing

There are the rare outdoor books that are so jam-packed with interesting stuff that you find yourself reaching for it whenever you get a spare minute to yourself. You find yourself taking it with you camping, hiking, fishing, even just walking. And the darn thing is so well written that you don't mind—in fact, you pick it up as much for pleasure as you do for information. Wisconsin outdoor writer John Bates has published just such a book.
> —Russell King, Council for Wisconsin Writers.

A Northwoods Companion
Spring and Summer
© 1997, Manitowish River Press

Exquisite phenology. Bates has provided the Harpers Index of North Country phenology. This North Country naturalist reveals the depth of experience necessary in knowing one's home or sense of place.
> —Clayton Russell, Outdoor Education Faculty, Northland College

This book will make you push back your computer screen, forget the e-mail and faxes, and put on your galloshes and go for a ramble. John Bates writes crisp prose with a touch of humor, and always the lilt and grace of his subject shines through...He brings the magic of the natural world alive.
> —Terry Daulton, Staff Biologist, Sigurd Olson Environmental Institute

Contributing author to:
Harvest Moon: A Wisconsin Outdoor Anthology
© 1993, Lost River Press

Order Form

Telephone: Call (715) 476-2828. Have your Visa or MasterCard ready.
Fax order: (715) 476-2818
E-Mail order: manitowish@centuryinter.net
Postal order: Manitowish River Press, 2263 Hwy. 47, Mercer, WI 54547.

Check the following books that you wish to order. You may return any book for a full refund, no questions asked, as long as it is still in good saleable condition (in other words, still like new - thank you.)

228

TITLE (BOOKS BY JOHN BATES)	PRICE	QUANTITY	TOTAL
Trailside Botany	$12.95	_____	_____
Seasonal Guide to the Natural Year for Minnesota, Michigan, Wisconsin	$16.95	_____	_____
A Northwoods Companion: spring and summer	$14.95	_____	_____
A Northwoods Companion: fall and winter	$14.95	_____	_____

Sales Tax: Please add 5.5% for books
     shipped to Wisconsin addresses   _____

Shipping: Book Rate: $2.50 for the first book,
     and $1 for each additional book.
     Air Mail: $4 for first book, $2 for each additional book.   _____

TOTAL

Payment:
Check _____ Credit Card: Visa _____ Mastercard _____
Card Number: _____
Name on Card _____ Exp. Date _____

If you would like to receive a copy of the current schedule for Trails North, John Bates' naturalist guide service, please check here _____.

Your Name _____ Street/P.O Box_____

City _____ State _____ Zip_____

Phone_____ Fax_____Email_____